THE BOOK THAT WAS DENIED
THE PULITZER PRIZE

Shortly before Christmas, 1966, after 18 months of intensive effort, Harrison E. Salisbury succeeded in becoming the first American correspondent ever to report from Hanoi.

Salisbury saw the sites of "accidental" bombings by precision American aircraft and viewed deadly prehistoric weapons used by the Vietcong today; he spoke to peasants, patriots and high government officials; visited hospitals, homes and schoolhouses; he even sat through fourteen acts at a Hanoi music hall . . .

The results? *A series of eye-witness reports that made the Defense Department backtrack. A storm of controversy that raged throughout the nation and the world. And, finally, a book that was nominated for the Pulitzer Prize by the Pulitzer Prize jury— a recommendation overruled in a high-level decision still the center of a fierce debate.*

From the observations that rocked the Pentagon to the fascinating human side of life in North Vietnam, here is the most exciting, factual and deeply troubling account of the enemy camp ever presented.

ABOUT THE AUTHOR

HARRISON E. SALISBURY is assistant managing editor for *The New York Times*. From 1949 to 1954, he was Moscow correspondent for the *Times*, and in 1955 he was awarded a Pulitzer Prize for his series of articles on the Soviet Union.

Mr. Salisbury is the author of a number of books, including *To Moscow—and Beyond, New Russia,* and *The Shook-Up Generation. Behind the Lines—Hanoi* enlarges on Mr. Salisbury's controversial series of dispatches from the North Vietnamese capital.

BEHIND THE LINES—
HANOI
BY HARRISON E. SALISBURY

BANTAM BOOKS
TORONTO · NEW YORK · LONDON

BEHIND THE LINES—HANOI

A Bantam Book / published by arrangement with
Harper & Row, Publishers, Incorporated

PRINTING HISTORY
Harper & Row edition published April 1967
Bantam edition published July 1967
2nd printing

Photos by Harrison E. Salisbury courtesy of
The New York Times Company.

Published simultaneously in the United States and Canada

Bantam Books are published by Bantam Books, Inc., a subsidiary
of Grosset & Dunlap, Inc. Its trade-mark, consisting of the words
"Bantam Books" and the portrayal of a bantam, is registered in the
United States Patent Office and in other countries. Marca Registrada.
Bantam Books, Inc., 271 Madison Avenue, New York, N.Y. 10016.

PRINTED IN THE UNITED STATES OF AMERICA

For Arthur and Iphigene Sulzberger

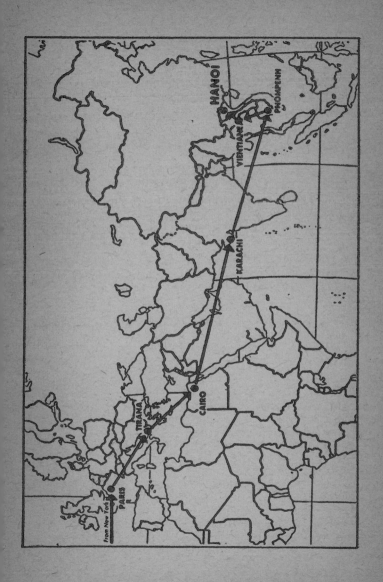

Contents

It was Saturday, a week before Christmas, and I walked down Fifth Avenue, pushing through the bright-faced throngs, the girls in their long boots of Courrèges white and Wyeth brown, the boys, tousle-haired, fresh, pink, moving with long loose strides, the crowds excited by the glitter in the windows, the pleasant clamor in the streets and the dazzle of the lights in the fading afternoon. I walked south through the crowd, feeling part of it and not part of it, for this was a Christmas that I would not share. In forty-eight hours I would be boarding a plane on a long journey that would take me to Hanoi and to a world of war that lay almost outside the margin of my perception, a world where the germinal issues of our day were being delineated in shapes and forms such as even Goya had not imagined, a world of primitive drama, new experience, new adventure and blinding conflict. I walked through the Christmas crowds, past the excavation of General Motors-to-be, past the shimmering elegance of the

Banque Continentale, its French tapestry and Circassian walnut the guarantee of affluence that made the dollar sign seem gauche, past the Sherry-Netherland with its faint aura of Chanel No. 5, past long-legged girls with short jackets of pink mutation mink, past the fountain of the Grand Army of the Republic, its jets spewing ribbons of electric light, past the great windows of the Plaza, golden at tea time, past F. A. O. Schwarz and the giant pandas, the giant giraffes, the giant tigers, the Playboy Club with television eyes, the luxury of Rizzoli's, all tender calf and morocco bindings, Chagalls laughing on the walls, black-haired girls with white clown faces, the golden sound floating out of Saks Fifth Avenue to halo the skaters on the Rockefeller rink.

New York, New York, Christmas, 1966. Beautiful, splendid, opulent, gay. A Great Society Christmas, an electronic Christmas, electronic carols by the Volunteers of America and murmuring electronic computers totaling the new volume figures, click-click-click. Peaceful America. Friendly America. Holiday-time America. Profitable America.

I walked right through the Chanel, the mink, the expensive ladies, the caroling transistors and into the Air France office for my ticket to Paris, where a Hanoi visa was waiting. Whether there would be any Christmas for me in 1966 I could not say. Word of the visa had arrived two days ago at a moment when I had virtually lost all hope that it would be forthcoming. I had added Hanoi to the list of countries at whose door I periodically knocked nearly a year and a half earlier, at the end of summer, 1965. For years I had spent much of my life visiting difficult, inaccessible, impossible countries—Communist countries for the most part. I had been the first correspondent to visit post-Stalin Siberia, the first into post-Stalin Central Asia. I had reopened the doors to Bulgaria and Rumania after the 1950 freeze. I was the first American after World War II to penetrate Albania (and no one else had made it since my visit of 1957). I was one of the few Westerners to travel to Outer Mongolia. For years I had sought admission to Communist China. Nothing had come of this, but I continued to cast my paper boats upon the water. Sometimes I reinforced them with cables to high officials in Peking, dispatched at what I thought might be propitious moments. There were two other hermit kingdoms on my list—North Vietnam and North Korea.

Korea had drifted further and further out of world interest

but Vietnam, bloody, desperate, nagging, Vietnam the quagmire, bottomless reservoir of trouble, breeder of tension, eater of manpower, omnipresent danger, loomed larger and larger over the American scene.

I began my campaign to go to North Vietnam by sending a letter to Premier Pham Van Dong proposing that Hanoi permit an American journalist, a representative of the country's greatest newspaper, to come and take a first-hand look at what was going on. Everything about Vietnam was controversial. Every step we took seemed inexorably to lead to another more fateful, increasing the American investment of manpower, of treasure, of matériel, of blood. Yet the more we poured in troops and guns and planes, the worse the mess seemed to get. People began to call it a "dirty little war," echoing Kipling's phrase. Dirty it might be, but little it no longer was. "Don't knock it," a cynical pilot said, "it's the only war we have." Grim words. Grim thought. But where was happiness about Vietnam? The President had won an election by setting his face firmly against deeper involvement in Vietnam. He had rejected Barry Goldwater's call for bombing of the North. He would not, he assured the American people, lead us into a land war on the continent of Asia. But by 1966 he had largely followed the rejected Goldwater formula. He had escalated and escalated again. The force level had risen from 1,364 at the end of 1961 to 9,865 a year later, to 15,500 by the time of President Kennedy's assassination, to 125,000 in August, 1965; and in December, 1966, it stood just under 400,000. Month by bloody month it rose, no longer by creeping steps, but by great leaping bounds. No longer was it a question of whether to escalate. It was a question of how much, how fast, and could we build the ports, harbor facilities, airfields, barracks, roads, utilities and PX's fast enough to accommodate the surging flood of manpower. We had more men in Vietnam than we had put into Korea. More men than we had committed to any foreign war except the two World Wars. Long since, we had crossed the Rubicon of action beyond the 17th parallel. No longer did we debate bombing the North. We bombed the North. We bombed and bombed and bombed. Here the tonnage figures matched the fabulous manpower rise—300,000 tons of bombs in 1966. We bombed *our* Vietnam more than the North, but rapidly the gap was being narrowed. Our bomb factories could not meet the voracious demands of our planes. Again and again the air offensive had to be curtailed or slowed while fresh tonnages of explosives were rushed to the loading points, sometimes by costly and seldom-announced airlifts.

And with the rise in American troop levels, with the rise in the intensity of bombing, came the rise in tension in the United States and the world. Nations in Asia and Europe watched the massive application of American military power in Vietnam with anxiety or open hostility. The Western European press turned critical. Thousands in England, in France, in Scandinavia massed for protest demonstrations. Friendly foreign offices bit their tongues and offered mild reproofs. In Moscow there were sharp words. Warning followed warning that the war in Vietnam meant an end to détente, trade and cultural contacts, an end to negotiations on disarmament. It meant nuclear proliferation. Incidents arose. *Hello, Dolly!* was banned in Moscow. A partial freeze settled on Soviet-American relations which the Russians said could not be lifted so long as we continued "aggression" against their Southeast Asian ally, North Vietnam.

At home criticism mounted in Congress, led by Senators Mansfield and Fulbright. Critics snapped and barked in the House. Some Republicans said Johnson was doing too much. Others said he was doing too little. The mood of the country soured. There was a growing distaste for Washington explanations, disbelief in official statements, the frightening emergence of the "credibility gap"—a public relations phrase which simply meant that people no longer believed what their government told them.

It was against this background that I had dispatched my requests for permission to visit Hanoi. They evoked no response, but that did not surprise me. Communist countries seldom telegraph a punch. You fire off your cablegram, and the first intimation that it has struck home may be a cryptic message left with your hotel porter that if you call at such and such a legation you will learn something to your advantage.

I had few hopes of getting a Hanoi visa. Of all the Communist countries North Vietnam seemed most securely battened down. There were no resident Western correspondents at that time. Visitors, except for the occasional journalist from *Pravda* or *L'Humanité*, had almost never been admitted. Not even many delegations from the Communist countries visited Vietnam. Hanoi was the lone wolf of the Marxist world. To be sure, everyone knew it was getting aid, and substantial aid at that, from China and Russia. But there was no public acknowledgment of the fact by Hanoi.

The first outward sign of a break in this sealed society came with the admission of the British journalist James Cameron, who spent four weeks in the North in the autumn of 1965 and wrote a series of articles which were reprinted by *The New York Times*. His admission gave me some hope. True, he was English. True, he sympathized with the cause of North Vietnam and sharply criticized American policy. Still it was a breakthrough. I returned to my typewriter and batted out another communication to Hanoi.

A little later the name of Staughton Lynd, a Yale professor, flashed across the horizon. Together with Thomas Hayden and Herbert Aptheker, an American Communist party official, Lynd turned up in Hanoi. The invitation had been issued to Aptheker the previous summer during a peace congress in Helsinki. He was told that he might bring some companions and chose the left-wing Hayden and the non-Communist Lynd, liberal, son of the Middletown Lynds, young, dynamic, enormously popular with the Yale students.

When Lynd returned from Hanoi I sought him out for any ideas he might have or any aid he might render. I also wrote to a number of Soviet newspapermen and other Communists, asking their assistance in gaining entry to North Vietnam. Some helped. Some did not. Some failed even to answer my letter.

So my campaign for admission to Hanoi had gone on, week after week and month after month, pursued without response from North Vietnam but with the patient hope that one cable, one letter, one intervention might strike some spark, might arrive at that particular moment when the authorities had decided at long last that they would end their policy of isolation and permit the world to see what the war looked like from their side of the lines.

In the spring of 1966 Clifton Daniel, managing editor of *The New York Times,* proposed a new plan of action. He suggested that I attempt a trip around the periphery of Communist China, viewing that country from its frontiers, attempting to piece together the Chinese puzzle by talking with the people who knew the Chinese best—their neighbors.

But this was not all. From the frontier points I would renew my efforts to gain admission to China—and to North

Vietnam. It was Clifton's thought that in places like Hong Kong, Tokyo, New Delhi, Rangoon, Moscow or Ulan Bator I might pick up helpful hints on getting into the forbidden lands. And, of course, there were Communist Chinese and North Vietnamese embassies or consulates where I could make personal representations. There are often, Clifton felt, nuances to a situation that are apparent close at hand but invisible from afar. And the exercise would serve as an excellent background for a deeper understanding of the complexities of Asian Communism, which now loomed so large. I had seen this Communism only from the north—from the Soviet side, from Soviet Central Asia, from eastern Siberia and Mongolia. Now Vietnam had risen to dominate the American scene. Who in America knew anything of Vietnamese Communism, of the nature of its regime? We possessed a few secondhand accounts from the French who had experienced the movement in its Indochina phase; we had some scholarly studies and a number of propagandistic and self-serving books written either to justify American policy or to glorify Ho Chi Minh. But our ignorance was abysmal. And on China the depth of misunderstanding was, if anything, even greater.

Should my journey fail to open the door to Peking or Hanoi, it should at least provide the readers of *The Times* with a picture of the most dangerous Communist manifestations in the contemporary world—the tough, belligerent North Vietnamese regime and surging, turbulent China.

As a preliminary I renewed my passport and that of my wife, Charlotte, who would accompany me on the trip. At the same time I obtained State Department clearance to visit the three Asian Communist countries which are off-limits to Americans—China, North Vietnam and North Korea. My interest in North Korea was minimal. But if permission to enter it came through, I wanted to take advantage of this.

Charlotte and I spent two and a half months on the periphery of China. We traveled from Hong Kong to Cambodia, to Thailand, to Laos, to Burma (breaking another barrier when I became the first American correspondent to win admission to that country in four years), to New Delhi, to Sikkim, to Moscow, to Irkutsk, Ulan Bator and then via eastern Siberia to Khabarovsk and Nakhodka and by steamer to Tokyo. At every point I made soundings of the prospects of entry into Hanoi and Peking.

Once I struck favorable signs. In Pnompenh, the Cambodian capital, I was received by the North Vietnamese consul and permitted to file visa applications for Charlotte and myself. The consul was a little surprised when I said my wife wished to accompany me. He did not think conditions in North Vietnam were suitable for women travelers. But he accepted the applications and strongly hinted that we might get a favorable response. Elated, we extended our stay in Cambodia. We visited the ruins of the ancient city of Angkor. We saw the jungle temples and we rode the elephants. We traveled up to the frontier and inspected villages which had been hit by American shelling and bombing in the "nasty little war" across the border in South Vietnam. We heard the thunderous roll of American bombs as the nightly cargo of high explosives dropped on "Zone D"—the complex of Vietcong strongholds that lies northwest of Saigon and southeast of the Cambodian frontier. We waited. But nothing happened. Finally the North Vietnamese consul reported that the visas would not be granted "at the present time." Yet he held out hope for the future. He did not know when. But surely before the end of the year the visit would be possible. I took this word with a grain of salt. Experience had taught me that once an opportunity passes it seldom is repeated. But there was nothing to do but continue our trip and hope for the best. On my return to New York I sent new letters and cablegrams, more in stubbornness than in expectation, reminding Hanoi of my deep and continuing interest. No reply was forthcoming.

Then through the intercession of another *Times* reporter, John Corry, I won a fine and unexpected supporter for my project—Anne Morrison, widow of Norman Morrison, the American Quaker who had burned himself to death before the Pentagon, sacrificing his life in an effort to arouse the conscience of America against the war in Vietnam. Morrison had become a saint in North Vietnam—much more than a hero. His name was reverenced and, I was told, every North Vietnamese child knew his story. Mrs. Morrison wrote a letter in my behalf. I do not know precisely how to evaluate its effects. But after I reached Hanoi and learned of the sanctity in which Morrison's memory was held, I came to feel that Mrs. Morrison's letter, simple and direct, had probably been my best credential in getting the visa. Not only was Morrison a shining light in North Vietnam, but his widow and child were equally venerated throughout the land. This I learned, of course, only later.

So the situation continued until November, when an idea occurred to me. There would, no doubt, be a Christmas truce of some kind in Vietnam. Perhaps that would be an appropriate time for a visit to Hanoi. I sent off another wire—and waited. No response.

Then, on the morning of December 15, Seymour Topping, the foreign editor of *The Times*, walked over to my desk and put a cablegram before me.

"Does this say what I think it does?" he asked.

I read it carefully. There was a slight garble in transmission, but I thought the meaning was plain.

"Yes," I said, "I think it does."

"You're in," he said.

"Well," I replied cautiously, "let's wait and see. First let's send a cable for clarification and see if it really does mean to pick up the visa in Paris."

The next day the clarification arrived. We had interpreted the original message correctly. The visa to Hanoi did, indeed, await me in Paris. I was to fly to Pnompenh from Paris and go into Hanoi via the International Control Commission plane.

The visa could hardly have arrived at a more auspicious moment. For weeks the Vietnam story had dawdled along without special excitement. Now suddenly it had leaped into commanding headlines again. On December 13 and 14, or so the North Vietnamese authorities contended, American planes had penetrated into the center of Hanoi and for the first time dropped bombs within the principal urban area as distinguished from the industrial outskirts. The United States angrily denied the charge. Indeed, Robert McCloskey, the State Department spokesman, said he did not know what was meant by the "city limits" of Hanoi.

Now, if all went well, I should reach Hanoi in time to make an eyewitness examination of the bombing charge. It should be possible to determine whether American planes had bombed the city or whether the North Vietnamese were just making propaganda as the Pentagon contended. The Defense Department declared that if damage had occurred within the city it must be due to misfiring of the powerful SAM's—the surface-to-air missiles that the North Vietnamese employed against American bombers.

It might not be easy, I realized, for a nonexpert to determine whether damage had been caused by a missile or a bomb. But I could try to find out. And I would, in any event, be the first American to make an on-the-scene inspection.

There was another dramatic aspect of the December 13-14 bombing. North Vietnamese officials contended that the attacks signaled a new step in American escalation. Now, they said, the United States was extending the bombing offensive right into the capital itself. It seemed possible that I would arrive in Hanoi at a significant turning point in the war.

So it was that I found myself hurrying down Fifth Avenue in the holiday twilight, hurrying to the Air France ticket office, hurrying to a camera shop to pick up film and flash-bulbs, hurrying to a little shop to buy a trinket for Charlotte, a tiny substitute for the Christmas we would miss.

We spent a quiet weekend before the take-off for Paris—a quick last trip to the tranquillity of the Connecticut hills, brown now, the oaks leaf-armored, elms gray-bare against a thin blue sky, the fields rusty with fall plowing and bright with the yellow of winter grass. I looked out the kitchen window at the sturdy apple tree on the sloping hill, its shoulder bent against the wind, a few frost-carmined, wizened crabs still catching the sun in the high branches, and beyond on the far hills slow-moving heavy cows beside the great red barns. This was our land, our America, weathered by the winters, burned by the suns, the product of hundreds of years of rich evolution, of generation after generation in which we had been free of the foreign invader or the threat of foreign conquest; this was the pride of our society, the product of our philosophy, of our own individual and stubborn American way of life. I wondered what meaning this scene might have to a small, alien, Asian nation fighting in its rice paddies against a foe whose only tangible presence was the quick flash of silver wings, the high-pitched whine of super-jet engines, the thunderous crash of bombs.

Could one reporter's skill bridge this chasm in experience, comprehend the totality of an Asian existence and an American life which hardly shared a single point?

I did not know. I could try. This thought and the problems that must be resolved were wedged deep in my mind as Charlotte and I sat with Clifton and Margaret Daniel in the black leather chairs of a corner table in the Oak Room of the Plaza Hotel.

We talked very little of Hanoi, but before the evening ended Clifton made a remark that seemed entirely reasonable.

My departure was a complete secret. Only six of my associates at *The Times* knew I was going. Nothing was to be said publicly until I actually had my visa, actually had arrived in Pnompenh, actually was ready to board the I.C.C. plane.

"Then," said Clifton, "send me a cable that you are taking off. You know that we don't usually go in for exploitation on *The Times*. But this is a little unusual. I think we ought to advertise a bit and let people know that we have a man in Hanoi."

It seemed like a good idea, and I promised to send Clifton a cablegram so that our promotion people could get to work. Neither of us realized that my first dispatch from Hanoi would have an impact far beyond that of any announcements we might make over WQXR, the radio station of *The New York Times,* or any ads we might run in the big Sunday paper.

My first problem was to locate the North Vietnamese Mission. I had arrived at Orly airport on a gray, chilly, dispirited morning. Paris was a Laocoön of traffic. The trip from the airport to the hotel in Rue Richelieu took an hour. We crawled through the Place de la Concorde. I had never seen such traffic. Not even the Long Island Expressway on a Sunday evening in July was so bad. Gone was the derring-do of the Paris taxi driver. No room for his dashing exploits. Only room to inch and crawl, to inch and crawl through the Concorde and then into the density of the Place de l'Opéra. In Paris, too, it was Christmas, the sidewalks as thick with pedestrians as the streets with cars. Rich, indulgent Paris, windows lavish with diamonds, emeralds and rubies, with silks and velvets, with pearls and sables, with rare champagnes and bibelots. Paris, self-centered, inner-motivated, preoccupied. Not with war, but with the holiday, with the shopping, with getting away. Three million Parisians, *Paris-*

Soir said, would be leaving the city in the next three days. Away from the gloom, the cold, the fog. To the south, to the seashore, to the Alps, to the skiing. Anywhere. Out of the gray city. By train. By plane. No parking in the vicinity of the *gares* for the next five days. Special police to handle the throngs. Hundreds of special trains. It was Noël in Paris, and that was all anyone cared about.

I checked in at the hotel, started out again and finally located the North Vietnamese Mission. It had moved. But not far. From Rue d'Assas to a building just off Rue d'Assas on Rue le Verrier. It lay just beyond the University in Montparnasse and only a short stroll from the Luxembourg Gardens. Patiently the taxi breasted the tides of traffic. Again we pushed through the Place de la Concorde and across the bridge to the Invalides. Then along the Boulevard Saint-Germain and finally, abruptly, suddenly, pulled up at a gray stone building in a gray stone street just beyond the Law Faculté. There was no plaque on the door. No sign. No notice. Across the street I saw a *flic,* his cape flowing smoothly from his shoulders, his mien studiously casual but his policeman's eyes beadily inspecting me as I reached up to the iron bell and rang. There was a long wait. I rang again. The *flic* now eyed me with open interest. Finally I heard steps and the door opened a crack. An elderly Vietnamese woman stood there. I said, in English, that I had come for a visa. She regarded me uncomprehendingly. I switched to French. She looked equally baffled. Finally she said, *"Non, non."* I said, "Visa." She said, *"Non, non."* An impasse. I heard the chatter of people somewhere inside and caught the strong odor of oriental cooking. It reminded me of the smell in the Burmese Embassy in Moscow in the days when the bachelor Burmese Ambassador and his staff of five young Burmese cooked their own meals and did their own housekeeping.

Finally the woman had an idea. She ran into the next room and came back with an alarm clock. Speaking in Vietnamese, she held up the clock and pointed to two o'clock. I got the idea. Come back at 2 P.M. I held up two fingers. She nodded her head vigorously.

I turned away and walked slowly around the corner and into Rue d'Assas, under the vigilant scrutiny of the *flic*. It was just 1:30. A half-hour to wait. Impossible to return to the hotel. I sauntered past the Law Faculté, the youngsters, boys and girls, coming out from their classes and walking arm in arm down the street. Not like the youngsters on Fifth Avenue. These had a casualness, an openness, a directness, that was lacking in the American boys and girls. The girls' hair flowed back over their dark sweaters, their figures moved easily, their skirts were mostly short but some wore them long. Each seemed equally chic. I felt that the style of the boys and girls was a product of their own life, their own taste, that behind their casual grace lay not competitive, strident Seventh Avenue but the whim and mood of real people.

I strolled down the street and through the gate into the Luxembourg Gardens, along a swept-sand *allée* and to a bench on a path where a schoolmistress was leading her class of twenty-eight nine- and ten-year-olds, their faces rosy with the raw wind, each in a blue serge coat and skirt, each with hair in pigtails.

I looked past the gray marble busts of forgotten goddesses and savants and thought how far I had already come from the electrical tensions of America. Yet here in France only a historical moment ago there had been a conflict, a division in society that halted only on the verge of civil war—a crisis which had its origin in the same soil that now was possessing the American spirit, preoccupying the American will, devouring the American substance.

For Vietnam had not been an American problem—until we made it so. It had been a French problem. A terrible problem. One that arose from the debris of the French Empire which lay about the world at the end of World War II. Indochina and Algeria. First Indochina and, when that slipped away in 1954, Algeria.

Why, when France finally called it quits in Indochina, had we picked up the commitment? We had done this by our own positive action. It was not a casual deed. Indochina was not our responsibility. We had not backed France—at least not very strongly—in her hour of crisis.

Like most Americans I knew only in the vaguest of ways how we had gotten involved in Indochina. I was aware that President Roosevelt, envisioning the end of World War II, had been antagonistic to the perpetuation of the British, Dutch and French colonial empires. He had, in fact, deliberately proposed steps which he hoped would make it impossible for the French to regain their hold in Indochina—a hold which they had lost to Japan in the first months of the war. Roosevelt had refused to aid the French to reassert their position in Indochina. He had favored there—as in all the Asian and African areas—the rise of independent nationalist regimes.

What had happened? Where had this great design for the liquidation of colonial empires gone awry? The British had set themselves resolutely to the task which Winston Churchill had said he would refuse to undertake—to "preside over the liquidation" of the British Empire. Despite Churchill's statement, the British accomplished India's independence, as well as that of Pakistan, of Burma, of what came to be Malaysia, of Ceylon. Indeed, in eastern Asia there were few visible remnants of empire except for Hong Kong. This had not been achieved with ease. But it had been carried through with resolution. By and large England had not contributed to the world's agony a portfolio of new irreconcilable problems. For the most part the British had accomplished their difficult task with a bonus—they had earned the goodwill and friendship of the colonial peoples whose rule they had renounced. It had been harder for the Dutch. They had tried to hang on. But this had not worked, and grudgingly and in bitterness they were thrust out of what we now know as Indonesia. Worst of all had been the experience of the French. By desperate means they had reimposed their rule on Indochina. But the cost was deadly. A bloody guerrilla war which drained France of treasure, of manpower, of prestige. A war which put a generation of French military men on the rack, a war which brought France to the precipice of economic debacle, a war which split the country socially and politically so savagely that its consequences would be felt for decades, a war which, to put it simply and bluntly, the French lost. A war which they could not win.

It was this savage, complex, impossible, distant, puzzling situation in which, somehow, we Americans had become involved. At first only in a small way. At first in such a small way that few even realized we had taken a stake in the conflict or the area, but which each year like some cancer had grown and grown until it now dominated the whole horizon of our concern.

I did not know how much of Vietnam I would get to see. But I hoped at least that out there on the ground I might gain some comprehension of what we were doing—and how we had gotten there. I confessed to myself as I sat on the Luxembourg Gardens bench and waited for the clock's hands to swing around to 2 P.M. that I did not know the answers. Nor, indeed, even many of the questions which must be asked.

Presently I walked slowly back to the building at the corner of Rue d'Assas and Rue le Verrier. The *flic* nodded to me as I stood once again before the tall door and rang the bell. Again there was a long wait, then the Vietnamese woman appeared and with a gesture which seemed to me half exasperated and half despondent waved me up a short flight of stairs and into a waiting room that reminded me of the waiting rooms of all the Communist embassies I have ever waited in—stark leather-covered davenports, overstuffed chairs, the inevitable glass-topped coffee table, the wall adorned with the portrait of the leader (in this case Ho Chi Minh), the dark wooden sideboard, the closed door, the long wait before someone appeared. When he did he proved to be a young consular officer, smiling and pleasant. He knew absolutely nothing about my visa. He had never heard of me, but he was very agreeable. I assured him I had received a cablegram that a visa was waiting for me in the consulate. He vanished to inquire, and I had another long wait in which to wonder whether, in the end, this would prove to be one more wild-goose chase.

But my fears were not justified. Presently he returned with another consular employee, a woman. It was true. They could issue the visa. If I would just fill out the form, the visa would be ready tomorrow or, perhaps, the next day. But this posed a serious complication. To catch the irregularly scheduled International Control Commission plane that flies to Hanoi from Pnompenh, the capital of Cambodia, I had to leave on the Air France plane in the morning. There was no time for delay. Moreover, I had not only to collect the North Vietnamese visa. I had to obtain a transit visa for Cambodia.

A great flurry arose, but in the end it was determined that the North Vietnamese visa could be ready by 5 P.M. Meanwhile I was to go to the Cambodian Consulate and see what arrangements I could make there. Under the interested stare of the policeman I found a taxicab and started the long trip across town to the Cambodian Mission—a forty-five-minute drive through the Christmas traffic, now more dense than ever. Nothing, I have found, is ever very simple with visas. Or so it seems. Trouble started the moment I filled out the Cambodian form. The young woman took a glance and handed it back. "No visas are being given to journalists. Particularly not to American journalists," she announced.

I had an answer ready. I whipped out a cablegram which I had received just before leaving New York from Prince Norodom Sihanouk's *chef de cabinet*. It said that His Highness the Prince, Cambodia's chief of state, had graciously consented to permit my transit of his country.

The atmosphere changed. Three Cambodian consular officials shook my hand and concurred that the cablegram was indubitably genuine. But, alas, they had no instructions. Possibly the consul had a cablegram about my cablegram. But he was out of town. Perhaps I could come back tomorrow.

Tomorrow, I explained, was no good. Tomorrow I would be aboard the Air France plane bound for Pnompenh. They had a suggestion. No doubt the essential cablegram was at the very moment en route from Pnompenh. The consulate would be open until 6 P.M. Perhaps I could return. I agreed. What else could I do?

Back, then, across the traffic stream to the North Vietnamese Consulate. Again the lengthy wait at the door under the scrutiny of the *flic*. Not often, I imagined, did he find an American spending the day coming and going at the Vietnamese Mission. What could the American be up to? Some mysterious piece of business, no doubt. Some plot, perhaps. Something subversive, almost certainly.

Within the mission—cordiality, bright smiles. The visa was ready. I looked at it curiously. There it was. Visa to Hanoi. For the first time, for the very first time, I began to have a feeling of reality. It seemed to me in that moment that the trip would actually come off. Before, it had still been in the realm of the unreal. I had not permitted myself to think that it would happen. Now, sitting in the severely plain and ugly waiting room of the house on Rue le Verrier, it seemed clear to me that I would in fact go to Hanoi. Several thoughts crossed my mind, strongly and urgently. Once you are there what will you do? What will you be able to do? How will they treat you? What manner of an expedition had I got myself into? After all, an American going to Hanoi, behind the enemy lines? I shook the thoughts out of my mind, thanked the smiling consular officials, slipped on my coat, descended the steps and went out the door. The *flic* could restrain himself no longer. He sauntered briskly across the street and asked me how I was getting on with my business. I shook my head negatively, muttered, *"Je ne parle pas français,"* and hurried off into Rue d'Assas. He looked at me with skeptical, troubled eyes. I wondered what kind of report he was going to be able to make. Something for the Sûreté to puzzle over, I felt sure. Well, it was not the first time, and it would not be the last. There would be a good deal of puzzling, I thought, in the various security and intelligence services of the world before my trip was over.

But there was the matter of the Cambodian visa. Back I plunged through the maze of cars to the Cambodian Mission. Up the halting *ascenseur* to the fourth floor. Smiles, pleasant greetings, friendly words—but no visa. No cablegram had been received. Come back tomorrow. Again my explanation. Tomorrow was too late. Much consultation. Nothing could be done. But a bright afterthought: Just go ahead to Pnompenh. There they will have instructions. You can get your visa at the airport. I heard those words with a sinking feeling. But there seemed no alternative but to go on. I could not wait for the missing instructions from Pnompenh to turn up.

I decided not to worry. By one means or another, certainly, I would manage to get to Hanoi. I had the North Vietnamese visa. Back at the hotel I examined it closely. It bore no time limit. It merely read for *"entrée"* and *"sortie."* Clifton Daniel had said: "Stay as long as you can. Write everything you can. Do everything you can. See everything you can." I thought in terms of a two-or-three-week stay. That should be possible with this visa. Perhaps longer—if I actually wanted to stay longer. On an impulse I took out one of my cameras, fitted it with a flashbulb, propped the visa up on the bed and took a picture of it. Undoubtedly the visa would be collected when I left Hanoi. Since it was on a separate piece of paper, there would be no mark in my passport, no tangible evidence that I had ever been in the North Vietnamese capital. Now, at least, I'd have a picture for a souvenir.

Enough worrying. I had the visa. I had my plane ticket. I went off to Les Halles with my *Times* colleagues, Henry Tanner and Richard Mooney, and their wives. We dined in the Pharamond, an exquisitely middle-class French restaurant, all old tiles of pears and pear trees, rich red mahogany and brass, a tight circular staircase rising in the center of the small room up which coats were whisked and below it a *cave* so narrow that a man must stoop to descend for the wines, tables for not more than thirty guests, the proprietor, a solid man with his photograph displayed over the cashier's desk, two waiters and two boys. The menu included *belons,* which tasted of copper, entrecôte, tangy and tender, pommes soufflés, crisp and crunchy, an apple tart and hot bitter coffee so chicory it made the hair rise on the back of my neck. When we left we found the street outside half blocked with boxes and crates and baskets and trucks, berries and melons and fruits and vegetables. Les Halles was beginning to go to work and the Pharamond was closing its doors. Our heels echoed on the granite paving as we walked to the cars. It would be, I thought, a long time before I would again experience the full-bodied measure of this French civilization—so close-grained, so complexly knit, so fiercely concentrated upon itself and upon the ritualistic assuagement of the senses—the tastes, the smells, the sights, the sensations, the satisfactions of the body (and the mind)—in a manner so various, so subtle, so sophisticated.

This was the France which had sat on the backs of the Vietnamese for two-thirds of a century. This was the France which in her power and her majesty had set the stage for the tragedy toward which I was making my way. This was the France which with the decline of her force had striven so stubbornly to hold on to the frayed vestige of empire in Southeast Asia. This was the France which now cynically, now passionately, watched us struggle with the legacy she had left in Indochina. I wondered what echoes of Paris might await me in Hanoi.

There were Christmas carols at Orly as I awaited the Pnompenh plane. Neat, intelligent-looking French schoolmistresses were taking hundreds of schoolchildren to see the exhibition of crèches—modernistic crèches which turned the Nativity into a "Happening," a Picassoesque crèche which depicted an elongated Christ child and Madonna in pastel blue and rose, traditional crèches from many lands and an exquisite antique from seventeenth-century Florence. Through the airport came the children, class after class, their eyes brown and sparkling, their little figures forming serpentines among the hurrying travelers.

Not many passengers turned up for the Pnompenh flight, and I sat with my typewriter and attaché case, bundled my cameras in my lap, and thought about Christmas. I hated being away. Not only missing Christmas with Charlotte but missing Christmas with Stephan, my nineteen-year-old son, and missing the wedding of my eldest son, Michael, and Susie

on New Year's Eve. Of course, the trip was important. I had
not had a more important assignment in my life. But it came
at a difficult, impossible moment. A time when I wanted to
be at home, when I should be at home. For a dozen reasons.
All of them good and all of them bound to those I loved, to
Charlotte and the boys and the rest of the children.

But I would not be at home. I was waiting for the Air
France plane to take off. One more holiday in a distant land.
There had been so many in the past. Wartime Christmases. A
miserable Christmas in Teheran waiting to go from Iran into
Russia in 1943. The Moscow Christmases—I could not bear
to think of them. But this was different. Would I be in Hanoi
for Christmas? Did they celebrate it there? I had no notion. I
had read that they had savagely persecuted the Roman Catholic Church. Perhaps there were no churches in Hanoi.

I pondered anew about my mission—it seemed obvious
that it implied more than the mere acceptance of an importu-
nate American correspondent who wanted to see North Vietnam. Why, actually, had the authorities decided to let me in?
What was the significance of their action? A Communist state
does not undertake such a move without a reason.

What might be that reason?

I could think of several. I knew that the principal concern
which North Vietnamese officials had expressed in the past
about letting me—or someone else—in was that the action
might be misunderstood, might be thought a sign of weak-
ness, a sign that they were slackening in their resolution to
fight the United States. I suspected that my visa had not
come through last June because just at that time they had
given a visa to Chester Ronning, the retired Canadian diplomat, a man who had made several unofficial trips to Hanoi
seeking to sound out various peace possibilities, a man deeply
respected in North Vietnam and China and a man who was
by coincidence the father-in-law of Seymour Topping, the
foreign editor of *The New York Times*. I had heard that the
North Vietnamese supposed that if they gave a visa to me at
the same time they gave one to Ronning the United States
would believe they were softening up. And this, they thought,
would make the United States hit them twice as hard.

I didn't know whether that reasoning was accurate or not.
But certainly they still wished to maintain an attitude of out-
ward strength and no compromise toward the United States.
From that standpoint the visa was to be understood as a show

of self-confidence: they were willing to let even an American journalist see what was going on behind their lines, how strong they were, how resolute their determination to fight to the end. But was this the whole story? I didn't think so. I thought that in reality this action was one of those curiously ambiguous signals which Communist regimes sometimes give—a signal of strength, to be sure, but also an action designed to create the image of a country which was more reasonable, more understandable, more down to earth than we had reason to believe. At long last the North Vietnamese had learned that the world pictured them as an oyster which could not be opened, as a people uninterested in the opinion or attitude of others.

But why should they now wish to change their image abroad? Only, I thought, because the war is shifting its ground. Either they fear it is moving into a new and wholly unmanageable stage—either they believe the United States is about to make the war total by moving its land forces north of the 17th parallel or by landing them on the North Vietnamese coast—or there may be factors on their side which are changing the equation of force. What could those factors be? I knew of two and they were interconnected. The first was China and the boiling, dangerous pot of China's "cultural revolution," the multitude of signs that China might explode, might blast through the ceiling, might fall apart in disastrous civil war. The other was the deadly quarrel between Moscow and Peking, which grew more harsh with every passing day.

Fearing the quarrel with China, believing that it might evolve into armed conflict, might not Moscow have finally given the private word to Hanoi that it was time to change, time to create an atmosphere in which negotiation and a negotiated settlement would be possible? I did not know. But this seemed possible. There was an associated thought. Perceiving the danger signals from Peking, the symptoms of possible internal disorder or a Chinese-Soviet clash which would disrupt the flow of supplies, might not Hanoi on its own and without a Moscow initiative be seeking to set the stage for a possible peaceful settlement?

I could not guess the answers yet. But I thought it would be surprising if I did not solve the puzzle when I got to Hanoi. These answers, at least, should be made patently clear.

I took out my diary and entered a notation of my thoughts:

I think my trip is supposed to convey an image of confidence, of hardihood in the face of U. S. bombing; of horror at what we have done; a positive image of North Vietnam but at the same time it is designed to bring peace or a truce or talks nearer, in part by assuring the U. S. and U. S. opinion that the present policy is not winning; in part by showing a reasonableness on the part of North Vietnam.

We were airborne now, moving up in a great circle through the dull gray cloud that overhung Paris, then out into the sunny openness of the upper atmosphere. The stewardess was making the usual announcements and I was only half listening. Suddenly I pricked up my ears. Something about Tirana. What did that mean? The scheduled route was Paris-Athens-Cairo-Teheran-Karachi-Pnompenh-Shanghai. I listened closely as she began the announcement in English. I had not been mistaken. We were bound for Albania. First stop Tirana. I could not conceive why. We flew on over the high cloud. Presently we were above the Alps with a fine view of Mont Blanc. Then down over Italy, across Florence, the Adriatic, lowering clouds and then down, down through endless overcast which broke only a few hundred feet above the ground as we flew above irrigated, closely cultivated fields toward the Tirana airport. The rain was spitting; the land looked poor, sulky and angry, the buildings gray and dismal in the downpour. Even the airport infield was irrigated and planted with rice or winter rye. Albania, I thought, must be short on food. As the aircraft came in for the landing, the stewardess hastily announced that the authorities would not permit anyone to leave the plane during our stay.

The plane scudded down the runway. It had been lengthened since I last was there in 1957. Then it was just as the Italians had built it when they took over from King Zog in 1939. I well remembered the unusual hexagonal paving blocks. Now these seemed to form but a tiny midsection of the long course.

Progress had come to Tirana in the form of a jet runway. I could see no other visible sign. The people looked sodden and miserable, huddled in their ponchos against the rain. As we taxied up to the apron before the low-lying airport building, little bands of dreary Albanian soldiers, their guns in hand, took up sentry duty all around the plane. No one, it was clear, was going to be permitted to touch foot on sacred Albanian soil. Good, I thought. I will not be tempted to violate the provisions of my passport. I had been cleared for travel to every nation in Europe and Asia—with the solitary exception of Albania.

I pressed my nose to the window and stared out at the rain and the bedraggled soldiers. No one else was in sight. Two Albanian customs officers, a dark little man and a snub-nosed blonde girl, came aboard. They had no business. No one was getting off at Tirana. But why, I puzzled, had the Air France liner halted here? There could be no traffic. It was not a scheduled stop. There seemed no answer to the question. We waited on the apron. No one came into sight. Presently a Czech airliner touched down and taxied over near us. Its door opened. No one got out. The Czech airliner sat quietly. So did we.

The scene was desolate except for a trim row of thirty MIG fighters parked some distance away. Two, I noticed, were poised on a feeder lane, ready to roar onto the main runway at a second's notice. Who did they think might attack? I was not a specialist in MIG's. But I presumed these must be old MIG-17's, relic of Soviet aid in the days before Tirana broke with Moscow and declared its undying allegiance to Peking.

An hour passed and nothing happened. Then I noticed people straggling out of the airport building and walking between two rows of shrubbery that led to the apron. They paused there. Bouquets were presented, kisses exchanged. There was much hugging. In twos and threes the passengers began to hurry across the concrete expanse in the rain and into the plane. On and on they came. I counted as they crowded through the first-class compartment and into the almost empty economy section, laden with bundles, some carrying violins, some accordions, some young men and some young women, all poorly dressed but their faces flushed with excitement and, I suspected, Albanian slivovitz. They came on and on. I counted ten, fifteen, twenty, thirty, forty passengers. And there was no stopping. The plane began to fill up. Somewhere over fifty I lost count. Later the Air France stewardess gave me the correct count—seventy-one. It was a company of Albanian singers and dancers and they were en route to China for a two-month tour. Air France was flying them on charter as far as Shanghai.

We flew on over the Mediterranean, and I watched them as they strolled through the airport at Cairo, inspecting the German cameras, the Japanese transistor radios, the Scotch

whisky, the French perfume, the postcards of the pyramids
and the transparencies of King Tut's tomb. No one who had
not been informed, seeing this group of men in shiny serge
suits, their poorly ironed collars, their thin wool scarfs, the
young women in their shirtwaists, their flowered cotton
dresses, their shabby coats and yellow imitation-leather hand-
bags, would have guessed that they were performing artists,
the cream, perhaps, of Albania's culture. He would have more
readily supposed them to be a group of poor emigrants not
unlike those who landed at Ellis Island a half-century ago.
Watching as they strolled about the dismal Cairo airport
waiting room, I guessed that perhaps fifty-five or sixty of
them were actual artists. The others, the men with shifty
glances, nervously hovering over the idling groups, hardly
masking their officiousness, were the plain-clothes police detachment, there to see that no Albanian kicked over the
traces, that none defected to the United Arab Republic or, a
bit later on, to Cambodia or even China.

It was, I thought, a striking measure of the radical disarray
into which the Communist world had fallen that the Alba-
nians were compelled to dig into their skimpy hoard of foreign exchange to pay the French to fly their song-and-dance
troupe to China, skirting the Soviet Union. Once the Alba-
nians would have traveled via Aeroflot, the Soviet line, on the
old and familiar route from Tirana to Moscow and then out
across the Siberian vastness.

If Communist regimes now had to use capitalist airlines
and pay hard currency to move cultural groups from one
Communist country to another, the differences within the
bloc could hardly be more serious. And if Hanoi had not yet
begun to take into account the effects this conflict might at
any moment have on its war effort, it was time that it did.

I slept through the long, long flight from Cairo across most
of Asia—across the deserts of Arabia, the wastes of Iran, the
mountains of India, the steaming Gulf of Bengal. When I
awakened I could see below a sandy coastline—Burma or
Thailand. Cambodia was not far distant.

The plane came down in the hot tropical sun at Pnompenh. The temperature was 100 degrees in the shade—as hot
as it had been when I was there in June, or hotter. I was
amazed. Now I would see how good the Cambodian Consulate's advice was. Whether, indeed, my transit visa was wait-

ing at the airport. I handed over my passport to the control officer.

"You have no visa," he said.

"I know," I replied. "I understand a transit visa is to be issued here. I am in transit to Hanoi."

He consulted his colleagues.

"We have no authorization," he said.

I whipped out my cablegram from the *chef de cabinet*.

"Ah," he said, "yes. But unfortunately we have not been advised."

I suggested that he might communicate with the *chef de cabinet*.

"Regrettably," he apologized, "the telephone to the airport is not working today."

Finally a brilliant thought dawned. They would get a car and go into the city and consult the *chef de cabinet*. Meantime I could go into the café and have a Coca-Cola. An hour and a half later word came through. The visa was ready. I picked up my baggage and made my way into town, to the cool depths of the Hotel Le Royale. Everything seemed in order—visas, transportation. The next morning, unless something interfered, the International Control Commission plane would pull in on its biweekly circuit from Saigon. I would clamber aboard and be on my way to Hanoi. The I.C.C. was a relic of the 1954 Geneva agreements. It was supposed to watch over the observance of the agreements in the four areas of North and South Vietnam, Cambodia and Laos.

I was lucky to have a reservation on the I.C.C. plane. It flew only three times every two weeks, and often, for one reason or another, the flight was canceled. I was to go on the Friday plane, and there would not be another for a week. Transportation to Hanoi seemed to me to be remarkably fragile. Last June when I had been in Cambodia there was direct service from Pnompenh to Hanoi via Royal Air Cambodge. But this had been discontinued because of the dangers of flying over Laos and North Vietnam amid the intensifying air activity. Service had been withdrawn after an Air Cambodge plane had been warned back from the approaches to Hanoi by two American F-105's presumably en route to attack objectives in the Hanoi area.

The only other air service to Hanoi of which I was aware was a Chinese feeder line which flew in from Nanning. It was, I understood, as irregular as the I.C.C. flight. Presumably it was the route used by Russians and other Communists. It was not, however, a practical way for Americans to fly to Hanoi because of Chinese objections to transit of their country by U.S. citizens. True, the Chinese permitted some to come in as guests of North Vietnam, but I did not believe they were likely to let an American correspondent travel via that route.

It seemed to me that Hanoi badly needed a more reliable air service than was provided by the itinerant I.C.C. plane or the limited Chinese service.

Exhausted after forty-eight hours of almost continuous travel, I threw myself on the cool bed at Le Royale but found I could not sleep. I rummaged through my attaché case for something to read and found a copy of Le Monde, which I had picked up in Paris. My eyes idly ran down the page and suddenly halted. There was a dispatch by a Le Monde correspondent, Jacques Decornoy, just back from Hanoi. I began to read with fascination. The U.S. bombing, he reported, was devastating the country. He had visited a small railroad town which had been wiped off the map. Nothing was left of it. The name of the town was Phuly. He had visited a textile center south of Hanoi which had been heavily damaged— great sections of the residential part of the city had been destroyed. The American bombs, he reported, were erasing substantial portions of the civilian life of North Vietnam along with military objectives. He told of having seen a section of the railroad running south from Hanoi. It had been smashed by American bombing. Within a few hours the freight was moving forward on bicycles.

I hoped that the reports of Le Monde's man would not take all the edge off my own correspondence. I folded the paper up and put it back in my attaché case. Later on it should be useful to compare his reports with what I myself might see.

The I.C.C. plane was late. I sat on the terrace at the Pnompenh airport and drank Coca-Cola and worried about the
flight. The plane had taken off from Saigon, Airport Control
said, but it was already an hour overdue and I wondered if
something had gone wrong. I was not alone as I sipped my
Coca-Cola. An officer of the North Vietnamese Embassy had
come to see me off and several East European diplomats
joined us. They had heard I was going to Hanoi and were
certain that my visit had some deep diplomatic significance.
They associated my trip with a message dispatched to Secretary General U Thant of the United Nations a few days earlier by U.S. Ambassador Arthur Goldberg, supporting the
Secretary General's efforts to try to mediate the conflict. Although I assured them that my trip was quite unofficial, that
the State Department had nothing to do with it, I realized
that they did not believe me. Certainly, they insisted, something will be forthcoming. They left no doubt of their deep

hopes that the visit would prove to be a positive step toward peace. Each expressed concern about the war and the great dangers it implied.

In the forefront of the diplomats' concern was China, and they did not attempt to conceal this. What might be the upshot of the rampaging "cultural revolution" and the Red Guards they did not pretend to know. But China lent a special atmosphere of crisis to Vietnam and the war. One of the diplomats had been in Peking and knew China well. But, he said, he did not think he would go back "until the dust settles." He had made a trip to his home capital in Eastern Europe during the autumn but deliberately avoided going by way of Peking. "It's too complicated there," he said.

I heard a bit of gossip which gave me cause for thought. A young African journalist had just visited Pnompenh and had applied for a visa to North Vietnam. He was a Communist and an ardent supporter of the Chinese line. Hanoi gently but firmly refused his request, telling him that the time was "not appropriate." Thus, at the moment when the North Vietnamese were preparing to welcome a correspondent from the capitalist West, a newsman from the country with which they were at war, they were rejecting an application from a man whose ideology, I would have thought, must come very close to their own. Was not the Vietnam war, as viewed from Peking, the opening phase of the great world revolutionary struggle which would spread from the jungles and mountains of Southeast Asia gradually around the globe, encompassing all of Asia, Africa and Latin America? And was not the young African in the vanguard of this struggle?

It was a small straw in the wind. But not an insignificant one. When a Communist country begins to admit enemy nationals and excludes some of its close friends and sympathizers, something important is afoot. The instinct of the East European diplomats seemed correct to me. My visit clearly had important implications.

We sat on the pleasant terrace and talked about Cambodia and the war. There seemed to have been little change since my visit six months earlier. Prince Sihanouk was still deeply concerned lest his country be sucked into the conflict or South Vietnam and Thailand join forces to attack and destroy Cambodia. He was at that moment at the frontier inspecting areas where constant skirmishing was in progress between Cambodian and Thai forces. Recently several high-ranking officers in the Khmer Serai, the Free Cambodia movement which the Prince contended was sponsored by South Vietnam and Thailand with tacit United States collaboration, had been captured and executed. There were recurrent episodes along the Cambodian borders, attacks by American planes and sometimes, it was said, by ground forces, recurrent charges by the United States that the Vietcong were crossing into Cambodia and using that country as a sanctuary for outfitting and recuperation, and indignant denials by the Cambodians. Charges that Cambodia was providing rice to the Vietcong had died away, probably because a sharply reduced rice crop in 1966 had left Cambodia with a severe shortage in export supplies. Since rice was the principal earner of Cambodian foreign exchange and since the Cambodian economy was in a shaky state, the likelihood of Cambodia's shipping rice to anyone not prepared to pay in hard currency was slim. Some rice, I heard, was still going to the Vietcong by the traditional smuggling routes down the Mekong River and across the frontier on Route Nationale No. 1. It was being paid for in hard cash. And, of course, large quantities of consumer goods from the Saigon black market and the United States Army PX depots were coming in across the border for sale to Cambodians.

Cambodia's most serious crisis, I heard, related to shortages of petroleum products—gasoline, oil and kerosene—that normally came up the Mekong River from Saigon. South Vietnam had put restrictions on Cambodia's Mekong shipping which might, it was said, severely pinch the economy. That these moves had had any effect thus far I strongly doubted, judging by the large numbers of Mercedes-Benzes, Renaults, Fiats, Chevrolets and Hillmans I saw in the Pnompenh streets.

Just before noon the I.C.C. plane touched down, a venerable silvery four-motored Constellation which, I was told, had been in service ever since the air route was established after the Geneva Conference of 1954. I boarded and we took off. There were a dozen other passengers—the No. 2 man in the French Consulate-General in Hanoi, bringing diplomatic pouches up from Saigon, two German-speaking Polish members of the I.C.C. returning to their posts in Vientiane, the administrative capital of Laos, four or five junior Indian staff members of the I.C.C., a young American student en route to Vientiane, several persons whose identity I could not immedi-

ately fix and a cheery Canadian staff sergeant who spent the
trip regaling me with stories about the I.C.C. plane's
narrow—and not so narrow—escapes. The sergeant made the
trip almost every week. He did not enjoy it. He would fly up
from Saigon and return on the same plane, leaving Hanoi
early the next morning. I learned for the first time that the
plane flew into Hanoi only after dark.

"It's much too dangerous in daylight," the sergeant said.
"We will fly to Vientiane and stay there until dusk. Then we
will go on to Hanoi—if we are lucky."

According to his account, almost everyone in northern
Laos and North Vietnam was armed with a rifle and shot at
any plane in the sky—regardless of whether or not it bore the
great "CIC" marking as did our Constellation.

"They shoot first," he said. "I don't think they even bother
to look. They just assume any plane in the sky is out to bomb
or strafe them. And they are usually right."

It was over this area early in 1966—the location never precisely ascertained—that the I.C.C. lost a sister plane to the
one in which we were flying. The aircraft was on its way
from Vientiane to Hanoi. About three-quarters of an hour
out of Hanoi it reported in. Then it vanished. No trace had
ever been found. It was presumed the aircraft was shot down
over the Laotian mountains.

There had been other incidents, the sergeant said. Not infrequently the plane turned back to Vientiane because bombing or air activity was in progress in and around Hanoi. The
night flight procedure had been adopted because American
air activity seldom occurred in North Vietnam after dark and
thus the prospect of involvement in a dogfight was reduced.
At night there was also less danger of gunfire from mountain-
eers or accidental attack by North Vietnamese ground batteries. The Chinese who flew in from Nanning, it was said,
followed the same precautions and never approached Hanoi
except under cover of darkness.

The Canadian sergeant's conversation hardly eased the tensions which I found rising as I drew nearer and nearer to the
object of my mission. A sad-eyed Vietnamese stewardess,
who had lost her husband on the companion I.C.C. plane
which had been shot down, served a lunch of fricasseed
chicken, and about 2:30 P.M. we landed at the Vientiane airport. It seemed hardly changed since I had last seen it in
June—the same three white I.C.C. helicopters stood on the

ramp and beside them a dozen Air America planes, little Piper Cubs, Swiss mountain aircraft, lumbering old fat-bellied transports. Air America was an acknowledged subsidiary of the C.I.A. There were military aircraft in half a dozen places, and I saw bays off at the edge of the field where neat squadrons, possibly bombers or fighter-bombers, were parked. There had been a great flood during the summer and the waters of the Mekong had covered the airfield to a depth of six or eight feet. But now operations were back to normal—the curious Laotian normal in which, under the mantle of "neutrality," some of the most savage air operations of the Southeast Asian war are carried out.

Within the airport building I saw the customary mix of American pilots, restless American wives, svelte Vietnamese girls and middle-aged American personnel. Outside along the access bays was parked a row of Mercedes-Benz sedans—the cars of Air America pilots. As the pilots came in from their missions, sleek little service trucks, just like those which operate at La Guardia or Kennedy, scooted out to the planes, took aboard the crews and whisked them back to the terminal. There they climbed into their Mercedes-Benzes and rolled off into town. Sometimes a wife and children waited in the car, waiting for daddy to come back from the afternoon's bombing to drive him into town for a nice cool beer in an air-conditioned villa.

"This is the strangest country in the world," a Polish diplomat observed as we sat in the airport. "I would not have believed such things could happen anywhere as happen every day in Laos."

I was sure that he was right. Later on, when I talked in Hanoi with a foreign Communist who had visited the Laotian hill country, who had seen the pro-Communist Pathet Lao forces there, who had experienced the attacks of American bombers, raining down explosives on a twenty-four-hour round-the clock schedule, I could only concur in his observation. The Communist told of visiting a Pathet Lao headquarters in the hill caves of northeastern Laos not far from Vietnam—he did not specify where and I did not ask. I guessed that it must be near the famous Ho Chi Minh Trail down which the North Vietnamese send supplies, men and munitions through the Laotian mountains to the Vietcong in South Vietnam.

"You cannot imagine what it was like in the headquarters

of these people," the Communist said. "Never is there any halt in the bombing. Not at night. Not by day. One day we were in the cave. The bombing went on and on. The toilet was in another cave only twenty yards away. We could not leave. We could not even run the twenty yards. It was too dangerous."

Within the caves, he said, the Pathet Lao had set up a hospital, a printing press, a small textile mill, a bakery, a shop for making arms and ammunition. Everything in the caves.

"Nothing else is safe," he said. According to him, the American planes came over on a constant schedule, a dozen varieties of planes, some of them the newly outfitted DC-3's laden with machine guns that pour a hurricane of fire into the ground.

"You can't imagine what they sound like," he said. "It's like a fireworks factory exploding. Such a racket. And so dangerous."

There were, he added, other American planes firing "bullpup" missiles—guided rockets for which the pilot codes instructions. He programs a missile and can fire it about four and a half miles from his target. The bullpup will make right angle turns, dive, rise and corner.

"They can even program the damn things to dive into a cave," the Communist declared. "Fortunately, it's not easy to hit the entrance."

There were bombers and fighter-bombers, he said, spraying the area of the caves with high explosives and with deadly antipersonnel weapons like the "lazy dog," which spews out three hundred individual bombs, each the size of a baseball. These fragment and fill the air with murderous steel particles.

"At night they come over in pairs," said the Communist. "One is a flare plane. It drops enormous flares on parachutes which light up the countryside as though it were daylight. That plane photographs the terrain. It also observes. If there is a sign of life, a movement on the ground, it signals a second plane, which sweeps in and lays down a carpet of steel and explosive. That goes on all night long, one pair of planes after another."

The people in the caves, he continued, venture out only at dusk and dawn. They must come out because they are dependent upon rice terraces and patches of sweet potato and other vegetables for food. Only at dusk and dawn, he declared, is it safe to hoe and transplant—and often it is not safe then.

"The planes come again and again, always taking pictures," the Communist said. "When they see a sign of agriculture, or a sign of trails being used, they zero in on that neighborhood and simply cover it with bombs. I can't imagine how much tonnage they are dropping up there in the hills. It must be colossal."

This was the other side of the picture which spread out before me on the long December afternoon as we waited for darkness so that we might resume our journey to Hanoi. The Communist perhaps exaggerated a bit about American air activity. But perhaps not. For the following month, on my return flight from Hanoi to Vientiane, we arrived over the airfield just before 6 A.M., but could not land. We circled in a broad traffic pattern, around and around, over the Mekong River, over the fields, over the countryside for a good half-hour, waiting for a break in the steady traffic—the bombers going out on their dawn runs or coming back, the reconnaissance planes, the little Piper Cubs, up to goodness knows what mission. We watched them take off and land as we flew in our circle. Finally we descended and taxied past the three white I.C.C. helicopters. They were parked as they had been when I first saw them in June. I had not known then what I now knew. That the I.C.C. no longer had pilots to fly them. They stood there under the wings of the big Air America planes, a symbol of the futility of the International Control Commission and the concept of a neutral Laos.

We took off from Vientiane about 5:30 P.M. I was interested to see that the A-28 bombers were on precisely the same schedule as when I was last at the airport in June. The same little group buzzed down the far runway and took off, one by one, toward the north for the late-afternoon bombing. Then came our turn. We flew a long dogleg to the north and then turned east. It was safer that way, the Canadian sergeant said. The light faded quickly and soon we were flying over mountainous country dimly seen in the light of the quarter-moon. The sergeant had made an acquisition in Vientiane. He had bought a fat goose which he was taking to his comrades in Hanoi—the five men who constituted the Canadian component of the I.C.C. mission there. It was a live goose and he had put it into one of the big scarlet Canadian canvas diplomatic pouches. Trussed though it was, it flopped and wriggled on the seat beside the sergeant.

"It's a Christmas goose," he said. "I doubt if they can get one in Hanoi." As I watched the goose tug and strain, my mind went back to World War II and a Christmas I spent flying from Cairo to Teheran, and to an American captain who bought some Christmas turkeys in Hamirabad, near Baghdad, and put them in gunnysacks aboard our DC-3. Once they had broken loose. I hoped the sergeant had better luck. A goose or turkey hunt in a pitching transport plane was not my idea of amusement.

We flew on steadily in the darkness. The air turned rough and I sensed that we were going over a mountain range. About 7:15 P.M. we began to lose altitude. I looked out the window and saw lights off to the left, lights picking out a pattern of streets. Hanoi was not quite blacked out, but it looked from the air more like a small, distant village than the metropolitan capital of a country. We turned sharply and came down swiftly in the harsh glare of portable field lights and a flare path which switched off before we had taxied to the end of the field. It was impossible to see whether any other aircraft were parked there. We turned and taxied slowly up to a low airport building, which was dimly lighted, and halted amid several large puddles. It had been raining and it had only just stopped. The aircraft engines died and the plane fell into total darkness. There was no auxiliary power generator to provide us with light.

I got up and groped for my typewriter and cameras. The rear door opened, and I could see by a flashlight in the stewardess's hand that two North Vietnamese border policemen had entered the cabin. They stood near the exit examining passports.

I made my way toward them, their dark faces thrown into deep shadow by the wavering flashlight. I handed them my passport and they looked at it curiously. I doubted that they had ever seen an American passport before. Patiently they leafed through it and then consulted a dog-eared list of typewritten names. Finally they smiled and waved me past. I walked over to the hatch and down the aluminum ladder. In the dusk I could see several men. Two of them detached themselves from the crowd and came up to me. One spoke softly: "Mis-ter Har-ri-son?"

"Yes," I responded.

"Welcome to Hanoi," the little man said and motioned me toward the murky depths of the air terminal.

Hanoi. I was behind the enemy lines.

We walked through the pleasantly cool, pleasantly fresh,
pleasantly fragrant night air and into the small terminal,
sparsely furnished with a few benches, some wooden tables, a
few chairs. The lights were flickering but the rooms were
scrupulously clean. Half a dozen border police and customs
officials awaited us with the usual customs and currency
forms. Meticulously I ticked off the items: no opium, no
firearms, no gold bars, no radio transmitters, no diamonds or
other precious stones. I was carrying two cameras, a typewriter, an alarm clock, a wrist watch, a thousand dollars in
traveler's checks, another thousand in currency. No problem
with any of these items. Cameras and black-and-white film
were permitted but not color film. The taking of color pictures was barred. Color film had to be turned over to customs, to be returned on my exit. The reason, it was explained, was that all film had to be developed in Hanoi be-

fore being taken out of the country and facilities for developing color film did not exist.

I was behind the enemy lines. But the formalities were not much more rigorous than they would have been coming in through customs at Kennedy. The two officials who had been assigned to meet me—one from the Foreign Ministry, one from the Journalists Association—talked easily and chattily in rather rusty English. They wanted to know when I had left New York. They asked about Charlotte. They had heard that she had applied for a visa in June and inquired why she had not accompanied me now. I explained that there had not been time, and besides, there were family responsibilities in New York: my eldest son was being married on New Year's Eve. I had come in spite of that, but she had had to stay behind.

The atmosphere grew homey. They asked about my family, the age of the children and what the weather was like in New York.

We spent twenty minutes filling out the forms, pulling the color film out of my bag and getting my passport stamped. Then we emerged into the night and got into a Soviet Volga—a medium-size car something like a ten-year-old Plymouth. The chauffeur touched the starter, the motor coughed, belching a kind of evil-smelling, low-quality gasoline I had not smelled since my wartime days in Russia, and we moved down a narrow lane, through the airport grounds and onto a busy road. Everything was dark and gloomy. There were small lamps dangling at street intersections, but the headlights of the cars were dimmed or obscured by shields designed to conceal the beams from overflying aircraft. I was almost instantly aware of the movement of people in the darkness, and I could see vague files of bicycles silently moving in both directions, throngs of burdened men and women and a steady flow of heavy-duty trucks, which I readily recognized as Soviet-made. We fell into the traffic pattern and moved slowly through what I guessed were the industrial suburbs of Hanoi. Presently I saw that we were parallel to a railroad line and that, black and darkened, with no lights showing, a train was proceeding alongside us. As we drew abreast of the locomotive I saw to my surprise that its headlight was not dimmed but cut a narrow beam through the darkness.

All around I felt the vibrant, pulsating city—traffic on the road, the railroad beside it, the hundreds of bicycles. Every truck seemed to have a canopy of jungle leaves and branches and many of the cyclists had leaves woven into their sun helmets—camouflage. It was the order of the day and of the night. Henceforth I was hardly to see a moving person and certainly no moving vehicles without camouflage of one kind or another, usually a thin spread of leaves plaited into a pullover rope fretwork.

Hanoi, I knew, was a city of 600,000 people with a metropolitan area population of about 1,100,000. The area between the airport and the city, I had been told, had been heavily bombed by the Americans. I strained my eyes in the gloom for some sight of damage. But I could make out nothing. The only thing I saw was stacks of spare rails, small mountains of ties and heaps of ballast all along the railroad. It was obvious that the North Vietnamese were ready for quick repairs if U.S. bombs disrupted the rail route.

Presently we began to move across what proved to be a very, very long bridge, with single lanes of traffic on the outside and a railroad track in the center—the Paul Doumer Bridge, or Long Bien Bridge as it is now called. We crawled bumper to bumper. The bridge, I later learned, is almost two miles long, including approaches and causeways, and crosses the Red River, the only bridge between the main portion of Hanoi and the north. It was also, as I later came to know, the most shining military objective in Hanoi but one which, thus far, had not been touched by U.S. bombers.

Finally we arrived at the end of the bridge and descended to the street level by a roundabout. The streets were only faintly illuminated but looked clean and neat as we proceeded under an arbor of trees, the traffic by no means so heavy in the city as it had been outside. Alongside the road from the airport I had seen an almost continuous series of slit trenches and shelters. Here in the city streets, dim though the light was, I spotted the circular concrete manhole shelters of which I had heard, the unique North Vietnamese contribution to air-raid protection. Each was just large enough for one Vietnamese, and they were spaced three or four feet apart along every boulevard and street in the city, round dark cavities with concrete lids.

There was a row of command cars, jeeps and black Volgas outside the hotel as we entered the wide, high-ceilinged lobby. I was told it was the Thong Nhat Hotel. Thong Nhat means "Reunification," and there in mosaic on the lobby floor were the initials "T.N." Only later did I learn that in French times the hotel had been known as the Metropole.

At the far end of the lobby with its rubber plants and lounges I saw a bar and a dozen people sitting over drinks and coffee. I took a good look now at my two escorts. They were very neat young men, both small, both wearing neat dark suits, clean white shirts, neat dark ties. They might have been a couple of young men just beginning their careers in Madison Avenue or Fleet Street. There was nothing sinister about their appearance. Indeed, they looked painfully normal.

We went up to my suite—not really a suite but an enormous chamber divided into two sections by folding screens. There were shuttered and curtained windows along one side that reached nearly twenty feet to the ceiling and a bathroom as big as a Pullman car. The bed was vast and draped in a flowing mosquito net. It seemed too cold for mosquitoes, but the young men said it was not and advised me to use the net. I decided they knew best. Hanoi, they told me, was an early-rising town. People got up at 5 or 5:30 A.M. and retired at 9:30 P.M.—just the hour my watch now showed. Perhaps that was why I had seen so little of the normal activity of the East as we rode through town, none of the bazaars, none of the constant movement, none of the street stalls, none of the people sitting, sprawling and playing in courtyards or doorways. Only the purposeful movement of truck convoys through the streets, other convoys being loaded and the throngs of bicycles moving in groups out of the city. The impression I had was of a city determined, rather grim, businesslike, with little time for relaxation, play or leisure.

My young men made a date with me for six o'clock the next morning and vanished. I ventured into the Grand Central of bathrooms, observed with wonder the toilet stationed one step up on a small platform, the bidet which seemed to have been constructed for the broadest of bottoms, the bathtub large enough to accommodate a whole family. I tried the hot water tap and after a minute the water ran hot. Hanoi was at war but it still managed amenities which I would not have expected to find. I washed and went down to a late dinner. I found the dining room empty but for two pretty waitresses wearing white silk blouses and the black sateen trousers that I soon learned were the uniforms of Vietnamese women. The headwaiter asked in French what I would have to drink. When I mentioned mineral water he appeared with a bottle of Borzhumi, a kind of Caucasian Vichy water I used to drink in Russia.

Dinner was excellent—a thick cream of chicken soup, a tender piece of rather bony fish fried in egg batter, a fricassee of chicken cooked with mushrooms, carrots and celery, a piece of French pastry with pink icing, whipped cream and maraschino cherry and a cup of very black, very strong, very good French coffee. The coffee delighted and amazed me and continued to delight and amaze me as long as I stayed in North Vietnam. I had nothing but good coffee there—as good as in France itself. It was, of course, a heritage of French culture and French industry. Coffee, I learned, was grown in Vietnam, having been introduced by the French. It was still produced and now, even in wartime, some exports flowed out, including some to France.

It was after ten when I finished dinner, and as I arose the headwaiter brought over a piece of paper on which he had written out the hours for meals: breakfast 6 A.M. to 8, lunch 11 to 1:30 and dinner 6 to 8.

I thanked him and made my way back to my room.

Though I was behind the enemy lines, yet it felt curiously familiar. It seemed so much like what I had encountered so often before in my years of traveling in Communist countries. The two men who met me had been pleasant, precise and quiet. Certainly no hint of any hostility. The hotel was not very much like a Soviet hotel. Much more like what I might have found in French Africa. A bit run-down perhaps. And yet the service was pleasant and rapid. The food was not distinguished but it was unmistakably French. Particularly the good French loaf. And if the butter was a little rancid—well, that could have been duplicated in Rangoon or New Delhi. I looked about the room. There was a big quart vacuum jug decorated with green and pink flowers, the kind I had seen so often in Mongolia and Siberia. It was one of the principal exports of the Chinese. Why they should concentrate on vacuum bottles I did not know, but they seemed to have cornered the Asian market. I looked at the brown wool blanket on my bed. The label was in Chinese characters. Beside the bed was a pair of straw slippers with green rubber soles. They were only half big enough for me. They, too, came from China. The soap on the bathroom shelf came from China. The tea service on my coffee table with its maple leaf design outlined in gold—that, too, was Chinese and the duplicate of the tea services I was to see in almost every institution I visited in Hanoi.

At 5 A.M. I awoke with a start. My room was deep in darkness. But outside, nearby, I heard a cock crowing. Then another. And another. It must be near dawn. The room was damp and cold and I was shivering. I got up to toss my topcoat on the bed and discovered to my dismay that I did not have it. It had been left on the I.C.C. plane. I saw it in my mind's eye—hanging on a coat rack just beside the two little border policemen. In my excitement I had gotten off the plane without it. Where might it now be? Surely the stewardess must have noticed it and left it for me—I hoped. For Hanoi was chilly. It was a thousand miles north of Saigon and often in winter suffered cold spells. I was going to need my topcoat with its fur liner.

My first business of the morning must be the recovery of the topcoat. So I resolved. But it is one thing to resolve, another to execute. It proved no easier to accomplish so simple a task in Hanoi than it might have been, for instance, in Moscow.

I mentioned my missing topcoat to my little men when they met me at 6 A.M. No problem, they assured me. They would contact the I.C.C. Undoubtedly the coat was there. The next day I inquired. Somehow they had not managed to communicate with the I.C.C. The following day the answer was the same. I finally took matters into my hands and went to the I.C.C. offices, located in the most imposing building in Hanoi, a great five-story structure which must once have housed a bank or a customs house under the French. It was like going into a ghost house. Or walking down echoing corridors in a Hitchcock movie. I wandered through great halls, lined with offices. My heels echoed in the empty vastness. The offices bore signs, but not a soul was to be seen. I mounted the wide staircase to the second floor. Here was a great sign: "STATION CHIEF." But within the office nothing. Finally I stumbled onto a pleasant young Indian having a cup of tea. He was, it turned out, the chairman of the I.C.C. section for Hanoi. I explained my problem. No problem at all, he assured me. He would just send a signal to Saigon. Two days later the plane came in. No coat. I shivered my way back to the hotel. Two days later the I.C.C. plane came in again. This time I sent an emissary to the airport to question the crew. The coat had been taken to Saigon. No instructions had been received as to its disposition.

I was in despair. I was also close to pneumonia. My Vietnamese friends took pity on me. They promised me a warm coat. It appeared. I put it on. The sleeves reached only to my elbows. The Vietnamese are constructed on a different frame than we are. They laughed. So did I between shivers. They brought me another coat the next day. The sleeves came down halfway between the elbow and the wrist. It looked ridiculous, but I wore it with pleasure. Finally, ten days after I had arrived, I returned to my hotel one night and found a bundle there—my coat. With an apologetic note. The coat had been brought up to Hanoi twice by the hospitable sergeant who had provided the Canadian mission with the Christmas goose. Each time it had been taken back because he could find no one with whom to leave it.

By this time the Hanoi cold snap had lifted a bit. But I put on my coat and resolutely wore it each day that remained of my stay.

But of all this I mercifully had no premonition that first morning at 5 A.M. when cockcrow found me shivering. I got up, made myself a hot cup of Nescafé with the water from my Chinese vacuum jug and prepared to see what life might be like behind the enemy lines.

No one without a strong stomach should visit the Museum of the Revolution in Hanoi. Particularly not at 6 A.M. of a chilly December morning. It is a chamber of horrors—horrors of life in colonial Indochina, horrors of warfare against the French, horrors of warfare against the Americans. And passing from one exhibit to another I had the feeling that to the North Vietnamese the horrors blended together until it was difficult for them to distinguish between those which had occurred in 1885 and those which were occurring today, between the atrocities in the jungle warfare of the nineteen-hundreds and the atrocities in the jungle warfare of 1966, between the enemy who wore a French uniform and the enemy who wore an American one. The name "Museum of the Revolution" was a misnomer. This was a Museum of the Revolution, to be sure. It was filled with faded photographs of street demonstrations in the nineteen-twenties, of the hangings and torturings of revolutionary strike leaders in the rub-

43

ber plantations, of manifestoes, leaflets and proclamations, proudly posed pictures of young men and women who composed the revolutionary committee, or the plenum, or the working cadre of one movement or another. It was all that. But basically it was a Museum of Vietnamese History, of Vietnamese nationalism, of the Vietnam nation, its ancient origins, its centuries of struggle for identity, for existence against one external threat after another.

First I was shown a detail map of Vietnam—all of Vietnam, North and South, with the minority nationalities picked out in mother of pearl. There were sixty of these minorities and they spattered the face of Vietnam like a case of measles. Then I was shown the prehistoric origins of the Vietnamese people—stone artifacts from Thanhhoa Province dating back, it was said, 300,000 years—axes and arrowheads.

"Notice how the arrowheads were fashioned in those times," said Director Ky. "You see how the head tapers and there is a strong indentation, then the arrowhead flares again. You know what that means? When the arrow goes in it can't be pulled out. Not unless you rip the flesh away. Our people in the mountains, the Montagnards, still use arrows made in this fashion. They cannot be pulled out once they pierce the flesh. A very useful weapon."

It was indeed. A useful, deadly weapon. I could see a man struggling to extract the head. It simply could not be done. Only a surgical operation would remove it. Each backward tug would only tear and lacerate the flesh and make a terrible wound more terrible.

He showed me another arrowhead—this one of copper, dating back to 208 B.C. It was fashioned on the same principle—a continuity in fighting technique which extended back almost three thousand centuries. A very long time. No wonder, I thought, this is so stubborn a war and fought with such frightful weapons. There was more—much more—of this kind of thing to be seen. There was a display of sharply pointed spikes set into wooden platforms. These had been buried along the trails followed by the barefooted French troops in the eighteen-seventies and 'eighties. In another room was a ghastly device—a kind of bird cage with movable cross-wires to which were fitted a set of jagged fishhooks. The bird cage was buried on a trail and covered with a light scattering of leaves. When a man came down the trail his leg would thrust down into the cage and the fishhooks would dig in. If he tried to lift his limb or struggle out, each pull would drive them deeper, more cruelly into the flesh. The barbs could not be removed except by a surgeon's knife. This was not a weapon of the past. This was a deadly device being set out that very day and every day in the jungle trails of the South where the Americans were seeking to flush out the Vietcong strongholds.

There were pictures of beheadings, of disembowelments, of stockades, of the "water cure," of men being buried alive and women being sliced to bits. Only by looking at the dates could one be certain whether an exhibit was historical or contemporary. The history of Vietnam was presented as one long record of torture, atrocity, killing, suffering and vengeance, and the longer I looked at the cruel parade, the stronger became my feeling that to a Vietnamese it must be almost impossible to distinguish one historic epoch from another—each blended into the other, each was equally cruel, equally ferocious.

But this was not the only impression that came through from the Museum of the Revolution.

The museum began with prehistory. But it quickly moved to the recorded wars and triumphs of Vietnam. The first heroes in the lengthy roll were Trung-Trac and Trung-Nhi—the legendary Trung sisters. Not mere folk heroes. Gods in the Vietnam iconography, twin Asian Joans of Arc. The Trung sisters lived just after the start of the Christian era—A.D. 40 is the generally accepted date. Vietnam then was under Chinese domination. The husband of Trung-Trac, a local lord, was killed by the Chinese. Trung-Trac and her sister, Trung-Nhi, rallied the populace and sallied forth against the Chinese. They drove them from the land and ascended the throne as queens. But the Chinese came back with a powerful punitive expedition. They defeated the Vietnamese, and the Trung sisters committed suicide. They entered the Vietnamese legends as gods. To this day they are worshiped. But by a curious anomaly—or perhaps not so curious—their worship was now stronger in the North than in the South. For the cult of the Trung sisters had been a special preoccupation of Madame Ngo Dinh Nhu, sister-in-law of the ill-fated Ngo Dinh Diem. She attempted to rally the Southern populace around the Trung sisters. Indeed, she seemed to act as though their spirit had been reincarnated in herself. She raised a great monument to the Trung sisters in the heart of Saigon.

With her brother-in-law's death and her own precipitate fall from power, the cult of the Trungs fell into disfavor in the South. The monument was toppled from its pedestal in a symbolic act of reprisal against Madame Nhu and to this day it remained vacant. Rare was the word of the Trung sisters now heard in South Vietnam. But in the North they were venerated and held an honorable place in the Museum of the Revolution.

The next hero to whom I was introduced was Than Hung Dao, a great commander of the thirteenth century. He was celebrated for defeating a horde of 300,000 Mongols who entered the country in 1288. Three times, so I was told, the Mongols drove south. Three times they were defeated and thrust back north by the powerful generals of the Tran dynasty.

In these times the Chinese maintained nominal suzerainty over Indochina, but it was loosely exercised. Vietnam was virtually independent under its own powerful dynasties. Finally, in the fifteenth century a new challenge arose from the Ming dynasty of China. This, too, was thrust back by a Viet hero, Nguyen Trai.

As they told the story of the battles against the Mongols and the Mings, they made it seem almost like a contemporary story. The Mings, for example, had entered the country with powerful forces to re-establish Chinese power. For ten years the struggle raged. Then finally the Mings confessed defeat. Graciously the victorious Vietnamese provided their defeated enemy with horses and supplies to enable them to return to China.

"We would do the same for the Americans," the director said suddenly, underlining the thought which had arisen in my mind.

From that time on, according to the museum's version, the Vietnamese people ruled themselves. True, tribute was paid to the Forbidden City every three years. But for practical purposes the Vietnamese ran their own affairs. Peking was far away. The Nguyen dynasty reigned on its own, governing a powerful, aggressive substate which extended its domination over the now-vanished Champa Kingdom and the Khmer, or Cambodian, people and finally pushed to the shores of the Gulf of Siam.

So matters stood until the middle of the nineteenth century. For two hundred years Indochina had had extensive trade with the British, the French and the Dutch. Missionaries from the West entered the region early. The Jesuits appeared in the sixteenth century, and decade after decade a steady progress of conversion to Christianity occurred which laid the foundation for today's strong Vietnam Catholic community.

Then in the mid-nineteenth century French power began to impinge on Vietnam. French naval vessels attacked Vietnam ports in the eighteen-forties. By 1859 the French had seized Saigon. The occupation of Cochin China (the south) was completed in 1867. Hanoi was captured in 1873, but the French relinquished it only to return and seize Hanoi and Haiphong in 1883 with a handful of men. By the treaty of August 25, 1883, the Nguyen dynasty submitted to French overlordship. A protectorate was established over Tonkin (the north) and Annam (the central region). So ended Vietnam's independence.

And so began Vietnam's struggle for independence. Guerrilla warfare started almost immediately.

Indeed, whatever the actual historical record might show, the version presented by the Museum of the Revolution dated the start of today's catastrophe from the French accession in 1883. The war began on August 25 of that year. It was still in progress. It had gone through many forms. For decades the enemy was the French. Then with World War II it became the Japanese. Then the French again and now the Americans. These were distinctions of nationality with little difference of principle so far as the museum was concerned. I was to find as I spoke later with the North Vietnamese that they found it extremely hard to tell where the war against the French ended and that against the Americans began.

Now the museum brought the story swiftly down to more modern times.

It capsulized the past with a cartoon showing the French colonists sitting with their moneybags atop a pyramid formed of the backs of the suffering Vietnamese people. The cartoon interested me. It interested me enormously. I had first seen it—or its counterpart—in Bukhara, in Soviet Central Asia, where the old Emir was shown sitting on the backs of his people in precisely this manner. Then, later, I had seen it in Ulan Bator, where the Mongol rulers were shown sitting on the backs of the Mongol people in the same pyramid. Now I found it here in Indochina. I wondered how many other colo-

nial peoples used this cartoon to simplify and epitomize for
their people the story of the past.

The pattern of the story changed. It began to narrow and
focus on Ho Chi Minh. He was shown early in his career.
The exhibits did not quite go back to Paris at the time of
World War I when Ho, as he himself has described it, was
making a living as a photographer's retoucher and as a paint-
er of freshly manufactured "Chinese antiquities." In those
times, as Ho has recalled, he was a rather ignorant and naïve
member of the French Socialist party, striving to gain some
comprehension of the nature of the great issues which were
shaking the world—Communism, Socialism, colonialism. His
interests, of course, as he later was to recall, centered
strongly and basically on colonialism. The attraction of Lenin
was for him Lenin's understanding of the colonial problem. It
was this which moved him onto the path that led to Communism and to his joining the French Communist party with its
founding in 1920.

Ho, son of a minor mandarin, was born Nguyen That
Than in northern Annam in 1890. The name by which the
world knows him, Ho Chi Minh, means "He Who Enlight-
ens." He chose it in adulthood, a not uncommon Vietnamese
custom. Ho's father was a nationalist, and Ho, too, was a nationalist from boyhood. He made his way to Europe before
World War I, working at a variety of jobs. Once he was a
pastry cook in London's Carlton Hotel. For a time he worked
on a French ship. He visited the United States. He appeared
at the Versailles Conference and tried without success to get
the statesmen of the world to grant Vietnam its independence.

The career of Ho and the struggle for Vietnam's independence became intertwined in the Revolution Museum with the
early nineteen-twenties. Here he was pictured attending the
Fifth Congress of the Comintern in 1924 and having his picture taken with Georgi Dimitriev, the famous Bulgarian revolutionary. Here he was shown founding the Indochinese
Communist party on February 18, 1930. And here was the
party's declaration of purpose:

To overthrow French imperialism, feudalism and the reactionary Vietnamese capitalist class.

To make Indochina completely independent.

To establish a worker-peasant and soldier government.

To confiscate all banks and other enterprises belonging to

the imperialists and put them under the control of the worker-peasant and soldier government.

To confiscate all the plantations and property belonging to the imperialists and the Vietnamese reactionary capitalist class and distribute them to the poor peasants.

And all the rest. Signed with the name Ho was then using: Nguyen Ai Quoc.

Not all of Ho Chi Minh's history was spelled out in the wall displays and glass cases of the museum. Probably not even he could remember every twist and turn of the story. He had been a member of the French Communist party, a member of the Comintern in its great revolutionary days, a student of revolutionary techniques and tactics in Moscow; then he had gone to China, and there he had been a member of the Chinese Communist party. He had worked with Chiang Kai-shek before Chiang broke with the Communists. He had gone underground and devoted himself to revolution in his native Indochina. He had been sentenced to death by the French but found refuge in Hong Kong. He had been in a dozen prisons. Much of World War II he spent in Chinese prisons, in Liuchow and Kweilin, suspected of being a French spy. He had returned to his own land in 1945. Here under glass was the very handful of earth which he had kissed.

And here was the Declaration of Independence of the Democratic Republic of Vietnam.

This was the document of which Ho himself was author, proclaimed on September 2, 1945, when the Vietminh, the nationalist-oriented, Communist-led Vietnamese independence movement, took over power from the defeated Japanese (the French were virtually nonexistent in the north). Here was the document as it was proclaimed by Ho:

All men are created equal. They are endowed by their Creator with certain inalienable rights, among these are Life, Liberty and the pursuit of Happiness.
This immortal statement was made in the Declaration of Independence of the United States of America in 1776. In a broader sense this means all the peoples on the earth are equal from birth, all the peoples have a right to live, to be happy and free. . . .

So the document read, opening with a paraphrase—virtually an exact quotation—from our own historic proclamation.

What, I wondered, could have happened to turn history so awry? Here was a country and leader which had, for whatever reason, clearly drawn in its founding hour upon the

very best of the American heritage. Yet here was a country
in which I was now an enemy behind the lines, a country engaged in deep and deadly warfare with the United States, a
country in arms against American power.

What had gone wrong?

Here, embedded in the Vietnamese Declaration of Independence, was another passage:

*We are convinced that the allied nations which at Teheran and
San Francisco have acknowledged the principles of self-determina-
tion and equality of nations will not refuse to acknowledge the
independence of Vietnam.*

*A people who have courageously opposed French domination
for more than eighty years, a people who have fought side by side
with the Allies against the Fascists during these last years, such a
people must be free and independent.*

Within this declaration there were echoes of many
things—of Ho's futile effort at Versailles to win recognition
and independence for his people, of the World War II collaboration of Ho and his organization with the O.S.S. and
with the Americans in the Indochinese underground, of the
fierce nationalism which constantly seemed to temper and
color Ho's Communism—to such an extent that not a few
Americans who knew him well during and after the war were
convinced that in a choice between Communism and nationalism Ho would choose nationalism—reluctantly, no doubt,
and with full hopes that Communism might succeed, but
nonetheless decisively.

Ho had negotiated with the French after the proclamation
of Vietnam's independence in that curious document with its
overtones of Thomas Jefferson and Woodrow Wilson. And an
agreement had been signed on March 6, 1946, whereby
France recognized Ho and his regime. It was a valid document. Ho had every reason to suppose that the long struggle—the eighty-year battle which his Declaration of Independence mentioned—had ended in success. But that went
glimmering. The agreement proved to be nothing more than
a piece of paper. It was never really accepted by the French,
and before the year was out France and Ho's regime had
slithered into violent combat. The French attacked Ho's new
republic, bombarding Haiphong and killing thousands of
Vietnamese in November of 1946, and a month later the
Vietnamese attacked the French in Hanoi.

The deadly, dangerous drift of Vietnam into civil war and

combat had begun, the slippery path that was to lead to one disaster after another, ending in the disaster of disasters at Dienbienphu.

Of all the events celebrated in the Museum of the Revolution this was the centerpiece—the crowning glory of Vietnam's resistance against France, the event which, I was soon to feel, had colored the Vietnamese psychology more than any other event in recent history.

Nothing equaled Dienbienphu and its victorious end on May 7, 1954—the day the Vietminh, Ho's rebel movement, and its brilliant General Vo Nguyen Giap crushed the massive strongpoint which had been painstakingly built up by the French in northern Vietnam, in the valley of Dienbienphu, obliterating the surviving 15,094 men in the surrounded, contracting and desperately defended *place d'armes*.

The annihilation of Dienbienphu led directly to France's signature on July 21, 1954, of the Geneva accords, bringing to an end the Vietnam war. It was this triumph of Vietnam arms and Vietnam strategy and Vietnam tactics over Western arms and power which had etched itself into the minds of North Vietnam's leaders and which had been, through their propaganda, etched into the minds of even the lowliest of North Vietnamese peasants.

What had been done once could be done again. Patience and fortitude. If we wait long enough the Americans will follow the same path as the French and Dienbienphu will repeat itself. So ran the philosophy, so ran the thinking. I was to hear it again and again, either explicitly or implicitly. It lay behind every call to sacrifice, every hardship, every defeat. North Vietnam could suffer through them. It could suffer the destruction of Hanoi. Of Haiphong. The devastation of its cities and villages and fields. Because at the end like a glittering rainbow lay the promise of a new Dienbienphu.

I was not convinced that this psychology was valid. I did not think the parallel between France and the United States ran true. Missing from the museum was any accurate exposition of how and why the United States had become involved in Indochina. It was a chapter which I knew was missing from the background of most Americans.

The United States had stood aloof from Vietnam during the postwar struggle between Ho and the French. It was not until the outbreak of the Korean War that American interest was suddenly triggered in Southeast Asia. Vietnam then

began to be seen as the "southern front" against China. It
was thought to be part of the same struggle against world
Communism to which we were so deeply committed in
Korea. We did not commit troops, but we began to provide
the French with matériel and supplies. We began to pick up
more and more of the check for the costly war. Korea gradually began to yield to American pressure, but in Vietnam
the French were pressed harder and harder. In the final
weeks before the Dienbienphu disaster the French urgently
called for American aid. Some American military men
wanted to mount an air strike to save the French, but President Eisenhower refused.

Reluctantly the United States acquiesced in the 1954 Geneva agreement but did not sign it. With partition of the
country U.S. support swiftly began to flow to the Saigon government of Diem. The gradual process of deeper and deeper
American involvement had begun. But even today it was not
like that of the French. The Americans fought not to stay in
Vietnam but to establish a stability there which would permit
them to get out.

I thought that Hanoi's reasoning, which held that the
United States was a mere continuation of France, was dangerous and delusive. And as the days went by, I told this to
many North Vietnamese officials. I did not believe they
should deceive themselves. History sometimes repeats itself.
But France was not the United States. Dienbienphu was not
likely to happen again, and they should not count on it.

Another lesson had been ingrained in North Vietnamese
minds—the lesson of distrust. This was born of North Vietnam's experience with France in 1946 and, however different
our motives had been, with the United States in 1954. The
Hanoi leaders felt that they had negotiated a valid end to
their struggle with the French in 1946 and that Paris welshed
on the agreement and utilized its terms to continue the war
by other means. They thought the same thing had happened
with the Geneva agreement in 1954. It had been signed, but
the United States, not a signatory but now a stand-in for
France, sought to overthrow its results and restore the *status
quo ante*. From this stemmed a deep and constant strain of
suspicion. Above all the North Vietnamese were wary of any
negotiations, of any new agreement which might, in their
view, turn out to be a new betrayal.

As my stay in Hanoi lengthened I came to feel, more and

more, that nothing was more important in North Vietnamese minds than these two impressions born of the past—the feeling of self-confidence arising from Dienbienphu and that of distrust stemming from 1946 and 1954. Before any end could be brought to the war these twin barriers in Hanoi's psychology had to be overcome. Not an easy task.

The first thing I asked to see in Hanoi was the bomb damage. Nothing, I felt, was more immediately important to Americans than to get a look at the results of the raids of December 13 and 14. What had been hit? What damage had been done? What had the United States been trying to do?

I was no specialist in air warfare, but I had seen much destruction during World War II. I had lived in London during the tail end of the blitz. I had seen the acres of devastation around the London docks and I had walked through the bombed-out areas of the East End. In those days I worked in Bouverie Street, just off Fleet Street, and each day I passed through the blitzed Law Courts. I often lunched at Blackfriars, a restaurant miraculously surviving in the ruins of the City, not far from St. Paul's. Later on in the Soviet Union I had seen the pulverized cities of Stalingrad, Kharkov and Sevastopol, and after the war I had inspected possibly the worst of all ruins, Warsaw's ghetto, transformed into a desert of broken brick and plaster in which it was hardly possible to imagine that human life had once existed.

Perhaps because of my experience with bomb damage on the colossal scale of Europe in World War II, I was not impressed by the magnitude of what I saw when I first viewed Pho Nguyen Thiep Street in the Hoan Kiem quarter of Hanoi, a five-minute drive from my hotel. This had been, quite obviously, an ordinary working-class street in an ordinary working-class section. It was rather narrow and on either side, as one could see by surviving structures, there had been one-, two- and three-story buildings of brick and stucco. The street, I was told, lay a little more than a hundred yards from the Central Market, and at one end, just beyond the damaged stretch, I saw a high brick viaduct along which railroad trains emerged from the Long Bien Bridge. The spot where I stood was 150 yards or so from the bridge approaches. Perhaps this accounted for the bombing or rocketing, but in any event it didn't say much for the "precision" of the attackers.

At about 3 P.M. on December 13, according to the people who lived on Pho Nguyen Thiep Street, a bomb or more likely a rocket, possibly a bullpup, had exploded just above their houses. It had caused thirteen houses on both sides of the street to collapse. The people told me that five persons had been killed and eleven injured. Thirty-nine families had been made homeless. This was their report. Not a very dramatic incident. The casualty figures were not impressive. It had been one of those sad little happenings which occur during a war, and, as an American, I could not repress a feeling of shock and futility. Why had it happened? Need it have occurred? No one in Pho Nguyen Thiep Street, certainly, had the faintest notion.

I talked with a young man who said his name was Tran Ngoc Trac. He was in his early twenties and told me he was a medical assistant, a kind of first-aid worker. He had lived in the house at No. 46 Pho Nguyen Thiep Street. On December 13 he had been taking an afternoon nap, and just before 3 P.M. he got up and was preparing to go to work when he heard the air-raid sirens. A radio announcer said that planes were about twenty-five kilometers, or a little more than fifteen miles, from Hanoi. He picked up his medical kit and walked out the door when he heard a plane directly overhead and dropped face down on the pavement. An instant later the bomb or rocket exploded and the house from which he had just emerged collapsed. He picked himself up and started to treat the victims. In House No. 48, he said, eleven families had lived but none were hurt seriously. In House No. 44 a woman and a child and a pregnant woman were killed. And at House No. 50 an old woman was killed.

I walked down the street, taking a few pictures. The houses from Nos. 36 to 50 had been destroyed or damaged, nine houses on one side of the street and four on the other. Just off the street through a narrow lane that led between two buildings was a small Buddhist shrine, the Phuc Lan Pagoda. It too had been badly damaged. The blast had knocked off the roof and caused some of the timbers to fall in. It had not, apparently, been used recently as a place of worship. There were children's school desks and textbooks scattered in the debris. But on December 13 there were no children in the pagoda since all schools had been evacuated from Hanoi.

Had the damage in Pho Nguyen Thiep Street been caused by bombs? This was a difficult question to answer. Had one of the SAM missiles misfired, as the Pentagon had contended, the blast, it seemed to me, would have been far more powerful, the damage far more impressive than this dismal destruction in this dirty little street. Was the smashing of the houses a deliberate act by an American flier? This hardly seemed likely in view of the proximity of the bridge. But the inhabitants of the street thought that they had been selected as the target of the American attack. The bombing would go down in history as one of the senseless accidents of war—death inflicted by a man who did not even know he was causing it.

As I was about to leave, Tran Ngoc Trac approached me again. Look, he said through an interpreter, here is a leaflet I found in our street after the attack. He showed me a dirty piece of paper. On it, the interpreter said, was a warning by the Americans: Don't live near a military target. Where, asked Tran Ngoc Trac, was the military target? I turned away without an answer.

The interpreter and I got into the car and drove a short distance to an embankment along the Red River. This, I was told, was Phuc Tan Street. It did not look like a street. It looked like a stretch of rubble—but even the rubble was not impressive. Here, it was said, there had stood about three hundred houses—obviously the simplest kind of huts, those constructed of mud and wattle with thatched roofs. Here and there had been a house of brick and plaster. This, the officials said, was another working-class quarter. A rather poor one, I judged, by the remains. Here, they said, at about the same hour as the destruction in Pho Nguyen Thiep Street a high-explosive bomb or bombs, possibly an air burst, had leveled the houses and killed four persons and injured ten. The toll seemed very light considering the area of destruction, which I estimated at roughly 220 yards by 75 yards. I was puzzled at this, but the officials said that most of the people had been at work and the casualties were largely elderly nonworkers and children left at home by working parents. The region, like all areas of the city, was studded with manhole-type concrete shelters. I walked through the rubble and wondered what had happened here. In the debris lay the artifacts of the poor man's life—earthen pots, half-burned straw pallets, bits of crockery, an old bedspring, a torn mosquito net. Could this damage have been caused by the misfiring of a missile? The damage was extensive enough, it seemed to me, to have been done by a missile, but before I left I found some evidence which indicated that a misfire was probably not to blame. Over near the river side of the destruction I saw three craters—not large ones. Each was probably eight or ten feet in diameter. They had unquestionably been made by falling bombs. The existence of the craters seemed to support the belief of the local residents that it was American bombs which had caused the damage.

In Phuc Tan Street the residents were certain that they had been attacked deliberately. I thought I understood why they felt like this. But after studying the geography of this location a question rose in my mind. Both Pho Nguyen Thiep Street and Phuc Tan Street lay adjacent to the western approaches of the Long Bien Bridge. Could these small and insignificant attacks have been made as a warning to Hanoi? To drive home to the government the vulnerability of the Long Bien Bridge should we really list it as an active military target? Possibly. It was not something which could ever be proved one way or the other. This was the great problem of trying to establish—from the ground—what the man at the controls of a twelve-hundred-mile-an-hour plane was actually trying to do. Was he dropping his bombs precisely? Or was he just being careless? Even the American command could not always be sure, and I did not see how the factor of sheer accidental destruction could be ruled out.

Later on I discussed the question with a member of the commission which had been set up by Bertrand Russell, the British philosopher, and which had come out to investigate the American bombing. The commission members were certainly not prejudiced in favor of the United States, for Lord Russell's group was seeking evidence of "war crimes" to be used at a planned mock trial of President Johnson and other American leaders. Yet one commission member, a Scottish professor, said after several days of inspection of bomb damage in many parts of North Vietnam that the factor of intent deeply troubled him.

"It is easy enough to report that there has been enormous destruction of civilian property and nonmilitary objectives," he said. "Anyone who travels in North Vietnam can see this. But is it intentional? This is the difficult question. How can we read the mind of the pilot who dropped the bombs or loosed the rockets? How can we know, for certain, what his orders were? How do we know from the ground what the airman high in the sky really thought he was doing?"

I found as I talked with diplomats who had gone through the raids of December 13 and 14 that many were strongly inclined to believe that the damage to civilian areas of Hanoi had been accidental. The American planes, they said, had been over the city for long periods of time—three-quarters of an hour on December 13. They had come in on their targets from many directions, crossing and recrossing Hanoi. They were met with a hurricane of fire, both from the powerful SAM's, which tore the high altitudes apart and drove the planes down to lower levels, and from conventional anti-aircraft batteries. The American fliers were attacking very small objectives—objectives which were located within zones of heavy AA protection. The targets were difficult and dangerous to attack. It was the belief of many diplomats in Hanoi, especially Western diplomats, that the American pilots in their efforts to evade the antiaircraft fire may well have loosed bombs and rockets off target, thus causing such destruction as occurred in Phuc Tan and Pho Nguyen Thiep streets.

I spent the afternoon looking at bomb damage. We drove through Hai Ba ward, another of Hanoi's central districts. There on Ngo Hue Street I saw a house or two which had been damaged, it was said, by a rocket in an attack on December 2. As I quickly learned, while the attacks of December 13 and 14 had made world headlines, there had been raids on December 2 and 4 in which damage also was done in the central areas of Hanoi. In Ngo Hue Street a woman ran out to our car and led us back to the half-destroyed frame of her house. There I saw her ten- or eleven-year-old daughter, her arms in bandages and casts, who was said to be just back from the hospital after the December 2 attack.

We drove a short distance out of town to Phuc Xa, a village. It was not much of a village—a small collection of thatched huts, the people engaged in market gardening, in growing berries and oranges, in raising pigs and poultry. At a casual glance nothing could have looked more ordinary, more normal, than Phuc Xa. But, the villagers said, appearances were deceiving.

On August 13, 1966, at 12:17 P.M., they said, a high-explosive bomb had burst over the village, destroying twenty-four houses, killing twenty-four persons and wounding twenty-three. The villagers believed that the plane had first aimed for the nearby dike along the Red River, then attacked them. One bomb had fallen on the dike and dug out a twenty-five-foot crater. The next one fell on their village.

Phuc Xa had been rebuilt in thirty-six days with the help of surrounding communities. Now in its center stood a small tile-roofed building which was a kind of museum. Here was preserved a fragment of a bomb which the villagers said was the one which had caused the destruction. It bore the loading date of July, 1966. "Imagine," the villagers said. "The bomb was loaded in July and within a month it fell here on this village." It was the first such expression I had heard. I was to hear this again and again in North Vietnam, the amazement of the Vietnamese at the efficiency and speed with which we could rush bombs from the assembly lines in the United States to drop over the rice paddies and towns of Vietnam.

In front of the "museum" was a small monument commemorating the attack. Beside it I saw a young woman with a hoe, working in a flower bed. As we walked about the village she followed us. I asked who she was. The village official glanced at her sadly and shook his head. She was, it seemed, the sole survivor of her family. Her father, her mother, her sister and her child had been in a hut, eating lunch when the bomb fell. It exploded directly over their hut. All but she had been killed. The monument had been erected on the spot where the hut stood.

Now she spent her time puttering about the garden. Her mind was not quite right.

What had happened here? The villagers were certain that an American pilot had deliberately attacked them. And, as far as they were concerned, it made no difference whether he thought he was attacking something else. It was their homes that had been destroyed, their families who had been killed.

To me it seemed unlikely that an American pilot had deliberately aimed for the village. But who really could know what he had intended to hit? Possibly he had been attacking the dikes. He might have been trying to knock out shipping in the Red River or an antiaircraft gun along the shore. Or he might have been dropping his bombs in evasive action in order to get away rapidly from a very hot corner.

This was war. This was air war. It was being waged with new, extremely rapid, extremely sensitive aircraft. They were trying to attack very small, very precise targets. Were they being sent on missions that were beyond their capability?

This was entirely possible. It would not be the first time that air commands had assigned such missions.

Later on my conviction deepened that the American planes, particularly the fighter-bombers, were subject to orders which lay on the far horizon of their capability. I saw, for example, the so-called Vandien truck park on the outskirts of Hanoi—listed as one of the major targets of our December 13 attack. It was not a formidable target when I viewed it from Route Nationale No. 1—just a half-dozen loading sheds, blasted by American bombs. But in attacking these sheds the bombers had wrecked what was called the Polish Friendship School, probably half a mile distant on the other side of the highway. It was perfectly plain what had happened. The planes had come sweeping in on the truck park, and the chain of bombs had continued in a straight line and hit the school as well. I could accept the bombing of the school as an accident. But I was not surprised to find that the North Vietnamese thought it was deliberate. What caused me to wonder was why the truck park had been singled out as a target in the first place. It certainly wasn't much. The action seemed even less understandable when I learned from a foreigner who had been down Route Nationale No. 1 just before the raid that there were only twelve or fourteen broken-down buses and trucks in the "park" undergoing repairs when it was hit. For this kind of target was it worth jeopardizing $2 million planes and the precious lives of American pilots? Was it worth zeroing in through the powerful SAM explosions and the blizzard of conventional ack-ack to destroy twelve or fourteen old motor vehicles that were already out of order? And in the process destroy a fine high school which was supported and aided by the Poles?

I could not believe this made military sense. It certainly made no political sense.

I wondered what kind of reconnaissance we had—whether our targeting authorities really knew what they were ordering the planes to do or whether, as in World War II, their data often were on the fuzzy side. I had read many claims of the remarkable increase in bombing accuracy since World War II. Such claims were hardly borne out by the on-the-spot results. Could it be that our reconnaissance photography also was something less than miraculous?

I did not know the answer to that question. But I could

begin to see quite clearly that there was a vast gap between the reality of the air war, as seen from the ground in Hanoi, and the bland, vague American communiqués with their re-iterated assumptions that our bombs were falling precisely upon "military objectives" and accomplishing our military purposes with some kind of surgical precision which for the first time in the history of war was crippling the enemy with-out hurting civilians or damaging civilian life.

Having seen the aerial bombardment in World War II, I had been skeptical from the start that our technology could have advanced so rapidly in the ensuing twenty years as to make this miracle possible. Now on the ground in Hanoi I saw my skepticism was well founded.

In the late afternoon we drove through the diplomatic quarters of the city, an area of pleasant boulevards lined with shade trees and spacious villas in parklike settings.

We turned a corner into a narrow street and came to an intersection where the property of four embassies—the So-viet, the Chinese, the Rumanian and the Polish—adjoined. Workmen were busy making repairs in the rear of the Chinese Embassy, replacing a damaged second- and third-story wall and putting new tiles on the roof. The damage, the Chinese asserted, had been caused by a rocket-firing Ameri-can aircraft in the December 14 attack. There was damage visible as well to the Rumanian Embassy.

Later I obtained from a Western diplomat in Hanoi an ac-count of what had happened. The account had been pieced together from conversations with personnel of all four embas-sies. What had happened, the diplomat said, was that shortly after the onset of the December 14 raid, with the planes ap-pearing over Hanoi simultaneously with the sounding of the sirens, a rocket—probably a bullpup—had been fired into the diplomatic quarter. It hit a tree just outside the Rumanian Embassy and its engine was later found there. The explosion was very strong. Several Rumanians occupying a shelter near the tree were hurled to the ground. A red-hot piece of metal was flung through the open window of the Rumanian mili-tary attaché's office. Other parts of the rocket smashed into the Chinese Embassy's rear wall and roof, causing the dam-age which I saw being repaired. Two Russians were standing under a canopy on a terrace at the rear of their embassy. Splinters fell at their feet. There was minor damage to the Polish Embassy.

This was not the only damage in the diplomatic quarter. The Canadian Mission of the I.C.C. was also hit, and one dry-humored member packed up the fragments and sent them back by I.C.C. courier to his American friends in Saigon with a note saying, "Look here, chaps, this is going a bit far."

It was inconceivable to me that an American plane had deliberately attacked Hanoi's diplomatic quarter. Clearly an accident must have occurred. But it was the kind of accident which could easily have caused deaths and injuries in the embassies, just as similar accidents took lives in Pho Nguyen Thiep Street and Phuc Tan Street. Had four members of the Chinese Embassy been killed and five members of the Soviet Embassy been wounded, the diplomatic repercussions would have been explosive. The damage to U.S.-Soviet relations would have been incalculable. The world would have rocked.

The risks which the United States was incurring by flying its high-speed, highly armed aircraft through the skies over Hanoi were clearly far greater than the military officers who drew up the flight plans and picked the targets had conceived or been willing to admit.

I had long heard that President Johnson himself approved every target and every operation in the vicinity of Hanoi and Haiphong. I wondered whether the military had been frank in the briefings they had given their Commander in Chief. I wondered whether they had spelled out the possible consequences of "accidents" in the diplomatic quarter of Hanoi. Or whether, as is not uncommon in wartime, they had been inclined to accentuate the positive and minimize the negative; whether in their deep commitment to the theory of air power they might not have overlooked some basic considerations of national welfare and American interest.

Christmas Eve was raw and dark, and when I emerged from the brightly lighted lobby of the Thong Nhat Hotel it took my eyes a moment to adjust. The city seemed deserted as we got into our Volga and started out, but suddenly I became aware that in the almost blacked-out streets there was a quickening presence of silently moving people, throngs on foot and throngs on quietly rolling bicycles, men with girls riding behind them, mothers with their babies, and dark as it was I could see that the women were wearing silks, not the usual black sateens. I felt an air of excitement. The dark masses of people grew thicker and thicker and finally the car was forced to halt and we got out to find ourselves surrounded by a huge crowd moving in one direction. We were swept around a corner into a large square, a rectangle really, before the Cathedral of St. Joseph. Gray and venerable-looking, the cathedral was outlined with strings of glowing light bulbs. Before it, halfway down the square, was a central island filled with flowers and shrubs. This, too, was decorated with strings of lights—red, yellow, green, blue—and set among the flowers were hundreds of little Vietnamese national flags, red with gold stars.

We moved ahead and came to a heavy rope barrier guarded by policemen and volunteers wearing red armbands. The barrier was not to prevent access to the square and the cathedral but to control the crowd and enable the police to admit people in orderly fashion. We made our way to the side, came through the barrier and walked more freely in the inner courtyard. As I came up to the cathedral itself I found that it, too, was decorated with thousands of little red Vietnamese flags and red bunting.

I walked up the great steps and entered. Within there was a blaze of lights. The pillars were festooned with oriental pine and to the right, just off the main aisle, was a large crèche, not yet illuminated. Preparations for Christmas Mass were still under way and only a handful of people were in the pews, mostly elderly women and small children. They were being permitted to come in early to avoid the crush. In addition, there was a handful of spectators like myself—half a dozen Vietnamese officials, an Italian who I learned was a correspondent for the Communist newspaper *L'Unità* and who was intensely interested to find this Roman Catholic observance in Hanoi, a couple of visitors from East Germany, two Russian correspondents who had never before seen a Christmas ceremony, a very blonde and buxom young woman who I was told had just arrived to represent Radio Moscow, and possibly a dozen church officials, each of whom wore a little pink and blue ribbon in his buttonhole. I looked closely at the ribbons. They bore the legend: "Noël, 1966."

When I emerged, the crowd in the square had vastly increased. The rope barrier had been taken down and several thousand people were moving freely up to the cathedral steps, and soon, it was obvious, the doors would be flung open and they would be admitted. There were police along the steps with bullhorns in their hands. They addressed the crowd, cautioning it to be orderly and not to shove or press forward. As I walked back through the throng I found more and more young men and young women in their best clothes, the girls in sleek silk slit dresses and each, it seemed, wearing a wisp of bright-hued crepe de Chine around her neck.

We re-entered the car and drove again through darkened

streets to the Church of St. Dominique, in the diplomatic quarter, a long building constructed in an oriental style with inscriptions in Chinese along the rafters. Here the scene was quieter. There were throngs outside, but they numbered in the scores rather than the thousands I had seen around the cathedral. The impression was that of a quiet neighborhood church, most of the parishioners standing outside and gossiping as they waited for the hour to draw closer to midnight. Within the church only a few children had taken their places. I talked a bit with the priest, a Vietnamese with a strong face and high cheekbones. He had been trained in a seminary in Hanoi and once, in times past, had visited Rome. Then I returned to the hotel, where a little Christmas celebration had been arranged by the Vietnamese Journalists Association.

Many thoughts filled my mind. I thought of home and New York, of Charlotte and the children, of the Christmas I had left behind. In New York it was still early on the Saturday before Christmas, people were frantically checking their lists of presents, wondering whether to make one last trip to Macy's. Were there enough decorations for the tree without getting anything new from the five-and-ten? What about the strings of lights? Where had the spare bulbs been put? How distant, how unreal these questions seemed in this wartime city, in this wartime country, in this atmosphere in which the very celebration of Christmas was so surprising. I remembered how I had wondered in New York whether I would find any Christmas at all in Hanoi. It had been my impression that the Church, the Roman Church, had been severely repressed in the North. And, for all I had seen this evening, that might still be true. I had gone to many a midnight Mass of the Russian Orthodox Church at Eastertime in Moscow. Thousands of the faithful had turned out for those celebrations. But at the same time the Soviet regime had persecuted the Orthodox Church fiercely and had conducted savage campaigns against other religious faiths—the Baptists, the Jews, the Roman Catholics and the Moslems.

At the festive table in the hotel, decked out with a great roast turkey sporting a red cabbage rose, a baked pike which had been decorated in pink and green, and huge logs of French pastry filled with maraschino cherries, orange particles and whipped cream, looking like a pastry cook's nightmare, I questioned the North Vietnamese about Christmas, about the Church.

Amid toasts to peace, to the end of American "aggression" and to the national unity and sovereignty of the Vietnamese people, my hosts insisted that Christmas had always been and still was a great Vietnamese holiday. There was nothing, they said, unusual about tonight's festivities except that they were a bit less gay due to lack of lights and the general harshness of wartime. But, as they noted, thousands of Hanoi residents had come back into the city, bringing their children with them, to rejoin their wives or husbands for the Christmas holiday. This had been made possible by the Christmas truce. And thousands of the persons whom I had seen that afternoon riding on bicycles into Hanoi were coming back for Christmas Eve.

Christmas was not as important a holiday in Vietnam as Tet, the lunar New Year, which would be celebrated at the end of January, but it was a great and festive occasion.

At midnight I bade farewell to my hosts and left the Christmas party. As I started up the staircase to my room, the vice chairman of the Vietnamese Cultural Committee hurried after me. "I hope you see Santa in your dreams," he said. "Good night."

The relationship of the Hanoi regime to the Church and to religion was a topic which I pursued. I had heard, of course, of the hundreds of thousands of Roman Catholics who had fled the North in 1954-55 at the time of Vietnam's partition. It had been my impression that the North had practically wiped out the Church at that time and that this had caused the exodus. "The Virgin Mary has gone to the South!"—this, I had been told, was what had been said in those days. Was it true?

I found that the situation was not so simple as I had supposed. Before my departure from North Vietnam I visited communities where almost everyone, including party officials, so far as I could discover, was a practicing Roman Catholic, and I talked with several priests about the position of the Church. Not everything emerged clearly from these talks. I still felt uncertain about some aspects of the 1954 exodus. I heard, for example, intense bitterness expressed both by Catholics and by government officials over the movement of Catholics to the South. They contended that false rumors and propaganda had been spread against the Communist regime. They attributed the campaign to the Americans, contending that Cardinal Spellman had directed it. The stories they told were so confused and so laden with passion and prejudice that I felt the tale had been oversimplified and now existed as a cartoonlike creation in their minds. Yet it seemed to have some foundation.

I discussed the question with Monsignor George Hussler, Secretary General of Caritas, the German Catholic welfare organization, who arrived in Hanoi during my visit. He was the first official Catholic representative to come to the North since the partition of the country. While his presence ostensibly related to relief work—his organization had long been providing funds to the North Vietnamese Red Cross and the National Liberation Front Red Cross as well as to the Red Cross of South Vietnam—it was a matter of greater consequence as well. It was a symbolic visit, designed to demonstrate to the North that the Vatican was sincere in its declarations for peace in Vietnam. It was intended to show Hanoi that whatever the situation had been in the past, the Catholic Church was no longer playing sides. Indeed, the Vatican had been at pains for several years to make this clear. Now, it seemed, the message might be getting through. It was no accident that immediately after leaving Hanoi, after discussions with high officials, including Ho Chi Minh, and representatives of the Catholic hierarchy, Monsignor Hussler went directly to Rome to report. Referring to the events of 1954, Monsignor Hussler shook his head sadly and told me, "The American Church has much on its conscience so far as the people of Vietnam are concerned."

But what was the status of Roman Catholicism in the North at present? Late in my visit I spent some time with the Rev. Ho Thanh Bien, the pastor of the Church of St. Dominique, whom I had first met on Christmas Eve. He told me that he was the deputy president of the Commission of Patriotic Catholics, a group which had been set up to maintain relations with and support the Hanoi Government. It actually antedated, if I understood him correctly, the establishment of the 1954 government under the Geneva accords.

I met with Father Bien and two Catholic lay members of this group, Vu Thai Hoa, editor in chief of the organization's newspaper, *Justice*, and Nguyen Van Dong, chairman of the commission, in their headquarters in a roomy villa in the center of Hanoi. It was one of the many interviews which I conducted at the unpleasant hour of 6 A.M., with the dawn just breaking and many cups of steaming China tea which did not quite take the chill out of the air.

Father Bien wore his cassock and a rather frayed black beret and smoked one cigarette after another. He explained that the organization had been started to aid the struggle against the French but had evolved into a group which handled lay relations between Catholics and the government.

So far as the Church was concerned, he said, connections with the Vatican had been maintained by correspondence but until the visit of Monsignor Hussler no representative had come from Rome nor had any member of the North Vietnamese hierarchy gone to Rome since 1954.

The senior bishop of North Vietnam was Trinh Nhu Khue, so designated by the Vatican in 1962. At the time of the split in the country six of the ten bishops in the North went to the South and along with them went most of the seminaries. Father Bien was bitter about this. He said that the French and the Americans wanted to reduce the people in the North to nothing but "silent seminaries." In his view it was the hope of the Americans to eliminate the Catholic Church in the North and concentrate it in the South. Before partition, according to his calculation, there were about two million Catholics in Vietnam, roughly divided between North and South. Perhaps as many as 500,000 or 600,000 Catholics went to the South during the alleged propaganda campaign against the Hanoi regime.

Since then, Father Bien said, the Vatican had helped rebuild the Church in the North. Six new bishops had been consecrated so that now all the dioceses had a bishop. The seminaries had been painfully re-established until there was one in each diocese—ten in all—but they had only about a hundred novitiates. There was a serious shortage of priests. Father Bien estimated that there were three to four hundred in the North. Monsignor Hussler put the figure a bit higher. Obviously precise statistics were lacking. In Hanoi there were only ten priests for twelve churches. Father Bien said that by his reckoning there were twenty thousand Catholics in Hanoi, explaining that Hanoi was not traditionally a Catholic center.

He contended that the government had not repressed religion, that it had assisted in providing funds for the rehabilitation of churches and seminaries. He said that young people openly attended services and that christenings and confirmations continued as in the past. As for catechismal instruction, he asserted, this was offered by the Church to schoolchildren during the Christmas and spring vacations. Religious teaching of youngsters also took place in regular Sunday classes, he said, and confirmation ceremonies were held twice a year. There were, he insisted, still convents, although he conceded that many nuns had gone to the South—had been forced to go to the South was his way of putting it.

Father Bien spoke sadly of the prospects of peace. He had just been reading in the Hanoi papers of Cardinal Spellman's Christmas prayers in Saigon—prayers for the victory of the American Army. Father Bien found this very disturbing. He hoped that there might be more unity of feeling between the Roman Catholics of Vietnam and their coreligionists in other parts of the world. Many Catholic churches, he said, had been bombed in the course of the United States air offensive in the North. He placed the number at 126. He asserted that two priests had been killed and one wounded and that several seminaries had also been damaged. He did not believe that God supported the American cause.

The other great faith of Vietnam, of course, was Buddhism. The Buddhists, I knew, had played a major role in the South. But I had heard little of their activities in the North. One afternoon I went to an extremely pretty small pagoda—the Quan Su Pagoda, only about two blocks from my hotel. It was set back behind a wall in a gravel-pathed courtyard and to the rear was a pleasant reception hall where I took tea with Thich Tri Do, head of the Unified Buddhist Association of Vietnam.

Behind him, hanging on the wall of the reception hall, was a portrait of Ho Chi Minh. Three Buddhist sects had been merged into the single association, he explained. Buddhism, he said, was the dominant church of Vietnam.

"We Buddists consider this one country," he declared. "For us there is no demarcation line between North and South."

The Buddhist Church, he said, had had freedom of contact between North and South until the Diem regime. Then the ties had been cut and had not been renewed because of the intensification of the war.

Thich Tri Do contended, as did his Roman Catholic colleagues, that his church was permitted freedom of worship by the Communist regime. He said there were two hundred pagodas in Hanoi and about five hundred monks practicing in the city. He said there were no hindrances to monks entering the faith and insisted that the government put up no barrier to relations between the Buddhists of North Vietnam and their coreligionists in other lands. However, when I pressed him as to what trips outside the country had been made by North Vietnamese Buddhists, he conceded that these had been few for the last two or three years "because of the war with the United States." Before this, he said, there had been frequent exchanges of visits with Buddhists in Cambodia, China, India and Japan.

He spoke at length of the destruction of pagodas during air raids. In the United States attacks of December 2, 4, 13 and 14 in the Hanoi region, he contended, ten pagodas had been damaged. In the country at large, he asserted, about one hundred pagodas had been destroyed by bombs, with the most severe destruction occurring, as might be expected, in the region of the Demilitarized Zone, along the North-South border, where the bombing had been heaviest. He estimated that ten monks had been killed.

He looked forward to the reunification of the country at the end of the war and to the reunification of the Buddhist churches in North and South Vietnam.

I had talked often enough with religious leaders in other Communist countries to know that one must always assess their remarks with care. After all, they had to live and work and carry on the faith under difficult conditions. There is no escape for the Church from Communism. The priests and the bonzes must stay with their flocks and try to keep alive the faith as best they can. This often means that they must make compromises to find a way of living with Communist rulers with whom they have no sympathy.

I also knew that in times of stress, such as war, Communist regimes were likely to relax their oppression of religion. Religion is a unifying force. Men turn to it in times of trouble. In the Soviet Union during World War II Stalin gave up his atheistic campaign and made a concordat with the Orthodox Church. He halted attacks on the Church and suppressed the League of Atheists and in return the Church gave full support to the war. Something very much like that might well be in progress in North Vietnam. The regime had need of all the country's strength in this moment of crisis. Surely, at present, the churches, both the Roman Catholic and the Buddhist, were standing with the government and with the people in what all saw as a threat to the nation's life. All were suffering from the American air offensive. The pagodas and the churches suffered along with the houses and the villages. It was what one must expect. But one had also to expect the corollary that in the face of common attack the men of God and the men of Marx would be drawn closer together in the single cause of mutual survival. This was a by-product of our bombing which the targeting experts of the Air Force would never be likely to understand.

At 4:30 on a chilly Christmas morning I found myself sitting in the dark and deserted lobby of the Thong Nhat Hotel. I shivered a little as the cold air swept in from the outside with the slow turn of the revolving door. It was, I thought, just about the hour when, as a kid, I had awakened in my icy bedroom and slithered out from under the warm covers to sneak into the parlor and see whether Santa Claus had really come and whether, after all, he had gotten the letter about the toy train. Four-thirty A.M. on Christmas morning was not an hour when anyone but Santa-excited children were apt to be awake. I was awake now only because I had been told the night before to be dressed and ready to leave on a trip to the south. I had asked to see the countryside and, specifically, some of the areas which had been attacked by American bombers, and I was being taken somewhere to the south— just where was not very clear to me.

I sat, waiting for my interpreter to appear. There was a

line of milky neon lights which ran around the molding of the lobby, but they had been turned off. I could see a small tropical pine which had been set up for the Christmas party in a green porcelain urn and decorated with wisps of red and white cellophane that looked as if they might have come from cigarette packages. Beyond the tree was the bar with its sign saying that it closed at 11 P.M., and behind the bar was an array of bottles. There was one of Gordon's gin. Another of Stolichnaya vodka. One of Bulgarian slivovitz and innumerable bottles of Vietnamese wine and spirits. Not a very appetizing display at this ghastly hour of the morning.

Presently the interpreter showed up and we got into the car and started out through the dark streets. There was little traffic in the city, but I was startled to see a solitary man beside a boulevard patiently digging a manhole air-raid shelter. I wondered whether it was his own project or whether he had been assigned to dig it in his free hours—the latter, I suspected.

We were driving out of Hanoi to the south, moving down Route Nationale No. 1, and the traffic thickened as we neared the outskirts of the city. It was raining lightly and had been raining more heavily a few hours earlier. There were few lights, but I could see that we were passing through an industrial area. We fell into a long line of truck traffic, mostly big military two-and-a-half-ton trucks turned out by the Likhachev factory of Moscow, a product I was very familiar with from my long years in the Soviet Union. They moved down the highway steadily with a variety of burdens—I could not make out exactly what because of the murk and because each truck was carefully camouflaged with a canopy of boughs and tropical leaves. This, I was to learn, was the constant dress of motor vehicles outside of Hanoi, and most of the vehicles inside the city had also acquired a permanent tropical decor. The black Volga in which I traveled was not camouflaged—not on this day, which was Christmas, when the truce supposedly was in effect. But on subsequent trips I learned to expect that the Volga would be decked out in a fishnet in which leaves would be inserted.

Camouflage was not confined to trucks and cars. Most North Vietnamese men wore pith sun helmets, women wore broad conical straw hats and schoolchildren wore a heavy plaited straw hat which was said to be almost impervious to shrapnel fragments, and all these headpieces were turned into a kind of bird's nest of leaves and twigs. Even bicycles were camouflaged and babies carried on their mothers' backs were sometimes decked out in leaves.

But such things were difficult to see in the darkness. Meanwhile, I was surprised at the heavy truck movement southward, but the longer I stayed in North Vietnam, the more familiar I became with the traffic pattern on the highways. The trucks formed up in convoys in Hanoi in the late afternoon. During the day they were scattered about, but toward dusk they collected at loading points and then began to roll out of the city as darkness fell. There was little or no movement of trucks or supplies southward except after dark. But once night came the highways bustled with movement which continued, so far as I could see, until dawn.

I watched the procession of trucks roll down the highway that chilly Christmas morning. They were using their headlights, although these were dim and hardly sufficient to see by. At first I thought that this was because of the Christmas truce and that normally they must proceed down the highway blacked out. But I was mistaken. They used dim lights in the northern part of North Vietnam because the Americans did not engage in night bombing there. I didn't know why that was, but it was our policy. In southern North Vietnam, however, bombing went on around the clock, with flare planes illuminating the targets at night. And in southern North Vietnam, I was told, the trucks drove blacked out. But it was also true that in that part of the country there was little reliance on trucks and more on bicycles or human backs.

On this first morning of mine on the highway the bulk of the movement was by truck. Occasionally we would encounter bicycle brigades or work brigades, possibly going out to perform specific tasks. All during the first hours the truck convoys steadily moved south. Not without occasional interruption. The murky weather, the slippery roads, the dim lighting caused accidents. In one ten-mile stretch there were two traffic jams due to truck collisions. Here and there I noticed trucks in ditches. It seemed obvious that there was a fairly heavy accident toll in the movement of supplies southward, leaving aside the damage which was done to the convoys by American bombing.

Gradually dawn came and I could see that we were traveling across flat, open rice-paddy country, crisscrossed with canals or streams. Alongside the highway for considerable distances ran the railroad, and with the arrival of daylight I could observe for the first time the substantial evidences of our bombing offensive and its results.

There were bomb craters beside the highway and frequently along the roadbed of the rail line, which was a light, single-track system, a bit narrower than the standard American gauge. The railroad was operating, and from time to time we passed freight trains with a string of small boxcars, looking a bit like toys in contrast to my mind's image of American rolling stock. Bridges had been one of the chief objectives of our air attacks, and nearly every one we crossed had been damaged. But in this area, not far from Hanoi, the bridges had been repaired by one means or another and we moved across them without much delay—although some had only one instead of two traffic lanes.

Not long after daylight we passed through a town that seemed to have been almost obliterated by bombs. "That's Phuly," my guide said. "We'll stop there on the way back." I caught only a glimpse of Phuly, but there seemed little to see. On both sides of the road there were ruins. Along one side I saw a twisted string of small boxcars.

On our return trip we stopped in Phuly and I had a good look at it. It was a long, narrow town about forty miles south of Hanoi that had once lain beside the main railroad. I say "once" advisedly. There was no more town of Phuly—at least so far as I could observe. It was all gone. Just ruins of buildings strung out along the highway. Of the market, which lay between the highway and the railroad, only a few gaping walls remained. An official said that the town had been attacked five times on October 1 and that there had been two more attacks the following day. On October 9, he continued, there had been nine more attacks. More than a thousand bombs had been dropped in the assaults, I was told, many of them five-hundred- and thousand-kilogram bombs. None of the raids, said the official, had ever been announced. Phuly had had a population of ten thousand before it was attacked. Now only a handful of people were left.

I could see one obvious military target in Phuly. There was a small siding, a few strips of track where, I supposed, cars were shunted off. I thought I understood what had happened here. The American planes had come in to take out the railroad and the siding. Along with the tracks the town had vanished. It would take a long time to restore the town, but the railroad was working again. Indeed, while I walked through the ruins a train slowly passed by.

It was possible, of course, that there were more military objectives in Phuly than were visible to my eye. There was a bridge across a river and the highway itself. Possibly there were depots of one sort or another. But whatever the targets were, they had hardly been very imposing. This was obvious from the insignificant wreckage.

The grim World War II joke came into my mind: "One of our cities is missing." Now it had happened here in North Vietnam. Not to a city but to an obscure railroad town.

For the full distance that the railroad paralleled the highway—and we struck off from Route Nationale No. 1 after a time—I saw heaps of the light steel rails which are used by the Vietnamese system, cords of railroad ties, sometimes neatly stacked, sometimes simply strewn across the countryside, newly crushed gravel and stone for repairing the roadbed and great tangles of steel rods which, I supposed, were used to strengthen the bed and possibly the highway— although for the most part the highway seemed to be kept in repair simply by filling in bomb craters with the clay soil which everywhere surrounded us.

The longer we drove, the more impressed I became with the quantity of railroad repair material at hand. I estimated after the trip, and the impression was strengthened on my other trips about the country, that the North Vietnamese had enough rails and other supplies available to construct a couple of more railroads, should they desire.

The railroad and the highway, running side by side across the completely flat terrain, crossing and recrossing canal after canal and river after river, represented a bombardier's dream. Nothing could be easier to locate and hit from the air. There was no possible way in which the rail and highway network could be concealed, no way in which the American planes could be confused. It was like flying over a relief map in which the targets were outlined in red neon lights. Not only was the network plainly visible from any altitude, but it was incredibly vulnerable because of the streams and canals, each of which had to be crossed by a bridge. Knock out one, two or three bridges and the whole transport system from the North could be immobilized.

I imagined the target planners at their conferences. Certainly, air power could readily interdict the movement of men and supplies from North to South—or impede it so decidedly as materially to affect the ability of the Vietcong and their parent organization, the National Liberation Front, to carry on the war.

Yet here I was traveling along this dream target for strategic bombing and I could see with my own eyes that the movement of men, materials, food and munitions had not been halted. How could this be? We had been attacking the North for two years, and our bombing operations in this area of the Hanoi-Haiphong complex had been in full progress for more than a year. We had certainly destroyed sections of the railroad time and again. I could see bridges that had been blasted beyond repair. I bumped over stretches of highway that had been relaid several times. Yet traffic was moving. It was moving in very large quantities. And this, I quickly learned, was not just because a Christmas truce was on. This was the normal pattern in the North. The traffic flowed out of Hanoi and Haiphong night after night after night. It rolled down the highway and down the railroad. Never, so far as I could learn, had it been seriously impeded. Difficulties, yes. Barriers, no.

The way this was accomplished was one of the most important aspects of the war. It provided the clue to North Vietnam's ability to continue fighting against the United States despite the massive air power we had mobilized.

The secret of the North Vietnamese success was not hard to grasp. It lay in a massive investment of manpower, labor and matériel and a careful utilization of national resources.

It was really no great trick to keep the highways open. They were usually, but not always, tar surfaced. They were simple roadways laid over the clay soil. If bombs cratered a highway, all that was needed was to round up a repair gang with shovels. The holes could be filled in and the road resurfaced in an hour or two.

More difficult were the bridges. But here I was impressed by the ingenuity and practicality of North Vietnam's solution. If a bridge was damaged but traffic could be handled on one lane, that single lane was kept open while the other was being repaired. If the bridge was completely knocked out, a pontoon was put into service. The pontoons could not have been simpler in concept or easier to put into place. They were made by lashing together the required number of shallow flat-bottomed wooden canal boats, of which there were countless numbers available along the canals and streams. These sturdy boats, three feet wide and perhaps sixteen feet long, made an excellent bridge. A surface of cut bamboo poles was laid across them, without even being lashed or nailed in many cases. Or, if available, a surface of bamboo planks. The trucks lumbered over the pontoons with a roar as their wheels hit the loose poles, but the pontoons seemed sturdy enough to bear the heavy traffic. In most cases where a permanent bridge was knocked out, two pontoons were pressed into service—one to handle traffic moving south, the other to accommodate the empty trucks returning north.

Foreigners who had watched the pontoons being put into place said this seldom took more than a couple of hours. The boats and bamboo poles were kept available at every bridge, the expectation being that sooner or later the bridge would be knocked out.

The problem of keeping the railroad operating was more difficult. Trains could not run across pontoons. To repair a steel-girdered railroad bridge was not a task of a few hours. If it could be done in a few days, that was fast action.

But here, too, native ingenuity was called into play. If the rail line was blocked by destruction of a bridge or trackage, bicycle brigades were called up. Five hundred men and women and their bicycles would be sent to the scene of the break. They would unload the stalled freight train, putting the cargo on the bikes. Each bicycle would handle a six-hundred-pound load, balanced across the frame with a bar. The bicycles would be wheeled, not ridden, over a pontoon bridge, and on the other side of the break a second train would be drawn up. The cargo would be reloaded and moved on south.

So much time, manpower and material were being invested in keeping the railroad in operation that I seriously pondered the military advisability of the effort. It seemed to me that allocating the same manpower and material to the trucking operation would be more efficient and economical. The truck route could not be interdicted for more than a short time, regardless of the intensity and frequency of American attacks. Why not abandon the railroad?

The answer was not readily forthcoming. It was obvious that the North Vietnamese took enormous pride in keeping the railroad going. It was a symbol of their ability to overcome the enormous technological advantage of the Americans. Just as a factor in morale perhaps it was felt that the sacrifice was worthwhile.

Another aspect was that Communist China was the principal provider of steel, rolling stock, angle irons, signal mechanisms and other equipment for the railroad. Indeed, it was said that Chinese railroad battalions were helping to maintain the sections of the line which came down across the Chinese frontier to the north. China had a special interest in keeping the railroad open, for trackage in North Vietnam provided the most convenient access between two Chinese cities, Nanning and Kunming.

There was another consideration. The railroad operated on coal which was provided by North Vietnam's own mines. And, if necessary, the boilers of the small old-fashioned locomotives could even be fired with wood. But trucks were utterly dependent upon gasoline and oil and every gallon had to be brought into North Vietnam by tanker from the Soviet Union or Rumania. Cut off the gasoline and oil and highway traffic would largely be limited to bicycles and human backs. Perhaps the railroad was kept in repair as a reserve against the possibility that the flow of fuel might be ended should we, as many in North Vietnam anticipated, ultimately begin a systematic bombing of Haiphong, the major North Vietnamese port.

Already our attacks on petroleum storage capacity had been one of our most successful military blows. Our initial attacks on Haiphong in early July, I was told, destroyed at a single blow the storage tanks there. Subsequent air strikes against small depots in the Hanoi and Haiphong area had eliminated all the consequential storage facilities in the country.

I could see the consequence of this as I drove across the countryside. Wherever I looked, or so it seemed, I saw strewn about the nearby fields or along the highways and cross lanes fifty-five-gallon steel drums, in which North Vietnam's petroleum supplies were now stored. The random dispersal of these drums by the thousands in city, town and rural rice paddy insured that they could not effectively be attacked by American air power. The dispersal, of course, was not without cost to Hanoi in manpower and matériel. It was inconvenient to have to collect the drums from rice paddies and village backyards whenever a convoy of trucks had to be fueled. But it was typical of the rough-and-ready techniques by which

North Vietnam managed to carry forward its war effort with no great interruption despite the incredible weight of American firepower.

Not merely gasoline and oil were dispersed over the countryside. As previously noted, railroad and highway building materials were scattered higgledy-piggledy in every direction, so that I was seldom out of sight of them. The only rule seemed to be to keep them fairly close to some road so that it would not be too difficult to reassemble them when needed.

And the same system was employed with other equipment. I saw crates and bits of machinery, large weapons cases, huge boxes which contained, I guessed, shells and munitions, hardware of the most diverse sort, simply staked out in fields, let down beside rural roads, cluttering paths that led to rice paddies—indeed, in all the time I rode about the countryside I think I was never more than two or three minutes out of sight of some kind of supplies and equipment which had come to rest in the most unlikely setting.

While I was in Hanoi an article appeared in an aviation publication by an Englishman named Norman Barrymaine describing a visit he had made to Haiphong. He told of quantities of supplies which, by his description, had been piled up along the highways. He attributed this to the disruption of transportation. The North Vietnamese were unable, he thought, to move their needed munitions and guns to the South. He painted a sad picture of the roads between Hanoi and Haiphong and said the peasants talked of the highway as the "road that was"—meaning it no longer could be traversed. It often took four days, he reported, to travel from Hanoi to Haiphong.

His portrait was almost diametrically opposite to the conclusions at which I arrived, although some of the elements were the same. The practice of storing military supplies in the open, dispersing them in fields and along roads, to protect them from enemy bombing, was not invented in Hanoi. It was widely used in World War II. I saw it in Russia, where, sometimes, it seemed that half the machinery and munitions in the country had been scattered into the fields. I saw it in the islands of the South Pacific and in the hedgerows of England. It was a common, sensible military precaution—especially if, as in North Vietnam, the enemy had absolute command of the air.

So far as the clogging of the roads between Hanoi and

Haiphong was concerned and the difficulty of moving supplies out of the area, my impressions did not jibe with Barrymaine's. Nor did his impressions accord with those of Western diplomats in Hanoi who moved between Hanoi and Haiphong freely without any special interruption. They had often been subjected to air attacks in the course of such trips and reported that the bridges not infrequently were knocked out. But they never had to spend several days on the trip.

The diplomats did report that trips from Hanoi to Haiphong, like almost every trip outside the North Vietnamese capital, were normally undertaken at night because of the dangers of American bombing. I met no one who had taken longer than three or four hours to make the forty-mile journey, unless delayed by many hours spent in air-raid shelters. One explanation of Barrymaine's impressions became clear much later when I heard he had spent only a day or so in Haiphong and had not been permitted to leave the harbor area.

There was no question that the Haiphong Harbor was badly jammed with shipping, that it was attempting to handle much more traffic than its facilities could accommodate, that ships were slow in being unloaded and that supplies accumulated on the docks and wharves despite every effort of the North Vietnamese to disperse them quickly lest the harbor be bombed.

But that was another story. That was a by-product of the Soviet-Chinese tensions. It had nothing to do with the effectiveness or noneffectiveness of American bombing.

After extensive examination of the results of the United States bombing attacks, after discussing the situation in detail with the North Vietnamese, with the Western diplomats in Hanoi and with the extremely well-informed and remarkably outspoken East European diplomats there, I concluded that the military consequences of the bombing were almost identical with those which had been achieved in North Korea.

In North Korea the United States Air Force had ruled the skies. It was able to bomb at will against the Chinese when they entered the Korean War, crossing the Yalu River. It was able to attack by day and night all the supply trails and roads down which the Chinese troops and their supplies poured. But it was never able to halt that Chinese stream. It inflicted heavy casualties, but it did not keep the Chinese from moving south.

The same story on different terrain, on terrain which was much more to our advantage than the difficult valleys and mountains of North Korea, was being spelled out in North Vietnam. Strategic air power or even tactical air power was not able to halt the movement of a determined, tough and skillful enemy. At best it could only slow down or make more difficult his movement of men and supplies. And, as I was soon to learn, there were countervailing factors which, from my viewpoint, canceled out the minor military value of the enormously expensive United States bombing effort.

Every war propels some obscure city or town into the lime-light, a community which has existed in respectable anonymity for hundreds of years and now suddenly is on everyone's lips. Chance, historical accident, is responsible for this. There was nothing about Guernica which would have caused anyone to predict that it would be a name to survive the fading memory of the Spanish Civil War. Coventry was an ordinary English Midlands cathedral town until it was blitzed by the Germans and Stalingrad was a dreary Soviet industrial city before the battle. No one would have guessed in 1939 that Rotterdam would become a headline name in 1940.

Before Christmas Day, 1966, I had never heard of Namdinh. Possibly I had read the name somewhere but, if so, I did not remember it. But after Christmas Day, 1966, I would never forget Namdinh. Nor, I think, would many other Americans. Namdinh became a catalyst, a kind of prism through which the United States bombing offensive in North

Vietnam took on human dimensions. For the first time we began to see beyond the barrier of meaningless military terminology, the banal vocabulary that turns reality into a kind of etymological stew.

Namdinh is not much to look at. We drove down to it along Route Nationale No. 1 but branched off the main highway fifteen or twenty miles north of the city and veered to the east. At one point we took a detour of several miles through paddies and small villages, traveling along a newly widened and improved road which ran for considerable distances along the top of levees or barriers which had been thrown up to separate the endless rice fields with their ever-flowing water. The detour was necessary because a bridge was out—destroyed in an American attack only a day or two earlier.

We came into Namdinh from the north, and almost all the streets we drove through bore signs of bomb damage. Because we had started out so early there had been no time for breakfast, and now I was invited to sit down in one room of what seemed to be a kind of municipal office to drink some tea, eat some bread and butter (which came from the hotel in Hanoi) and have some tangerines and fragrant small bananas.

Two local officials briefed me about Namdinh, and from them I learned that it was a textile city of about ninety thousand people before most of them had been evacuated. They said Namdinh had been repeatedly subjected to United States attack—fifty-one or fifty-two raids up to that moment, including four on December 23. There had been, I was told, American reconnaissance planes over the city during the night, and thus far on Christmas morning the alert had sounded twice.

Nguyen Tien Canh, a member of the Namdinh Municipal Council, a small alert man dressed for the cold weather in a blue quilted jacket, said that Namdinh was the third largest city in North Vietnam and was situated about twenty miles from the Gulf of Tonkin. He described it as a center for the production of consumer goods, particularly textiles. Its large textile plant normally employed thirteen thousand workers, 70 percent of whom were women. About ten thousand residents were engaged in handicraft production. The principal industries, in addition to the big cotton textile works, were a silk mill, a fruit canning factory, a farm tool plant, a rice mill and a cooperative which made thread.

Namdinh might be North Vietnam's third largest city, but if this was all it produced, it hardly sounded like a prime target. The officials, including the Mayor, a petite woman named Tran Thi Doan, who had been a textile worker herself, insisted that so far as they were aware the city possessed no military objectives whatever.

Of course, definitions of military objectives are apt to differ between the civilians who live in a town and the men in the planes dropping the bombs. The residents of Namdinh reinforced their contention that the city could not be considered an important target area by insisting that it had never been mentioned as a target of attack in a United States communiqué.

The question whether Namdinh possessed significant military objectives and whether it had been mentioned in a communiqué later became the focus of a brush-fire controversy, touched off in Washington by the Pentagon. The Pentagon insisted that Namdinh, in contradiction to the portrait painted by its inhabitants, was a formidable military objective. It possessed a railroad line, a main highway, river transshipment facilities, naval facilities, oil storage dumps and other impressive installations. It was not correct to say it had not been mentioned as a United States target. By careful researching of available records it was found that on three separate occasions in the spring of 1966 the name Namdinh had been pronounced by the United States military briefing officer in Saigon. The briefing officer's references to Namdinh took several days to unearth and then were forthcoming only upon the inquiry and insistence of correspondents in Washington.* The mentions of Namdinh by the briefing officer, moreover, had been so inconsequential that the name of the city had never appeared in any *New York Times* war dispatch out of Saigon. Indeed, *The New York Times* Index showed only one reference to Namdinh more recent than 1954—a mention of the city in an article by James Cameron, the British journalist who visited North Vietnam in 1965.

This was hardly surprising. Like most of the "military objectives" which I was to see in North Vietnam, Namdinh seemed much more imposing in the language of a Pentagon spokesman than when viewed with the naked eye.

It was not a big city. It never had been. Now, under the effects of wartime evacuation, it was largely abandoned. There was little traffic in the streets. Once, the city officials contended, there had been 3 senior high schools, 6 junior highs and 20 primary schools with a total of 24,060 pupils. Not all of these institutions and children had been evacuated. There were still 172 primary school classes, 78 junior high

---

* Neil Sheehan says that the communiqués about the Namdinh bombings were issued on April 29, May 19, and June 1, and the bombings took place the previous days. The communiqué of April 29 said the bombings were directed against the Namdinh railroad. The communiqué of May 19 said the Namdinh railroad was bombed. The communiqué of June 1 said the bombings were directed against the Namdinh naval facility and railroad yard.

and 8 senior high school classes in the city. There had been a school for training medical assistants, a vocational school, a trade school for construction workers and two normal schools. All these had been transferred to the countryside.

The textile factory, according to the officials, was still operating but had been hit in nineteen attacks. When we drove through the battered area of the plant, it immediately became apparent that the term "operating" was a euphemism. I saw one unit where it was obvious that some activity was being carried on since a pipe was emitting steam. It was equally obvious from the shattered walls, windows and roofs of most of the textile sheds that the bulk of the plant had been abandoned.

The silk mill had been destroyed, and no pretense was made that it was still working. The thread cooperative had been devastated along with half the buildings on the street where it stood.

After my dispatches began appearing in *The Times,* Arthur Sylvester, then the chief spokesman for the Pentagon, urged that I walk down the main street of Namdinh, where, he said, I would find a large antiaircraft installation. I only wished I could have taken him with me on the stroll. My car had passed down the main street and turned at an intersection. No antiaircraft installation was in sight that day. Nor was one in sight on New Year's Day when some other visitors were in Namdinh. The nearest thing to a military installation which I saw on Namdinh's main street was a rather pretty militia woman, or traffic officer. She had a small revolver on her hip, but I doubted that it would have been effective against a supersonic attack bomber.

I got a thorough lesson in American air technology in Namdinh. I was not familiar with the names and types of the current generation of United States fighting aircraft. But everyone in Namdinh knew them by heart. They rattled off the designations—F-105's, F4H's, RB-57's, A3Z's, A4A's, A6A's. According to the residents of the city, the chief weight of attacks came from aircraft based on the Seventh Fleet carriers which stood offshore in the Gulf of Tonkin. Namdinh, they said, was a favorite target of the Seventh Fleet. The people were equally familiar with the technology of bombs. They spoke of MK81's, MK83's, MK84's, 70-mm. rockets and bullpups the way American teen-agers mention the latest pop recording artists.

According to the inhabitants of Namdinh, the first serious raid on their city occurred June 28, 1965. This was carried out by two F-105's and two F4H's, they said, and took place about 7:30 on a cloudy morning. Two bullpup missiles had been fired into the area of the textile plant, they asserted, and ten persons, including three children, had been killed and twelve wounded.

Many attacks, they said, had occurred at night, although U.S. planes do not usually attack at night in the North, and on occasion as many as twenty-seven planes had participated.

One of the worst attacks I was told, had hit Hang Thao (Silk Street) at about 6:30 A.M., April 14. This was a heavily populated thoroughfare, and normally there were 17,680 people living in the quarter. However, because of evacuation only 2,300 remained. The bombs fell just at the moment when factories were changing shifts, and 49 people were said to have been killed and 135 wounded. It was also asserted that 240 houses were destroyed.

Another bad attack was launched in Hoang Van Thu Street, the residents said, not far from Silk Street, on May 18. Normally this section had a population in the thousands, but evacuation had brought the number down to 230. It had been an area of busy shops in the center of the Chinese quarter. Nearby was the big Roman Catholic church and many temples. At 11:04 A.M. two F4H planes emerged from the clouds, according to the residents. It was raining and had been raining for some time. Water was deep in the streets and many shelters were overflowing. Eight bombs, they said, fell in the area in a south-to-north bombing run. People were unable to get into shelters and some who did were drowned. There were thirteen killed and eleven wounded in the attack, I was told.

We drove about Namdinh, through the textile area, and stopped in Silk Street. For blocks and blocks I could see nothing but desolation. Residential housing, stores, all the buildings were destroyed, damaged or abandoned. I felt that I was walking through the city of a vanished civilization. Here and there a handful of young men and women were at work, patiently pulling down lumber from broken houses and neatly stacking it. Many of the streets were so devastated that no one could live in them. Others had simply been abandoned in the wholesale evacuation.

I saw only one enterprise which seemed to be functioning

at close to the normal rate. This was the rice mill. All about it were evidences of bomb damage. The mill itself had been hit, but no vital portion had been struck. As we walked up to it, two young women workers were practicing military calisthenics, racing over a series of low hurdles, rifles in hand, then throwing themselves sprawling on the earth at the end of the course and taking aim at imaginary targets. Inside the mill I saw stacked beside almost every production post a rifle. Some were propped beside open windows. Each worker had his tin helmet and a first-aid kit. Air-raid shelters were built into the plant on the ground floor, some of them concrete embrasures under the milling machinery. At the sound of the air-raid sirens the workers would grab their rifles and take up posts at the windows and on the roof to fire back at the American planes. Those who had no guns went into the shelters.

It was not only the city of Namdinh which had been savagely damaged. The area of destruction continued outside the city. We drove out along the Dao River dike and came upon a band of a thousand or more young men and women constructing a great supplementary dike to hold back the waters of the Dao from Namdinh. This construction work had been undertaken, the officials said, because of repeated American attacks on the Dao dike system. Six bombs had hit the dikes on May 31 and July 14, they said. I saw several large craters and filled-in portions of the dike which indicated their story had some substance. There was no doubt in the minds of the Namdinh officials—and the Namdinh citizens—that the dikes were being deliberately attacked by United States aircraft. The danger to the city from such attacks was extreme. The whole of Namdinh is six, eight or even fourteen feet below water level during the rainy season. A breach of the levees would destroy the community. So seriously did the North Vietnamese regard this danger that they not only were building the massive new earthen wall outside the city. They had constructed supplementary dikes running right through Namdinh itself as partial insurance against a breach.

As I walked through Silk Street and saw the battered tower of the cathedral with its strings of red pennants and its white star of Bethlehem mounted for Christmas, looking out over a sea of destruction, I could not help but think of other scenes of wartime desolation, the earliest of which I had seen as a child in the London *Illustrated News* and the *Midweek Pictorial:* the shattered walls of Ypres and Rheims, the gaping craters I walked past every London morning between Park Lane and the North Audley Street mess, the chasms where workers' apartments once stood around Leningrad's Narva gates, the Evangelical church in Berlin's Kurfurstendamm which might serve as a memorial of all war's desolation for all time.

Now it had happened to another city, a remote city in a remote country, a city whose name meant nothing to practically anyone in the whole of the United States, a city so obscure that we would have to hunt for it on the map of a country whose name most of us could not pronounce.

What earthly meaning could be extracted from this destruction? What military purpose was it serving?

It was hard to comprehend as I sat in the air-raid shelter outside the Namdinh municipal headquarters talking with the Mayor, a woman whose petite figure suggested an age much closer to twenty than forty. Hardly had we gotten back from looking at the Dao River levees than the air alert sounded, at 2:26 P.M. We went to the bunker and sat there looking out at the sunshine which had just succeeded the day-long clouds.

A great deal of Namdinh, said Mayor Doan, had disappeared—probably 13 percent of the city's housing, residences for 12,464 people. Casualties had been, considering everything, remarkably low—only 89 killed and 405 wounded, she said. But, of course, she added, 80 percent of the city's population had been evacuated and not many more than fifteen thousand people remained in Namdinh. My impression that it was a ghost city was borne out by her statistics.

Why had Namdinh been attacked so heavily and so often?

"The Americans think they can touch our hearts," said Nguyen Tien Canh, meaning that the Americans thought they could intimidate the population. It was his belief that by a silent unannounced assault on Namdinh the United States was seeking to give North Vietnam an object lesson. This is what we can do to Hanoi if we wish—that was supposed to be the moral. So the officials of Namdinh thought.

There was no way for me to know whether their belief had any justification. All I knew was that Namdinh had taken a remarkable weight of high explosive and steel. The people of Namdinh and their residential areas had suffered heavy punishment—regardless of what might or might not be the intent of our military strategists.

I wondered as I sat in the shelter waiting for the all-clear—which finally sounded at 2:47 P.M.—whether there might be some vital military objective in Namdinh which was not visible to my eye, some secret installation which we were relentlessly trying to destroy or cripple. It seemed unlikely, but the whole story of Namdinh had a quality of unreality, like some terrible dream in a Dada painting. One could almost imagine our bombers coming again and again and again, attacking and attacking, trying to hit some phantom which ever eluded them because it never had existed.

I put my thoughts down on paper when I returned to Hanoi on Christmas evening and sent a dispatch off to *The New York Times* which shocked the Pentagon and produced a rash of denials, assaults on my personal reliability and hastily fabricated explanations. But after all the statements and all the verbal brickbats had been hurled, the mystery of Namdinh remained. For even by the Pentagon's least strict definition there were no very remarkable targets in Namdinh. True, materials going south passed through the city. True, there was a railroad, a (small) freight yard, an area along the river bank where boat and barge cargo was sorted out and reshipped. But it didn't amount to much. This, I was to come to find, was one of the tragedies of the Vietnam war, and perhaps the fatal fallacy in our whole bombing policy. When you totaled all the "military objectives" in North Vietnam, they didn't total much. The best of them from the military standpoint were the roads and railroads. We were hitting these with a tremendous amount of muscle. But the stuff still went through. North Vietnam was paying a tragic price in order that the architects of our bombing policy might prove its validity. But I wondered whether, in the end, the heaviest price might not be that paid by us Americans for our stubborn pursuit of a military theory which seemed to have little connection with reality. Would we not in the end suffer more deeply for permitting this folly to continue than the poor, battered, destitute people and their habitations upon which we insisted on imposing the grandiose title of "military objective"?

One morning I visited the March 8th Textile Factory on the outskirts of Hanoi, a big cotton-fabricating plant whose name honored International Women's Day, celebrated on March 8 in Communist countries. Construction of the factory had begun on March 8, 1960, and the plant had gone into partial production on March 8, 1963. It had not been finished until March 8, 1965, shortly after the launching of the American air offensive in North Vietnam, and by that time some of its units already were being evacuated to other parts of the country.

On the morning I visited the plant, a very dismal morning which even the customary cups of hot China tea did little to brighten, it was not operating at a very high level of efficiency. As we walked through the shops, some of them half empty due to the evacuation of workers and machinery, the girls were huddled in groups, gossiping and laughing.

They hardly looked up when the deputy director of the factory strolled through with a foreign visitor.

The plant had employed seven thousand workers, 70 percent of them women, at the peak of its production, but now two-thirds of them had been evacuated, along with various units of the factory, to villages thirty-five to sixty miles from Hanoi. Although the deputy director, Mai Xu Tan But, insisted that production was being maintained at normal levels, this hardly seemed credible to me.

Working conditions in this plant were equal or superior to those in most industries in Hanoi. The women worked an eight-hour day with a half-hour lunch break. The factory was on a three-shift basis. Workers averaged three dong a day in pay and got a 20 percent premium for night work. The base pay was two dong a day, and the rest was incentive payments and premiums for good production. The deputy director earned 145 dong a month, which was very high by North Vietnamese standards. Average pay for a worker in North Vietnam ran about 70 dong a month and few officials earned more than 150 dong. It was hard to calculate the purchasing power of the dong. It bore a nominal value of 3.53 to the dollar, but I doubted that this had much relationship to reality. The workers in this factory, according to Mr. But, averaged 78 dong a month and spent about one-third of their wages on basic items. Some were extremely inexpensive. The plant provided housing at a cost of only 1 percent of wages. Free transportation to and from work was provided, either by bus or bicycle, so that the principal outlays were for food and clothing, both of which were strictly rationed. Electricity, however, was very costly, and many workers did not have electric lights in their apartments.

The factory offered free medical and social services, but these facilities, it was said, had been evacuated to the provinces. The machinery in the plant came mostly from China, but some items were of Soviet origin. Possibly reflecting the factory's dependence upon the two great Communist countries, the director's office was decorated not only with the customary portrait of Ho Chi Minh, before which stood a tall vase of salmon-pink gladioli, but also with colored photographs of the Kremlin and the Tien An Men Square in Peking.

There was another exhibit in the plant which I found duplicated in most institutions I visited in North Vietnam. Next to a case in which cotton goods manufactured by the factory were displayed, there was a small heap of bomb fragments, pieces of American rockets and other military debris. This had been picked up, the director said, after the December 13 bombing of Hanoi. At least one rocket had exploded on or just above the glass roof of one large plant building, I was told, shattering the glass and doing minor damage. As we walked through the loom rooms, the patched-up roof and shards of glass on the cement floor provided visible evidence of the recent attack.

The partial evacuation of the March 8th textile plant was typical of industries in Hanoi. Some elements of almost every enterprise in the city had been moved out of the capital in the government's program of "preparing for the worst"— preparing for a sustained American bombardment of Hanoi and Haiphong.

North Vietnam had been deliberately conditioned to expect this escalation of the war. Not because President Ho Chi Minh wanted the war to be stepped up to this level but because he and his colleagues felt that escalation was the consistent pattern of American strategy, reflecting what Hanoi regarded as the frustration of U.S. officers at their inability to compel the North Vietnamese to yield.

As one North Vietnamese told me, the Americans first began to bomb just north of the 17th parallel. Then they extended their attacks to the 19th, to the 20th, to the 21st parallels. They ranged into the northern, the northwestern and the northeastern parts of the country. In July, 1966, they penetrated the areas of Hanoi and Haiphong. Now bombing was going ahead in every region, every province of North Vietnam. In these circumstances it was natural to prepare for the worst—the systematic bombing of Hanoi and Haiphong.

The country would fight on despite the attacks on the capital and its principal port. This was the determination of the leadership, and it was this for which the populace was being prepared.

Plans had been completed for the removal from Hanoi of all industries and facilities which could be moved. Some enterprises, it was conceded, could not be evacuated and would have to be abandoned or else try to operate under saturation bombing conditions in the event the war took this turn.

As to the future of Hanoi, the North Vietnamese displayed remarkable aplomb. They expected that their capital would be wiped out. They were not despondent. They already had in preparation architectural plans for the construction of a new capital. They would not rebuild Hanoi, at least not as a seat of government. They had picked a new site not far distant where the new capital would be erected once the war was over. After all, they said, Hanoi is a small old ugly city. It symbolizes the French occupation. After the war we will build our own capital. In fact, we have been thinking of doing this in any event.

It was true that Hanoi was run-down and shabby. The only buildings which looked fresh, bright and newly painted were the Presidential Palace, which had been the Governor General's residence, and the impressive Government Guest House, another palace that dated from French colonial times.

Half of Hanoi's population was supposed to have been evacuated to the countryside, but many of the evacuees flowed back into the city, week by week and month by month. This was particularly true of wives or husbands who found separation difficult and unpleasant. As for children, they were all supposed to have been sent from the city. But many remained. It was the personal responsibility of parents to evacuate their children and find someone in the country with whom they could live. Obviously this had not been done systematically or consistently.

Except for the finery displayed on Christmas Eve, the people's clothing had little of the brightness and color which we associate with street life in the East. The women wore their black sateen trousers, white shirtwaists and, in the currently cool weather, a cotton-padded jacket. The dull and shabby garments reflected the basic shortages which existed and which the North Vietnamese made no attempt to conceal. "Our girls don't look so pretty this year," one young man told me.

The shops were a discouragement. Some had closed. Others would have been better off closing for there was little on their shelves to buy. A special store had been established for the diplomatic colony to give foreigners access to the best of such consumer goods as were available. A visit to the diplomatic store was a commentary on the shortages which existed in the ordinary shops.

One afternoon I went to the diplomatic store, just across from the lovely Lake of the Restored Sword in the heart of Hanoi. What did I find there? The list was depressing:

Crudely cut women's slips and panties in bilious shades of

blue and pink rayon, printed handkerchiefs in blue and brown squares resembling those sold in Moscow's Stoleshnikov haberdashery stores in 1951, Chinese soap, white candles, little tin kerosene lanterns, a push-pull clown with a bell attached (from China), playing cards (from the Soviet Union), and can openers.

Another room was devoted to what passed for art goods or, I suppose, things you might buy for presents. Here I found lacquer ware of North Vietnamese manufacture, rather poorly done, cigarette boxes of wood and carved stone, rubber boots from Hanoi, plastic raincoats from China in pink and blue shades and plastic shopping bags, also in pink and blue.

On the day I visited the shop the items which seemed to be attracting the most attention were the plastic raincoats and raincapes and the rubber boots.

The section of the diplomatic store which did the most business was the food department. Here I found many diplomats shopping. Here I met some of my Soviet newspaper colleagues, and here I saw some Russians—burly men, tieless, with a rugged outdoor look about them—buying Moskovskaya vodka. They looked like, and probably were, construction workers from eastern Siberia, sent down to Hanoi to carry out some special tasks. I did not believe they were military men for they did not have the disciplined, close-shaven bearing of the Soviet Army officer.

What was there to buy in the food section? Bulgarian plum jam, jars of pickled Russian cucumbers and pickled Russian cabbage, Borzhumi mineral water, two kinds of Russian vodka (Moskovskaya and Stolichnaya), very large and fancy boxes of chocolate from China, gumdrops, Rumanian brandy, canned Russian crabmeat, Chinese powdered milk, Chinese tea, Chinese English-style tea biscuits in English-style tin boxes with English labels (very expensive) and, most improbable of all, half a dozen old boxes of Colman's mustard.

What could the Hanoi citizen buy in his own shops? Not very much.

Because of the severe shortages, many basic items of food and clothing no longer were being distributed through stores. The products were being delivered directly to the citizens through the factory or office in which they worked or at the apartment or neighborhood in which they lived.

This was not merely a matter of insuring equality in the

division of scarce items. It also related to the dispersion of supplies to minimize losses from bombing. For example, the food supply of the country had been radically decentralized. Each province and each locality now had taken on responsibility for distribution rather than vesting it all in central Hanoi agencies. Supplies were sent directly to provincial centers and it was up to the provinces to see that their people were provided for.

What were the rations? The most important was rice. Rice was the basic diet of Vietnam. So long as the rice ration was maintained, or so Western diplomats thought, North Vietnamese morale and fighting capability would not be seriously affected. The ration ranged from 8 kilograms to 20 kilograms a month, depending on the category of person—the smaller rations for evacuees, children and the aged, the larger for production workers.

The average was said to be 13 kilos, with students getting 15 and production workers 18 to 20. Persons evacuated to rural areas received 8 kilos, the theory being that they could more easily supplement their diet from local food resources. Apparently the ration had been maintained fairly well—in March of 1964 it was said to have averaged 14 kilograms a month. But there had been cuts in other kinds of food. Actually, in December, 1966, 10 percent of the ration was being provided in maize. The cost of the rationed rice, I was told, was very low—4 dong for 10 kilos.

Sugar was rationed at the rate of ½ to 1 kilo a month, depending on the recipient's category. The meat ration was 300 to 500 grams (10.5 to 17.5 ounces), and might be provided in the form of lard or fat.

Vegetables and fruit could be bought in the open market in fairly large quantities. Chicken was on sale (but not always) in government stores at 4 dong a kilo. In the peasant market it sold for double that price, or 8 dong.

The tightest item was meat. Although the basic diet of the Vietnamese is rice, they customarily eat it with meat or fish as well as vegetables. The ordinary North Vietnamese was getting very little meat under wartime conditions.

Clothing was also short. It was rationed at the equivalent of five or six yards of cloth per person per year, not much more than a cotton shirt and cotton trousers for a man or one dress for a woman.

Supplies of some essential items often vanished for a week

or two at a time. This was also true of cigarettes, matches, soap and paper. In the countryside salt was often difficult to obtain.

So far as I was able to discover, there was not much of a black market. Peasants could sell part of their produce freely for whatever the traffic would bear. But they were compelled to deliver to the state at state-fixed prices the bulk of their output. However, like peasants in any Communist country, they managed to keep enough food for their own needs and always had some to sell to city dwellers at prices that were two, or three or four times those of the state markets. Eggs, for example, were almost impossible to get in state stores, but were always available from peasants at high prices.

Despite short supplies, the government had cut some prices—largely, I thought, for purposes of morale. Bicycles, for instance, had been reduced by 30 percent. They now sold for about 200 dong. The price was the same for both Hanoi-built bikes and Chinese bicycles. The Hanoi factory had been scheduled to reach a production of 100,000 bikes in 1965, but the war had prevented it from attaining this goal. Now, with the enormous strain of moving men and material, the Chinese imports were vital in keeping North Vietnam's transportation running.

Bikes were not sold freely. To buy one required a special permit, issued through your factory or organization. On the black market a 200-dong Chinese bike fetched 1,000 dong. One evening, walking through the dark Hanoi streets, I encountered a crowd of some two hundred men and women quietly standing with their bicycles. I thought they were being dispatched to the South. Then I saw two large trucks crammed with new bicycles. The people had assembled to turn in their old worn-out bikes for new ones.

The best present you could give your girl friend in Hanoi, I was told, was not a box of candy, a bouquet of roses or even a diamond ring. It was a new bicycle chain. This and other spare bike parts constituted one of the major shortages in the country. The North Vietnamese were remarkably law-abiding people. Foreigners thought nothing of leaving a hundred dollars in cash in a bureau drawer. No servant would touch it. But bikes were different. No one left a bike without a padlock on the wheel, for bicycles were the one thing the North Vietnamese stole.

Bikes were not the only items on which prices were cut.

Medical supplies, medicines and bandages were reduced 50 percent. Radios were cut 30 percent to a range of 100 to 200 dong. But I did not find them to be very common. An official proudly told me that Hanoi did not jam the Voice of America. "We like our people to hear the V.O.A.," he said. "They can see what lies the Americans tell. For instance, it was very amusing for the people of Hanoi to hear the V.O.A. deny there had been any raids on their city on December 13 and 14."

There was not much ease or relaxation about life in Hanoi. I missed the vibrant street activity of oriental cities like Bangkok or Pnompenh or even Vientiane. Eastern diplomats frequently took breathers in Vientiane—which by any other standard would hardly have been considered a lively capital.

The tenor of life in Hanoi reflected the inevitable consequences of war. The old State Opera House, which had been the pride of the French capital and of which the North Vietnamese were very fond, was closed because the government would not permit so large a group of people to congregate in any one place. It was the same with church services. Mass was permitted only at 6 A.M. and 6 P.M. The shopping and commercial life of the city had been turned upside down. Shops opened now at 5 A.M. They closed at 8 A.M. They did not open again, for the most part, until late afternoon. The city assumed a semivacant aspect. There were no taxis. Only officials had the use of cars, and these were not too plentiful, mostly Russian Volgas or old Pobedas. There were streetcars, old and badly in need of new paint, battered buses in jungle camouflage and quite a few pedicabs, but they seemed as much used for the transportation of bulky bundles and light freight as for the conveyance of people.

Yet life went on. There were beer parlors and bars which began to fill up in the late afternoon and which were jammed by 6 P.M., with hundreds of bicycles parked outside. There were many small restaurants. And around the lovely little lakes which form islands of greenery in the midst of the city there were still waterside cafés. Young people strolled through the parks along the lake fronts and idled away the late afternoon, eating a kind of sweet bun filled with onion fragments and drinking delicious *café au lait* or Hanoi beer. (Hanoi was very proud of its beer, which it insisted was the best in the East.) There were flower stands around the lakes and pretty girls to sell bouquets to flustered young men hurrying back from the front to visit their sweethearts.

And in the last days of my stay I saw along the sidewalks, again and again, men and women patiently chopping pumpkins into great mounds of thin slices. This was to make the traditional sweetmeat for Tet, the lunar New Year, which lay only three weeks off—candied pumpkin meat.

The war was on. North Vietnam was engaged in a struggle for life or death. But the holiday preparations went forward as, I imagined, they had a thousand or two thousand years ago. And when Tet arrived the city would be given over to the holiday spirit. I wished that I might have stayed to see it. For Tet was the great festival of Vietnam.

"It is so lovely," a Frenchwoman said to me. "At Tet they close off some of the principal streets to all traffic. You can only walk in them. The streets are nearly hip-deep in flowers. For now the flowers will be coming in from all over the country."

The first flowers of the tropical spring came with Tet. Everyone in Hanoi would be in the streets, walking through the drifts of flowers, drawing in the heady perfumes, enjoying once again the renewal of the earth's spirit.

Hanoi might be preparing for the worst. But the lovely Hanoi women, with their supple figures, their grace, the elegance of their movements, would dress again in their finest silks. There would be flowers in their hair and they would walk, waist-deep in blossoms, as they had for past centuries, with their admiring men at their sides.

It was true that, as Ho Chi Minh had warned his people, they must prepare for the worst. But they would also enjoy the present—and the past—at least for a fleeting interlude. Tet had been celebrated long before this war, long before the Communists, and, I thought, long after the memory of this war has joined the legends of the wars with the Mongols and the Mings, Tet will remain as the great manifestation of the spirit and tradition of the Vietnamese people.

The crow of a village cock and the bark of a stray village dog ushered in 1967 to me. I was deep in the North
Vietnamese countryside, eighty-five miles south of Hanoi,
sleeping on a straw mattress in a wooden slatted bed in the
clay-floored headquarters of the An Hoa farm commune.

On New Year's Eve, after dark, we had left Hanoi and
driven in our camouflaged Volga sedan south along Route
Nationale No. 1. Dark though it was, I could see fresh bomb
damage since my last expedition down the highway, a week
earlier. I also saw new repairs—some of the bridges which
had been out of service a week ago now were back in use.

We drove slowly through the night. The truck convoys
were heavy, as usual, but the pace was steady. At intervals
along the highway and on the outskirts of each city, including
Hanoi, there were sentry posts and sentries who carefully
checked the papers of each passing vehicle. At bridges and
detours control officers directed the traffic, sometimes sending

North Vietnam Premier Pham Van Dong answers questions on many aspects of war and peace put to him by Harrison Salisbury. The interview and conversation took place in the Presidential Palace in Hanoi. This picture was taken by the palace photographer.

THE FOLLOWING PHOTOGRAPHS WERE TAKEN BY THE AUTHOR DURING HIS TRAVELS BEHIND THE ENEMY LINES

Movie posters on a Hanoi street. One advertises film about Nguyen Van Troi, who attempted to kill Secretary McNamara in Saigon.

A view of Phatdiem Cathedral with its oriental-style architecture. It escaped damage during the heavy air attacks in the region.

A Hanoi child with his pull-toy poses for Harrison Salisbury.

A beauty parlor in Hanoi. On the rear wall a portrait of Ho Chi Minh stares benevolently down at the women under the dryers.

Woman with a *don ganh,* or carrying pole, a common sight in North Vietnam. Behind her is Hanoi's Lake of the Restored Sword.

Peasant women going to church in the Phatdiem area. Bombs struck many churches here.

Interior view of Thuongkiem Cathedral. This church in Phatdiem area was badly damaged.

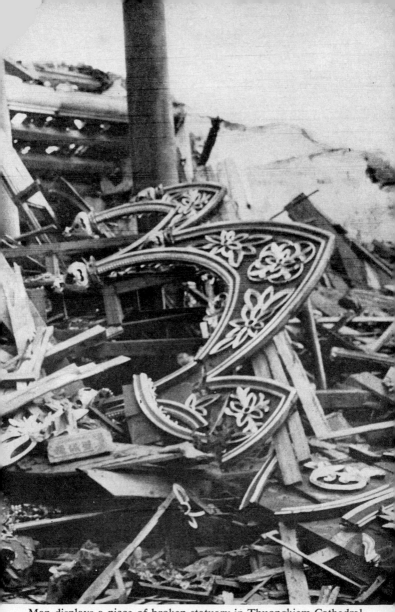

Man displays a piece of broken statuary in Thuongkiem Cathedral.

Individual air-raid shelters line a lakeside boulevard in Hanoi.

Vu Cat, lay leader of the Roman Catholic community in Phatdiem area village, holds up his injured son.

Women building concrete air-raid shelters on one of Hanoi's main streets. Each holds one person.

An air-raid bunker in downtown Hanoi situated along a lake shore.

low-priority vehicles (like ours) on the detours while permitting high-priority freight to move across single-track bridges.

We passed again through Phuly, and again the walls of its destroyed buildings formed a jagged silhouette against the starlighted sky.

It was nearly 10 P.M. when we turned off the highway and moved down a narrow dirt road along a seemingly endless canal, trying to find the place where we were to spend the night. It was not easy. The countryside was in darkness and I saw not a light showing, but several church towers were silhouetted against the sky. We halted before one, and two more were visible, one across the canal and one some distance away. My guides went in search of the local authorities. Finally they were located and we were directed on to the An Hoa headquarters, a one-story brick-and-plaster building with whitewashed walls and a hard clay floor. It was all one room, about forty feet long and fifteen feet wide, but it had been divided into three sections by blankets pinned up on ropes. A farmer's kerosene lantern flickered as we sat down for a cup of strong green tea at a rough plank table covered with flowered cotton cloth. On one wall there was painted in red letters the slogan in Vietnamese: "Defeat the American Imperialist Aggressors." On the opposite wall the slogan was: "Hail the Workers Party of Vietnam."

I had come down to this area to get some idea of what the countryside was like. Hanoi was not North Vietnam. North Vietnam was essentially a poor Asian peasant country, living by the cultivation of rice and other agricultural products. I was eager to see how the people were faring, for this, in essence, held the key to North Vietnam's war effort. What were the people like? Had their life been affected by the war? Did they support the government? And what kind of rule had the Communists created?

An Hoa was one of a large number of collective farming or communal village associations in the heart of a densely settled agricultural region called Phatdiem, in which the population was overwhelmingly Roman Catholic. That was the explanation of the churches which I saw on our blacked-out arrival and the many, many more which I saw on the New Year's weekend. Indeed, I was never beyond sight of a Roman Catholic church during the weekend, and usually there were four or five gray-towered edifices rising above the rice-paddy fields and turning the landscape into a kind of oriental Barbizon.

When the cock's crow awakened me on New Year's morning I was shivering. I had only a thin single blanket atop my straw mattress, and although I had lain down to sleep fully dressed and flung a coat over the bed, it was far from comfortable. I opened my eyes and looked about. The room was still in darkest gloom. It seemed a strange way to begin the new year, and I thought of the old Russian superstition that what you do on New Year's determines your life for the whole year. I hoped that this did not mean I was going to spend my whole year behind the lines in Vietnam or, even more improbably, sleeping on a straw pallet in a clay-floored hut.

Musing over these thoughts I fell asleep again, only to be awakened by the iron bells of the nearest church summoning the faithful to 6 A.M. Mass. There was no point in trying to sleep longer. I threw back the heavy mosquito netting (I found that despite the cold the Vietnamese religiously used their mosquito nets—danger of malaria must be real) and ventured out. The morning was still dark and gray with mist hanging over the rice paddies but my companions were rising. I smelled wood smoke from the cookhouse and the village was coming to life.

Fortunately, there was hot water from the night before in one of the Chinese vacuum bottles. I made some tea to keep me going until a great breakfast was put before me—four eggs, fried in deep grease, white bread, brought from Hanoi, and a hot, sweet infusion of coffee and milk—very tasty, very warming. There were oranges and bananas as well. The fruit was grown by the commune, and they were proud of it. They called the bananas "bananas for a king" and were certain they were the best in Vietnam. They were equally proud of their rice, which they called "rice for a king." It was white, flaky and excellent. If not the best rice in the world, it certainly was very good.

Rice and the rice paddies were the life of An Hoa and of the whole Phatdiem area. This was one of the richest agricultural regions in North Vietnam, lying in the heart of the Red River delta. The peasants cultivated fruit, sweet potatoes and what they called water potatoes and many other vegetables in addition to their basic crop of rice. The courtyards of the peasant huts were filled with golden and purple cocks and clucking chickens. I saw ducks and geese waddling in the ponds, and the canals were almost as laden with fish as the paddies were with rice. The Gulf of Tonkin was less than ten miles away and, until the Seventh Fleet had brought fishing activity to a halt by strafing of all boats along the coast, the diet of the Phatdiem peasants had been enriched by daily catches of sea fish. Now the fishermen seldom ventured out. Their boats were wrecked, and the danger of being spotted on the water by American armed reconnaissance planes was too great.

The average production of paddy rice per hectare, according to the officials, was 5.9 tons. They said this was a substantial gain which had been achieved only in 1965. Their district was one of twenty in the North which were said to have met their production quotas in 1966. In Hanoi I was told that the average rice yield in the North had risen through improved techniques from three to five tons per hectare.

The truth was, as I came to learn, that rice production in 1966 was badly off in North Vietnam. Just how badly, however, it was hard to establish. Rice production in all the Southeast Asian producing countries was down in 1966 because of floods in midsummer and droughts earlier in the year. How seriously had this affected North Vietnam? I could get no precise estimate. One official told me that 1965 rice production was 6 percent higher than 1964, but he professed to have no figures on 1966. I was not alone in the difficulty of getting accurate food estimates. A Russian turned up at an embassy party on New Year's Day. He was suffering from a terrible hangover. A friend commiserated with him. "The hangover is bad," he replied, "but I have worse trouble. Today is the day I'm supposed to put in my report on Vietnam's agricultural production for 1966." His friend asked him what his problem was. "I haven't got any figures," he said. "You don't know these people. It's impossible to get any reliable statistics from them."

The Russian's problem was the same which I had encountered in the long Stalinist years in Moscow when the Russians put out all figures in terms of percentage gains or losses compared with earlier years. But you never could be certain of what the base might be.

The North Vietnamese economic figures were almost entirely reported in percentage terms. Agricultural figures seemed to be virtually nonexistent in recent years. Specialists trying to put together a picture of North Vietnam's economy found it like doing a jigsaw puzzle with only half the pieces. The best figures were those of Soviet studies, but even these left gaping holes.

I learned later that the Russians, basing their arithmetic on their own calculations, estimated that the North Vietnamese rice crop was short by 20 to 25 percent of normal and that, in consequence, North Vietnam would require from 600,000 to 800,000 tons of rice in 1967. This would have to be provided in the main by China. One estimate of the 1966 North Vietnamese crop which I heard was 2.5 million tons. I doubted that any of these figures were accurate.

However, it was clearly not only bad weather which had caused the shortfall in the Vietnamese crop. It was also the war. For peaceful as the countryside now appeared as I looked out across the paddies to a single file of women in their conical straw hats, their formal black clothes, their beteled lips (on their way to New Year's Mass), it was not really peaceful at all. Just beyond the doorstep of the An Hoa building where I was staying there were air-raid bunkers, rather poorly built of earth, supported by a bamboo framework, and with connecting trenches, badly eroded by the rain. As I looked out at the gray, weathered churches I could see that some towers were pockmarked by shrapnel, and as I spent my day traveling through the network of canals and hedgerows that constituted the Phatdiem complex of villages, I saw that the countryside had suffered almost as extensively as the towns and highway networks from the American attacks.

The first incident of war in the region, I was told by Vu Xuan Tuong, a young party official of the local District Committee (who later revealed to me that he was a Catholic), was the shooting down of a C-47 transport plane on July 1, 1961. The plane, he said, was carrying a party of South Vietnamese commandos. The survivors were put on trial. The first air attack in their region had occurred June 18, 1965, he declared, and since that time there had been about 150. The town of Phatdiem itself, with a population of about five thousand, had been largely evacuated as a result of bombing, and almost every rural agricultural community in the area had been hit at one time or another. One of the worst, he said, was an attack on the village of Kien Tiony on April 24,

1966, in which seventy-two persons were killed and forty-six wounded.

But attacks were not confined to villages. Individual peasants working in the fields or threshing in their courtyards had been strafed, I was told. Most of the air activity in the vicinity was attributed to the Seventh Fleet and A6A, A4A and F4H attack aircraft. The planes usually came in straight over the sea, flashed over the villages and fields and bombed directly without circling around, or so it seemed to the villagers. There were many attacks reported on people on highways and roads, and on more than one occasion children had seen what they thought was a whole flight of little planes descending from a big plane. The "little planes" were aerial bombs with their aerostatic vanes.

I walked through the narrow lanes, visited the blasted villages, stood on the doorways of thatched huts where wounded children and injured adults were recovering. I inspected the St. Francis Xavier Cathedral, bombed into a shattered hulk on April 24, 1966.

I took a picture of Vu Cat, head of the Catholic community at Phuvinh village, with his little son who lost a leg when a bomb fell on November 2 and wiped out the tiny community, killing fourteen persons. Vu Cat, a sad, serious man, escaped with his life because he was at the church preparing for evening Mass. His wife and five of the children were killed. A second boy, sixteen-year-old Vu Tuong, who was tending a water buffalo, escaped. I saw a village hospital set up in half a dozen thatched huts where the victims of the latest air attacks were being treated, among them a woman who was unable to speak because a bit of shrapnel had coursed through her neck and a twelve-year-old boy named Van Thin who had lost part of one foot and part of a hand. I visited a village of thatched huts which had disintegrated under American bombs and a cemetery where, improbably, a string of bombs had been dropped, overturning headstones and setting the monuments askew.

It was as easy to see bomb damage in the countryside as it was in the towns, and it was not difficult to understand that life in the North Vietnamese villages had been disrupted badly by the war.

One thing struck my eye. Wherever I went in the Phatdiem area I rarely found a substantial building which had not been strafed. There was a row of stores in Phatdiem facing a large

canal. They were two- or three-story buildings, with store
fronts on the road and living quarters above. Almost every
building had been damaged. A movie theater across the canal
had been bombed. The beautiful oriental-style cathedral at
Phatdiem had not been hit but was no longer being used because of the danger of permitting people to congregate in
such large numbers. The churches whose towers rose above
the landscape had suffered repeated damage. So often was it
the case that bombs had fallen on the more substantial buildings in the countryside that the thought was inescapable that
they must have been considered targets. Otherwise why had
so many been attacked? It was plain enough from the ground
that these buildings, though they might seem substantial from
the air, were serving no military purpose. I wondered whether
it might be that the targeting authorities, hunting vainly over
the dreary rural scene for something to attack, had decided
that substantial buildings *must* have some military significance.

Vu Xuan Tuong told me that the villages had ceased using
the two or three brick school houses which had been built in
recent years because of the danger that, being substantial
buildings, they would be bombed. The children and the
schools were moved into thatched huts, where the classes
were carried on. He said that there had been thirteen attacks
on the dikes and ten on sluices. Although American authorities insisted that dikes and water control works had never
been listed as targets, the evidence in the Phatdiem region (as
in the Namdinh region) was that bombs repeatedly fell on
such works. What was the explanation for that? Was it nothing but one accident piled on top of another all over North
Vietnam? I would not expect anyone in North Vietnam to
believe that. The Pentagon claimed that we had perfected an
incredibly accurate bombing technique. But we could not
have it both ways. Either we could not control the placement
of our bombs or we were bombing civilian targets, possibly
on the faulty assumption that they were military.

In the whole of Ninhbinh Province, according to Nguyen
Xuan Luong, deputy editor of the Ninhbinh newspaper, there
was a population of about 500,000. In the Phatdiem area the
population was eighty thousand. It had been reduced by ten
thousand when the Catholic exodus to the South occurred in
1954-55, but the deficit had since been restored by natural increase.

In the province at large, Luong said, there had been 1,400 United States bombing missions in 1965 and up to December 15, 1966, 2,338 missions, including 303 at night. He estimated that 24 attacks had been carried out on what he described as "military" targets, 31 on "economic" targets and the rest at random. He did not specify how he defined military and economic targets. Of the 123 agricultural communes in the province, 96 had felt the weight of American bombs and rockets, he said, and each of the 24 towns and the provincial capital had been hit. The capital, Ninhbinh, had been hit so heavily that it was virtually abandoned. His newspaper, for instance, continued to publish. But the printing plant was no longer in Ninhbinh.

The American attacks, he calculated, had struck twenty markets, stores and cooperatives, five hospitals, ten village medical stations and ten churches and pagodas. Up to December 15 the United States was estimated to have dropped 6,347 bombs in the province, and the weight of bombs was estimated at fourteen times higher in 1966 than in 1965. He credited the North Vietnamese military with having shot down forty-one American planes up to December 1. The population was said to have brought down three with rifle fire.

The intensity of the United States attack on the area surprised me, although I could see one explanation for it. Ninhbinh was an important junction point. Ninhbinh and Namdinh were the two principal cities of the mid-south region of North Vietnam. One cause for the repeated attacks in the Phatdiem area might be that Seventh Fleet planes flying to and from missions to Ninhbinh and Namdinh must traverse this farming community. It was possible that the United States planes jettisoned leftover bombs on the way back from missions or exhausted their rocket stocks over this area. Or possibly planes which had difficulty in returning to base might lighten their loads in the Phatdiem area. There were antiaircraft installations in this region to protect the approaches to Ninhbinh and Namdinh and no doubt the Americans attacked them on occasion.

Yet when all this had been taken into account, the fact remained that an astonishing amount of high explosives was falling on a simple, quiet, rice-growing area. And when this was taken into consideration, it was no wonder that North Vietnam's agricultural output had declined, with all the dangerous consequences for the prosecution of the war which that implied. Peasants could not be expected to turn out as much rice if their villages were being attacked and if they were constantly being called out by the local authorities to assist in repairing bombed-out roads and railroads.

The United States, I understood, estimated that the equivalent of 300,000 people had been diverted to maintenance work. I wondered whether the figure might not be higher. Not in the form of permanent stand-by crews but in terms of occasionally diverted labor.

All day long I wandered through the countryside. The New Year's Day weather was fine. The peasants gathered green manure. They spread thatch out to dry along the roadsides. They poured out their rice for threshing in the hard clay courtyards and the women dyed grass reeds for weaving. Basketry was one of the great handicraft arts of the area. It was a peaceful scene, one which might have been duplicated in a dozen Asian countries.

I visited half a dozen churches and was eager to talk with the local parish priests, but not until after nightfall did I have the opportunity. Finally at 7 P.M. Father Nguyen The Vi, pastor of the An Hoa church, returned to his parish. He had been busy since early morning saying Mass in various small churches. He had 850 parishioners in his own church and served three other localities. He had served his church since 1936. He was a serious, quiet man, concerned for his faith and about the damage which the war was wreaking. He talked of Ninhbinh, a great Catholic center since the seventeenth century, and of the church there. The Americans, in other times, he said, had contributed to the church in Ninhbinh and had provided funds for a cemetery. There in the cemetery were buried two Catholic nuns who had died a barbarous death in some earlier Vietnam war, and now, he related, American bombs had fallen on the cemetery and damaged a monument erected to the nuns' memory with funds provided from the United States. He hoped that American Catholics might know of this and, perhaps, help out their coreligionists in some manner in this difficult hour. He was pleased that I had come and pleased that he had a kerosene lamp. "Usually, you know," he said, "the blackout is complete. Even in the church we can only use a tiny candle. After dark no lights must show. This lantern is a real pleasure."

I rode back through the night to Hanoi deeply troubled.

The New Year's truce had ended. Already the bombing and the fighting had begun again. I had seen towns and cities savagely damaged by the American air offensive. But, perhaps in a way, the punishment to the rural community was even more serious. It had a deeper effect than anything else on the war potential of North Vietnam, although I had never heard this mentioned by the Pentagon strategists. By forcing a diversion of manpower from agriculture to other tasks, our bombing had severely affected North Vietnam's capacity for feeding itself—a serious handicap to a nation at war.

But by what means had this been accomplished? In part, of course, by bombardment of means of transport and the diversion of labor to maintenance work. But this was not the whole story. There were the thousands of tons of bombs that fell on the countryside, on the fields, on the villages, on the peasant huts, on the peasants in the fields and on the roads.

Accidents, all accidents. This was our version. This might well be the literal truth. But how to make it credible to the peasants of North Vietnam?

No American wandering through the village of Xuan Dinh, a few miles outside of Hanoi, would have noticed anything unusual except, perhaps, for the network of trenches and the earthen blast barriers which had been erected at the entrances of some of the plaster-walled huts.

Certainly no American familiar with the pastel cinder blocks and picture windows of the suburban American high school would have recognized these thatched cottages as the North Vietnamese counterpart of a Westchester community high school. But what I was to see, or so I was told by the school officials, was not just an ordinary suburban school. It was the top-ranking high school in the whole of North Vietnam.

The school was situated in the Tu Liem District, a dozen miles outside Hanoi, in a countryside of many villages, pleasant little rice paddies, duck ponds and orange groves. We drove out across the Long Bien Bridge, past the airport at Gialam and then through a network of winding country roads and almost continuous villages until we came to a spot where the car halted. I could see no school but, in fact, I was right in the middle of it. The school had been dispersed for the safety of the pupils into a series of huts and buildings scattered through a farming community of about five thousand people. It was one of three senior high schools in the district—two of them having been opened especially to accommodate evacuated children from Hanoi.

The school which I was visiting had 710 pupils, of whom 300 had been evacuated from Hanoi, largely the children of officials and workers in Hanoi industry. There had been nine or ten classes before the evacuees arrived. Now there were sixteen. One of the principal problems was teachers. Not all of the Hanoi teachers were able to move to the countryside, and many rural schools, this one included, were shorthanded.

Here in Xuan Dinh the younger children, in many instances, were living in huts under the supervision of teachers who saw that they were fed and cared for. Many older youngsters had set up hostels and did their own cooking. The government provided money for room and board, and the children had a special allowance from the state to pay for textbooks.

There were not enough facilities to accommodate all the pupils and the school was on a two-shift basis. It was what was called a "third-grade" school for children in the 15-to-17-year age group. It provided three years of schooling and most of the youngsters were headed for higher education. There were two other categories of schools, primary schools for children 7 to 11 and secondary for those from 11 to 15.

This school was top-rated because the percentage of its pupils passing their college entrance exams was the highest in Hanoi. Hundreds of students had gone from this high school to the university, either the Polytechnic in Hanoi, which had been created with Soviet assistance, or one of the higher-level institutes. North Vietnam had 35 higher educational institutions. The total had risen from 27 in 1965. There were 46,000 students in these institutions, against 35,000 in 1965.

Not a few youngsters from Xuan Dinh went on to college in foreign countries, some to the Soviet Union, some to China, some to Eastern Europe. None had ever gone to universities in the West. Those who had been studying in China had been compelled to return a few months before when the

Chinese closed all their schools as part of the great "cultural revolution" in order to revise their curriculums. This brought several hundred North Vietnamese students back home. China had given training to 4,200 students and workers in the five years ending in 1960. The total increased sharply in the subsequent five years.

But Xuan Dinh youngsters not only went on to higher education. Now many were going straight into the army. Last year several had become fighter pilots. Others joined the navy and the antiaircraft defenses.

Nor was schoolwork their only interest. Many were assisting the agricultural cooperatives in handling livestock and machines. Some were giving literacy classes in the evening to older peasants. All were engaging in military training and military sports. In addition, they had the usual sports activities of youngsters everywhere—football, tennis, volleyball, swimming and track and field events. They had song and dance groups, and at harvest time amateur performers went out into the countryside to entertain the peasants. It was a busy life.

We went from classroom to classroom, and I inspected the trench network that connected the various huts. The youngsters and teachers could move by trench, if necessary, for hundreds of feet. The entrances to the thatched huts were guarded by shoulder-high walls of earth, reinforced with bamboo, to minimize blast effects if bombs fell nearby. Under each desk of the dirt-floored schoolrooms was a foxhole into which a youngster could slide in an instant. Each boy and girl had his fragmentation helmet—the heavy plaited-straw hat which the teachers assured me was impervious to fragments from the antipersonnel bombs which occasionally fell in the area.

The school itself had not been touched by bombing. But, the teachers said, on August 13, 1966, an air attack occurred near the school and some youngsters were injured when they were buried in a shelter in which they had taken refuge. Others lost their clothes and books.

The problem of carrying on education in wartime conditions was not an easy one. The Minister of Education, Nguyen Van Huyen, a serious man who wore a blue serge business suit, told me of the problems. He had been engaged in educational work for more than twenty years. Under the

French the country, by his estimate, was about 90 percent illiterate and in some areas illiteracy was almost 100 percent. The university in Hanoi had 600 students and there were 300,000 pupils in the schools of all Indochina and only 500 or 600 graduates per year from the high schools. There were 70 students in the medical college, with 15 graduates per year.

The task of the Ho Chi Minh Government from 1945 to 1954, the minister said, had been primarily a fight against illiteracy. By 1958, the regime felt, this battle was largely won. Beginning in 1956 North Vietnam's schools had been placed on a ten-year basis, with four years in primary school, three in secondary school and three in high school. In the current school year, 1966-67, there were 3,340,000 pupils in the system against a 1964-65 figure of 2,900,000. This year there were 2,410,000 in primary schools, 810,000 in secondary and about 100,000 in high school. This compared with 2,160,000, 670,000 and 80,000 in the respective categories the previous year.

The teaching staff numbered 90,000. This year, the minister said, kindergarten classes had been widely extended. There were 230,000 in kindergarten compared with 120,000 in 1965. There were also 900,000 in what he called ABC classes—preschool courses in which youngsters were being taught to read and write before entering school. The ABC classes, he thought, were unique to North Vietnam. He had never heard of another country with this system. I told him of American preschool classes with some pride.

But the war had made all the educational problems twice as difficult. Education had been harnessed to the war effort insofar as possible.

"The battle against the United States is very fierce," he said. "We must train our people to be capable of fighting more effectively day by day. We must be resourceful. We must work to increase production through people who are trained in science and technique. One reason why we have been able to increase our rice yields is that we have educated our people in improved farming methods."

The American bombing offensive had severely handicapped the whole educational process, the minister said. Many schools had been bombed.

"I say this with great pain and emotion to an American,"

he said. "But I believe the American people must know about it. Almost hourly the fate of our children is jeopardized. Many have died and others have been injured."

The minister spoke in sadness. He had some difficulty in mastering his feelings. He said that there really was no way to protect the schools from American bombs. If the bombs dropped near or even beside the schools, the pupils had some protection. But no protection was possible against a direct hit.

He mentioned a raid on October 21, 1966, in which the Thuy Dan school in Thaibinh Province was hit. The school, about sixty-five miles south of Hanoi, was in a large rice field. Four bombs were dropped. One hit a shelter, he said, and thirty pupils and a teacher were killed. While our fliers were not trying to hit schools, the fact was that schools were being hit in attacks on other targets or in jettisoning bombs.

In the Hanoi bombing of December 2 the Polish Friendship High School was damaged. Sixteen bombs fell around the school, but the pupils and teachers fortunately were in their shelters. Six pupils and two teachers were injured when a shelter collapsed, but all were saved. In the more severe attacks of December 13 and 14 the Polish Friendship School was damaged so severely that it could no longer be used.

The Polish Friendship School was one of many educational institutions in North Vietnam which were under the patronage of a Communist country. The Poles had provided much equipment for the school. Groups of Polish children and educators visited the school, and there were return visits to Poland. Other schools had arrangements with other Communist countries. For instance, the East Germans assisted the Hanoi Pedagogical Institute. The Hungarians assisted a second teachers' training school. Kharkov University aided the Polytechnic University. The Poles provided the laboratory equipment for the school near Vandien. They also sent films, microscopes, textbooks and other educational materials to the institution.

"We have great anxiety about the loss of life of our children," the minister said. "And about their nervous systems. The first thing they teach in kindergarten is how to get quickly into a shelter and how to maintain a shelter in good condition."

It seemed to me that his anxiety was well founded. There could not but be serious effects upon youngsters conditioned to this dangerous and difficult mode of existence.

While all children were supposed to have been evacuated from Hanoi, he conceded that many younger children had remained because their parents had not made arrangements for their care elsewhere. The university had been evacuated in 1965. Each faculty had been sent to a different locale. It had about 2,500 students in 1966 and the Pedagogical Institute 5,000. The university students, he said, were supposed to combine study and actual work. They were expected to raise 10 percent of their food from the beginning and later on to provide 20 to 30 percent from garden stuffs and animal husbandry.

The question of the health and safety of the children was not merely one for the Education Ministry. The Health Ministry was devoting much time and thought to the problem.

A disproportionate number of casualties in bombing was caused among young children due to the difficulty in getting them to observe proper air-raid security. They did not understand the danger of the attacks and often did not go to shelters unless adults saw to it.

This situation was made plain in a visit to the Hanoi city surgical clinic. The doctors had received fourteen children as a result of the December 13-14 raids, of whom one was dead on arrival and another died in the hospital. The principal source of wounds among these youngsters was bomb fragments, some of them minute, which pierced various sensitive organs. There was a ten-month-old girl who had suffered a cerebral hemorrhage from a fragment in the brain. A year-old boy had a small fragment in his skull. An eight-month-old baby had a fragment in the rear of its nose and many fragments in its legs. An eight-year-old girl had been wounded December 13 in a hamlet near Hanoi. She and her four-year-old brother were playing in front of their house. A bomb fell in the courtyard and her brother was killed instantly. She got a fragment in her spine and was paralyzed from the chest down. A sixteen-year-old girl had been working in a field where a fragmentation bomb fell. A particle entered through her left rib and lodged in her liver.

The clinic's surgeons showed me X-rays of these cases and pointed to the difficult medical problems involved in surgical removal of the small pellets of steel and other metal. One of their X-rays disclosed that a man had one fragmentation ball lodged in his hip and two in his legs.

The city surgical clinic was one of the municipal institutions which was to remain in Hanoi regardless of what happened to the city. Its primary function now was to care for air-raid victims, and if Hanoi was generally attacked it would be hard-pressed to meet the demands with its 120 beds.

Dr. Nguyen Dan Tin, Deputy Minister of Health, said that the problem of public health in North Vietnam had been greatly complicated by the bombing offensive. Between February, 1965, and June, 1966, he calculated, 180 medical establishments had been hit by bombing. He was sincerely convinced that medical establishments had been deliberately targeted by the United States bombing specialists.

"The United States says it bombs with precision," he said. "Therefore I assume these attacks were deliberate."

He mentioned a series of raids on the famous Vietnamese leprosarium at Quyuh Lap. The leprosarium was the pride of the North Vietnamese regime. It boasted 2,600 beds. On July 16, 1965, according to the North Vietnamese, it was attacked by American planes. It was attacked repeatedly (thirty-nine times in all) and, in the view of Hanoi, intentionally. The charge of deliberate destruction of the leprosarium was formally denied by the United States and the subject had given rise to bitter recriminations. But, the deputy minister said, the fact was that the leprosarium had been obliterated. It no longer could be used. The lepers had been moved to other locations. Whatever might have been the reason, the most outstanding public health facility in the country had been erased from the land.

This, the deputy minister insisted, was not an isolated example. In every part of the country he pointed to hospitals and clinics which had been damaged or put out of action by United States bombing.

Despite these blows North Vietnam was continuing to make progress in the field of public health. Or so he said. He painted a miserable picture of disease and desolation in the country under the French. There were then, he said, only forty-seven hospitals and nine maternity homes and one doctor per 180,000 population. Now all villages in the Red River delta region had medical stations and 80 percent of the mountain districts as well. Diseases like smallpox, cholera and poliomyelitis were virtually eliminated. North Vietnam produced its own Sabin vaccine. There had been a threat of a polio epidemic in 1959, but widespread use of the vaccine nipped it in the bud. Trachoma and malaria had been radically reduced, and the North Vietnamese had had great success in cutting back tuberculosis through use of BCG vaccine which they produced themselves. In 1958, 2.5 percent of the population had TB. By 1964 the percentage was down to 0.8 percent.

Great strides had been made in cutting infant and maternal mortality. The maternal mortality rate was 2 percent before the Hanoi regime was established. By 1964 it had been cut to 0.04. Infant mortality had been reduced from 30 percent before 1954 to 2.58 percent in 1964.

But the sharp cut in infant mortality and maternal mortality had produced another problem—population increase. The population of the North was seventeen million, that of the South fourteen million. The general death rate had been 20 per 1,000 under the French. Now it was 6.5. The birth rate had been 4.7 percent, now it was 3.5. The population increase was 2.9 percent. In Hanoi a vigorous birth control campaign had cut the city's rate to 2.2. But this was still too high. This was one of North Vietnam's major public health problems.

As for its public health achievements, these had been made possible through a broad increase in medical training. Ten times as many physicians were being trained today as ten years ago. Now they were able to carry out many kinds of advanced surgery—heart surgery, lung surgery and liver surgery—which had never been done before in North Vietnam. They were trying to combine the best aspects of traditional medical custom and European practice. They had to make some compromises. They used, for instance, dead BCG serum because of the lack of refrigeration. They now were producing their own cholera, typhus and diphtheria antitoxins.

But with all their advances they had enormous distances to travel to bring public health standards up to Western levels.

"The war is the great problem," the deputy minister said. "Now we have had to put everything else to one side. We must develop serums against shock. So many of the wounded are sent into deep shock from loss of blood. We have no blood banks. We have no way of keeping blood refrigerated. Somehow we have to find simple ways of doing things. It's not like America. Someday when the war is over we can go back to building up again instead of finding ways to work in temporary shelters or bomb-damaged ruins."

At one point in my long conversation with Premier Pham Van Dong he swung around, drew up his legs and almost threw them over the arm of his chair in order to face me directly.

He was talking about the Vietnamese people and trying to explain why the Vietnamese fought so well in the North and so poorly, as he phrased it, in the South.

"Why, on the other side, are they so bad," he asked, "and on our side so talented, so supremely talented—talented without precedent?"

He thought that never in history had there been a people's war which had been fought with such brilliance. He thought that even the Americans would have to agree to that.

The answer which the Premier gave to his own question seemed to me so pertinent, so vital to an understanding of the nature of the war as seen in North Vietnam and to an understanding of how the war is carried on there, that it is worth quoting in full.

"From our point of view," the premier said, "it is a sacred war [*une guerre sacrée*] for Independence, Freedom, Life. It stands for everything, this war, for this generation and for future generations. That's why we are determined to fight this war and win this war. Our victory stems from this very resoluteness. That is the key to the solution of all our problems. I think that this is something very difficult for you to understand. Not only for you. I say this to a lot of our friends in Europe. They don't understand. They are afraid of the American strength. They don't see how we resist an expeditionary corps of 400,000 men, well equipped with weapons, and the nearby Seventh Fleet. And they are concerned that we could not win the war. But now we are being victorious and we are telling them that finally we will win. They admit that truth but they don't understand."

Premier Dong looked me straight in the eye as he spoke these words, his face gripped by an inner intensity of feeling. He paused for the translation and then added with a little grin:

"I have no hope of convincing you, but I must tell you this because it is very important."

I left Hanoi positive that, indeed, this was the most important aspect of the war so far as North Vietnam was concerned—the spirit of the North Vietnamese people and the spirit with which they were fighting the war. There was no doubt in my mind that without this spirit their chances of successfully opposing the mass of American technology would be slight, regardless of how much matériel was shipped in by China and the Soviet Union.

I was equally convinced that Premier Dong was correct in saying that this was a phenomenon difficult for outsiders to understand. I knew, certainly, that it was not well understood by the Russians. Nor, I thought, by the East European Communists. They brought to North Vietnam a narrow and even an alien concept of the country. They applied to it formulas based on European Marxism or the pragmatic kind of state capitalism which was sprouting up in the ruins of Stalinist Communism. They did not feel at home in North Vietnam. They did not react as the North Vietnamese did. They were like cost accountants surveying a bankrupt business. They wanted to liquidate. Hanoi simply refused to pay any attention to the red ink and went on fighting.

Out of what was born this amalgam of patriotism and *élan?* That it existed I had not the faintest doubt. One evening I went to a small, rather run-down movie theater not far from the center of Hanoi. It was no longer being used as a movie house. Instead, it was given over to a kind of variety hall performance, songs, dances and skits. Of the fourteen acts twelve were devoted to epics of bravery. In one a group of ferrymen pulled their craft across a river in the face of fierce attack by United States planes. Several were killed, but they shot down an American aircraft. In a dance number a Red Cross nurse whose husband had been killed tore from her head the traditional Vietnamese white mourning veil and used it to bind up the wounds of an antiaircraft gunner. In another a Vietcong detachment stormed an American strongpoint and captured it despite terrible losses. There were few touches of humor, but in one tableau a twelve-year-old Vietcong lad captured a ferocious American captain, frightening away some would-be G.I. rescuers with a fake hand grenade made from a coconut.

That act brought down the house. The audience was almost entirely made up of youngsters, mostly boys of sixteen to twenty-one, many of them in uniform or semiuniform. Most of them were involved in the war. The only other note of lightness in the evening was a song by a group of maidens wearing the costumes of the Meo minority. They sang to the strains of long-necked, three-stringed mandolins a song about shooting down an American plane and before the chorus was over proclaimed that they had shot down not one but three. It didn't seem to me that the solemn-faced boys, taking a breather from the front or antiaircraft duty, quite believed that the beautiful young ladies were such crack shots.

The theme of the songs and the ballets was patriotism. The portraits of heroism were simple and humorless. The audience, judging by the intense and serious expressions I saw on the faces around me, took the tableaux with complete literalness. They lived the little sketches of war—their war. These were their heroes. They saw nothing naïve or made-up about these schoolboy vignettes. They themselves were mostly schoolboys. North Vietnam was a very young country. This, in large measure, was a teen-age war. I was impressed by the fact that again and again the same theme was repeated—that of fighting back against the American bombers, of shooting down American aircraft. This was the most important note. The antiaircraft gunners were glorified. Truck drivers who got their trucks south with loads of munitions and supplies despite the air bombardment were glorified. So were the crews of railroad trains. I did not count the number of United States planes shot down on the stage that night, but it made an impressive total.

This, of course, was one of the major preoccupations of the government. But it went further than that. Everyone had a sense of participation in the battle because so many people had been issued rifles and actually shot back at the American aircraft. Of course, they did not often get a plane. But it did happen, sometimes, and this was hailed as the feat of feats. Second only to the actual capture of an American airman. Villages vied for the honor of capturing a United States pilot, and when such an event actually occurred, the peasants came from miles around to view the American and to hail the brave captors. The papers were constantly writing about peasants who, armed only with poles and pitchforks, managed to take into custody American fliers. The wall newspapers and cartoonists found this a favorite subject for caricature. Special commemorative stamps had been issued when, by North Vietnamese count, the 500th U.S. plane was destroyed. Another stamp marked the 1,000th plane, and one commemorating the 1,500th victory had just come out. The Hanoi tabulation had now passed the 1,600 mark. The American official total was just under 500.

The North Vietnamese were proud of their conservativeness in claiming air victories. They said they had to present very detailed evidence before a tally would be registered, and they were fond of telling how President Ho Chi Minh had once rejected a count of planes shot down and given the North Vietnamese credit for only five planes, instead of the seven which they reported. Later on the United States communiqué, it was said, admitted eight losses. *"That's* how conservative we are," they stressed. One source of the discrepancy between Hanoi and Washington tabulations was the fact that Hanoi included drones and pilotless planes in its total whereas the Americans did not. However, the over-all disparity between the two tabulations was narrowed in February, 1967, when a careful estimate of American plane losses in the Southeast Asian war theater, including North Vietnam,

South Vietnam and Laos, based on Pentagon figures, by *The New York Times* military analyst, Hanson Baldwin, put the total losses of both combat and noncombat aircraft at 1,750.

The North Vietnamese liked to point to the fact that so many of them were bearing arms. The numbers were very great. Sometimes it seemed to me that every other person on the street was carrying a gun over his shoulder or strapped to his or her back. When the air alert sounded, rifles appeared in every hand. Petite little waitresses at the hotel instantly donned tin helmets, grabbed their rifles and rushed to the rooftops. Some foreign diplomats thought they were more in danger of stray bullets from the rifle barrage than from stray bombs from the United States planes.

"Where else have you ever seen this?" a party official asked me. "Can you imagine the regime in the South giving guns to all its people? They'd never dare. Here you can see for yourself that the people support their government. If they didn't, they have the weapons in their hands with which to change it."

Some of the East European Communists agreed with this. They pointed out that they had not witnessed anything like this in any other Communist country. Nor had I.

There was no doubt in my mind that by issuing guns to the people and by encouraging them to fire back at the Americans the government had gone far to solidify the morale of the people, to give them a feeling that they were fighting back, that they were not defenseless against the advanced technology of the Americans.

The government deliberately chose simple images around which to build its patriotic appeal. For instance, there was the island of Con Co. I had never heard of Con Co before, but I got to know it very well in North Vietnam. It was a small island, lying about a mile or so off the coast in the Gulf of Tonkin near the demarcation line. It was principally important as a radar observation point and for its antiaircraft installations. The island had been subjected to round-the-clock bombardment by the planes of the Seventh Fleet but had held out against every attack. The heroic achievements of the Con Co gunners were heralded in songs, in ballets and in a documentary motion picture. To be a gunner on Con Co Island was the equivalent, in North Vietnamese terms, of service in a Guards division in England, and the defense of the island took on a significance in North Vietnam's war mythology akin to that of Corregidor in the Pacific. When I visited the high school students at Xuan Dinh, I found that one of their ambitions was to serve on Con Co Island.

Another symbol of the war was the Ham Rong Bridge, which crossed the Ma River at Thanhhoa, about a hundred miles south of Hanoi. This bridge was one of the most important in North Vietnam. It carried both highway and railroad traffic from north to south. It had been attacked hundreds of times by United States bombers and had been hit many, many times. But as late as January, 1967, it had never been put out of action. The bridge was defended by strong antiaircraft batteries, and the losses of the United States Air Force in the attacks were considerable. The North Vietnamese contended that they had shot down sixty-nine planes in the battle of the bridge.

The gunners protecting this bridge were national heroes in North Vietnam. In this strange war in which there was no direct ground contact between Americans and the people of North Vietnam, the "battles" were those which arose out of antiaircraft actions.

Of the heroes celebrated in Hanoi none, it seemed to me, more perfectly suited the North Vietnamese temperament than Nguyen Van Troi. I could not recall having heard the name of Nguyen Van Troi before I arrived in Hanoi. Once there, it seemed to be on every lip. His picture looked down at me from movie posters. I saw it in great letters over the theater marquees. I saw his name on books in the windows of bookstores, and I found his portrait in museums and on calendars. Nguyen Van Troi was a Saigon teen-ager who had made an attempt on the life of Defense Secretary McNamara during a visit in 1965. He had been seized as he attempted to shoot the Secretary and, after trial, was sentenced to death and executed. Now he had become a cult in North Vietnam. The legend of the youngster who, singlehanded, attempted to take the life of the man who (with President Johnson and Secretary of State Rusk) symbolized the American enemy fitted the North Vietnamese temperament. Here was a young man who sacrificed himself in a desperate act of patriotism against overwhelming odds. What better way to die?

Indeed, the glorification of this youngster and his deed provided a clue to the temperament and morale of North Vietnam. Constantly I felt echoes of the Irish rebellion. Here was the same hotheaded, all-or-nothing, do-or-die, no-compromise, death-before-dishonor spirit which had characterized the Easter rising. It reminded me, too, of the maximalist young Narodniks in Russia, the idealistic, anarchistic, patriotic zealots of the nineteenth century who casually threw away their lives in one desperate attempt after another to bring down the Russian Empire with a single bomb or a single bullet imprecisely directed against the Czar or his principal ministers.

The North Vietnamese were amazed that I had never heard of Nguyen Van Troi. His was one of the most important names in their world, along with that of Norman Morrison, the gentle, idealistic young American whose act of freely giving his own life in a heroic gesture to arouse his fellow Americans had won the adoration of the people.

The symbols of the war were simple. Many of them seemed like cartoons to me. Yet I could see that they appealed to the youngsters on whom the brunt of the war fell. And in that very youth, I thought, lay part of the secret of North Vietnam's firm will. The youngsters did not take seriously the possibility of defeat. They really were not able accurately to calculate the odds on victory. They simply took it for granted that they would win. How, they did not know or think about.

The spirit of these youngsters certainly had not been crushed by our air bombardment or the long years of war. They had been born into a world at war. They lived in a world at war. Their life was war. They could not imagine another existence. A friend of mine was talking with some youngsters about what life would be like if peace came. Suddenly one of them said: "Peace! What will we do without the war? What will our lives be like?" There was in that sudden exclamation a sense of emptiness, of loss of purpose. The youngsters lived and breathed war. If peace came, the transition would not be easy.

Youth, too, might be the explanation, at least in part, for the stubbornness and cockiness that I encountered in North Vietnam. These were not people who easily bowed their heads. The odds might be long, but this did not cause them to modify their attitudes. So far as the teen-agers were concerned, they were certain they would triumph over the U.S. Nothing that anyone might tell them about the impossibility

of achieving victory against the weight of American weaponry really sank in.

It seemed to me that Dienbienphu and its legend played an
important role in this psychology. To the youngster in the
army, in the antiaircraft unit or in the bicycle brigade, there
was not much difference between the American enemy he
was now fighting and the French enemy which his father
fought a dozen or more years ago. The French war had
ended in Dienbienphu—a brilliant North Vietnamese victory,
a crushing French defeat. What had happened in 1954 could
happen again—*would* happen again. Of this the average
North Vietnamese had no doubt. Times might now be hard,
but in the end there would be an American Dienbienphu. He
didn't quite know how it would be accomplished, but he was
sure of it. Dienbienphu occupied in the North Vietnamese
mind the place of Waterloo, of Cornwallis's surrender, of Stalingrad. It was the epitome of victory. It was the name of one
of Hanoi's principal streets. It was celebrated in countless
pictures, sculptures and exhibitions. It was the name of a
brand of cigarettes. It was honored in a special room in the
Museum of the Revolution and in the North Vietnamese
Army Museum. Pictures of Dienbienphu held a central place
in the Museum of Fine Arts. Every youngster in Hanoi could
tell you the story, exactly how the battle was planned and
how it was won.

I seldom talked with any North Vietnamese without some
reference coming into the conversation of the people's pre-
paredness to fight ten, fifteen, even twenty years in order to
achieve victory. At first I thought that such expressions might
reflect government propaganda and that the individuals had
been coached to talk like this. But when I found Catholic
priests and Buddhists saying the same thing in much the same
words as simple peasants in the villages of the Phatdiem area,
I began to realize that this was a national psychology. It
might have been inspired by the regime, but it certainly was
entirely natural. And, I believed, it suited the North Vietnamese temperament. This spirit of stubborn determination,
of fierce national patriotism, combined with a kind of teen-
aged dare-deviltry, was characteristic of so many of the individuals with whom I talked. No one had put them up to this.
This was their way of talking and acting. It came naturally.
They were a warm, direct people, very simple, and this be-

came clear when they talked about themselves and the war. They often spoke of heroism and of their willingness to die for their country. They said they were no more willing to die than other people but that if one must die the best way was to die fighting for Vietnam.

"We do not fear death," one North Vietnamese told me. "We try to stay alive and to fight the enemy. We do not wish to die unnecessarily. It is important to stay alive because we have so much to do—we have to grow rice and we have to fight at the same time. We think that heroism is both courage and creation."

When this spirit was translated into action it produced remarkable results. A Communist visitor who had been with the North Vietnamese Air Force said he could not imagine other people carrying on under similar conditions.

"Imagine!" this man said. "Their pilots get up at 4 A.M. They go out into the rice paddies and work for three or four hours standing in cold water up to the hips. Then they come in and fly their planes against the Americans. I've never heard of such people."

Even in their evacuation and dispersal programs they refused to speak of terms of retreat.

"We have a word for that," an official told me. "It's 'sotan.' It doesn't really mean evacuation. It's more like regrouping in order to fight better and to reduce losses and to repair damage which has been suffered in combat. It's not a passive word—it's an active word."

One North Vietnamese official contrasted the attitudes of American youth (as he understood them) with those of the North Vietnamese youngsters.

"We don't underestimate American youth," he said. "If the American youth had to fight and defend the United States, they would fight very well. But American youth have been sent over here to fight a war which they do not understand and which is not a just war. So they do not fight like our youth do. The Americans have good weapons and fine techniques, but they cannot cope with our soldiers because they do not have the kind of spirit which we possess."

The patriotic fever in North Vietnam was lashed by other stimuli—atrocity propaganda, for instance—propaganda so crude and blood-curdling that I found it hard to take the venomous tales seriously. But I soon found that these savage and revolting accounts had an appeal for the North Viet-

namese people. At least I saw them crowding around the wall
bulletins and reading the detailed versions published by the
newspapers. These were atrocity stories of the most primitive
kind—tales of disembowelments, mass rapings, deliberate
killing of unborn and newborn children, cannibalism, fetish-
ism and weird variants for which I could not find any anthro-
pological category. Pictures of beheadings, torturings, disfig-
urations of men, women and children were a common sight
in the press and in the many exhibitions devoted to the war. I
had no doubt that in the savage hand-to-hand jungle combat
in the South there were atrocities. The exhibitions which I
had seen in the Museum of the Revolution prepared me to
believe that this was in the tradition of Southeast Asian combat. And I was aware that even in supposedly sophisticated
societies it was only too easy to believe the worst about your
enemy.

To what extent this fanned the flames of hatred in the
North Vietnamese national consciousness it was difficult to
say. But I was struck by one fact. I would not have been surprised to encounter demonstrations of hostility against myself. After all, I was the enemy. I was behind the lines. I was
the only representative of the enemy many of these people
had ever seen. If some North Vietnamese had shaken his fist
at me, scowled, made savage remarks or spat at me, I would
not have been surprised. I was certain that a North Vietnamese appearing in Washington would not receive a very
cordial welcome. Yet in the time of my stay in North Vietnam nothing like this happened. I was so struck by the generally warm and cordial reception and the absence of hostility
that I questioned other foreigners resident in Hanoi about it.
Had they ever encountered exhibitions of bad feeling? They
said they had not. I asked North Vietnamese officials about
this and they quickly attributed it to the government's "correct" propaganda policy.

"Our people know very well that those responsible for this
war are the government leaders in Washington—President
Johnson, Rusk and McNamara," I was told. "They know that
the American people in general are good and kind. We have
no war against the American people as a whole—just the war
criminals in Washington."

That was, of course, the propaganda line. But I doubted it
was the whole explanation. I wondered if, perhaps, the explanation might lie in the fact that this was such a strange war.

The North Vietnamese never really saw their enemy (any more than our airmen saw theirs). They saw the planes but not the soldiers. It was so different from other wars. The North Vietnamese could hate Johnson, Rusk and McNamara because they saw cartoons of them on the walls and heard their names. But it was difficult to hate the mysterious and invisible ordinary American.

One thing was certain. As the war had gone on, the spirit of the people, their general will to resist, their support of the war, had increased.

A Communist diplomat who had been in Hanoi for two or three years told me that he had been much struck by the steady growth in nationalist feeling as the war had intensified, particularly since the launching of the United States air attacks. He said he thought that the bombings had stimulated mass patriotic spirit, for now all the people felt that they were in it together. There was no front, no rear—just one war.

"I think something like this happened in England," he said, "in the days when the German Air Force attacked the British. As a Communist I have been interested to see the ideological propaganda gradually being replaced by national patriotic appeal. Maybe you remember something like this in the Soviet Union during the critical days of the German attack."

I did indeed. I remembered the patriotism in England. And here in this remote, backward, pitifully poor Asian country it appeared that the same kind of patriotic miracle was being wrought again—and this time as a by-product of our own ill-conceived military tactics.

One day while I was in Hanoi I was invited by a member of the Foreign Ministry to take lunch with him at the Bo-Ho Restaurant. Bo-Ho means "lakeside" and the restaurant is on the boulevard that circles the Lake of the Restored Sword, one of the most beautiful of the small lakes which lie right in the heart of Hanoi. Each lake is surrounded by parks and broad avenues and, even in wartime, there were many plantings of flowers and shrubs. There were tiny islands close to the shores of the lakes and these were connected by old stone bridges and on the islands stood small but beautiful ancient Buddhist shrines.

The Bo-Ho Restaurant in normal times probably catered to a general clientele. But now, in wartime, it seemed to be closed to the ordinary populace. At least it was the day I went there. There was a large government luncheon going on in the principal dining room, and we were admitted only after a rather extended conversation between my Foreign

Ministry host and the maître d'hôtel or the plain-clothes policeman (or possibly he was a combination of both) on duty at the entrance. Finally, however, we were ushered up to a private suite where a lengthy Vietnamese feast was produced—many meat dishes, chicken, pork, veal, beef; two or three kinds of fish; fresh crisp vegetables; a very tasty soup of translucent Chinese noodles and greens; and, finally, sticky rice and an excessively sweet and gelatinous dessert which I could not recognize and decided not to eat. We drank many cups of tea during the luncheon and finally retired to an adjoining room for coffee and liqueurs. My host had the liqueur and I the coffee.

The meal was the best I had during my stay in North Vietnam, but the conversation interested me more. My host had invited me not from motives of hospitality but to engage me in a lengthy discussion about the United States. It was one of several such conversations which I had in Hanoi, and, in a sense, they were perhaps the most revealing talks (except that with Premier Pham Van Dong) which I had in the course of my stay. They were revealing because of what they told me about North Vietnamese attitudes toward the United States, the kind of information which the North Vietnamese had—and didn't have—and the hopes and fears which they entertained.

The subjects we covered that day were, in themselves, a fascinating selection: United States economic problems, the guns-versus-butter controversy, the Great Society program, the drain of gold to Europe, inflationary tendencies, full employment, United States draft laws, relations between the United States and its European allies, the consequences of further withdrawal of American troops from the European theater, prospects for a tax increase, the decline in purchasing power of the dollar, the strength of hawks and doves in the new Congress, the divisions on the Vietnam question in the Republican party and in the Democratic party, the problems which Mr. Johnson would encounter with the new Congress, the attitude of the banking community toward the war, controversies between industrial interests on war questions, the divisions of opinion (if any) within the Joint Chiefs of Staff, the views of Secretaries Rusk and McNamara and whether there were significant differences between them, pressures for escalation of the war, the possibilities of the Republicans in the 1968 election, the personal background of President Johnson, strains on the NATO alliance, questions of Asian relations and of Asia's relations vis-à-vis the Soviet Union and China, the possible forms which escalation might take—land operations across the 17th parallel, amphibious landings of the Inchon type or more massive bombing—U.S. Air Force strategy, the general influence of American public opinion on the conduct of the war, how conversations looking to a settlement of the war might be started, what the basis might be of such discussions and in what capital they could take place, why the United States supported the Ky Government in South Vietnam, how political stability might be achieved in the South and, if talks started, whether they were likely to break off.

It seemed to me that the discussion covered the range of Hanoi's hopes and fears, and as the talk evolved I thought I could begin to understand the lines of thought which emerged in North Vietnamese circles as they tried to evaluate the future.

One group of questions clustered about the American economy. The diplomat found it impossible to understand how the United States could continue to finance the Vietnam war without raising taxes and without suffering severe inflation, a rise in the cost of living and a reduction in purchasing power. He had read of President Johnson's budget dilemmas, and it seemed to him that they could not be resolved without serious consequences. Would not the American workingman revolt if he found it more and more difficult to stretch his pay envelope to cover the cost of food and clothing? How could the President continue a policy of guns and butter? Would he not be compelled to cut back on butter, and if he did so, would not this produce opposition in Congress? The diplomat talked a great deal about the President's Great Society program. He could not see how the President could continue this program and also finance the war in Vietnam. And if the White House had to abandon the Great Society, my host felt certain that political resentment would sweep the country. Certainly, the diplomat insisted, the United States could not escalate the war in Vietnam with all the rise in costs that would involve and not abandon much of the present program of social legislation.

He cross-examined me closely on the United States' loss of gold. He seemed to think this was undermining the American economy and that it might produce a run on the banks.

The more he talked about the economic problems of the United States and their relationship to Vietnam, the more certain I felt that he was seeking to draw an analogy between the situation in which the French found themselves in the years after 1945-46 and the position which the United States now occupied.

France in the postwar period had failed to re-establish her authority in Vietnam at least in part because she ran out of steam. She ran out of money to finance the war. The French economy could not stand the joint burden of the war and of postwar reconstruction. The French gold reserves were threatened. The country went into an inflationary spin. The French workingman was faced with serious problems in the rise in living costs and the decline in the value of his franc.

But the French parallel did not hold true for the United States, as I explained to my host in great detail. I pointed out that the United States had an economic base far broader than that of France. The United States produced about half of the world's industrial output. The American economy was so remarkably prolific that it had thus far been able with only minimum strain to mount the war in Vietnam and continue to satisfy consumer demands. There was no shortage of consumer goods in America. True, prices had risen slightly in the last year. There had been some unusual increases in food items. But these were not big. They were not on the order of those which had occurred in France. They had, in fact, tapered off, and it did not seem likely that 1967 would bring a new rise. As for the gold drain, it was going on but at a rather small rate and it was not the kind of drain that France had suffered. Much of the gold was going abroad to be deposited to American accounts or to finance American investments overseas. The true balance of American assets, if the overseas assets were included, would show an enormous rise and a remarkable expansion of net worth rather than the reverse.

American industry was luxuriating. The American worker didn't like to pay higher prices. But his own wages were going up remarkably. I told my host of a visit I had paid to Detroit only a week before leaving for Hanoi and how the heads of the great automobile companies, Ford and General Motors, had said that in 1967 the automobile workers' union would be negotiating for a contract which would give them five dollars an hour—not five dollars a day, as was the case with the famous Ford contract of World War I, but five dollars an hour. I said that in all probability this new high wage structure would be established and that with wages like this a good deal of inflation could be absorbed without anyone's feeling it. I tried to bring home to him what five dollars an hour meant in purchasing power. But this was impossible. The five dollars earned in an hour by the Detroit production worker was probably more than the seventy dong which were earned in a month by the worker in one of the North Vietnamese factories.

But what kind of prices did the Ford worker have to pay? the diplomat asked—what did he pay for a car, for example? I said that cars sold for such a wide range of prices that it was hard to give him much idea. But it was possible to buy a secondhand car for $200 or $300, just for transportation to and from work. I saw him trying to figure out the equivalent in dong. It was a calculation beyond any kind of mathematics for it was like trying to compare the economy of medieval England with that of present-day America. It took the Hanoi worker nearly three months to earn enough dong to buy a bicycle. It took the Detroit worker less than a week and a half to earn enough to buy a used car—considerably less if he was on overtime. How could I make the American economy understandable in North Vietnamese terms? In those terms it just didn't make any sense.

As for the argument that the President could not continue a policy of guns-and-butter or that he would have to cut back the Great Society program, I said that it seemed to me that there was no real barrier to guns-and-butter, provided there was no radical escalation in military expenditures. Thus far the policy had been maintained. The Vietnam war was beginning to be very costly in absolute terms, but as a percentage of the gross national product or even of the total budget it was not of that magnitude. The war would, of course, have an effect on the Great Society program. But it seemed to me that, rather than having to abandon it, the President simply would not be able to expand it as rapidly as he had hoped.

We had a long discussion of the United States draft laws because my host was convinced that the President was going to have great difficulty in getting Congress to give him authority for a general national mobilization. I tried to explain our complicated and (as I thought) unfair draft law. I don't believe I succeeded. I did not know its complexities well enough myself. But I demonstrated to him that the President could, if he chose, continue to conduct the war with the powers he now possessed. In any event, he did not need to have a struggle with Congress on this issue if he did not wish one.

We discussed differences in opinion between various economic interests. The Foreign Ministry man had the classic Marxist concept that the war was supported and instigated by big industrial and financial interests. I told him I thought this was not the case; that there were very large interests which opposed the war on the simple grounds that it was bad for their business. The auto makers, for example, could make much more money if they could sell ten million automobiles in the domestic market than if their output was cut back to eight million and their military profits somewhat increased. True, some electronics and aircraft manufacturers were making money out of the war. But they did not call the tune in industrial or political America.

The diplomat talked a good deal about our European allies and the effect on them of pulling out more troops from Europe and sending them to the Far East. Weren't they afraid of the Soviet Union? What would happen to NATO? I told him I thought that there was no real concern in Europe now about the Soviet Union. West Germany, of course, would not like a further reduction in our European garrison. The other allies probably didn't care. I told him that my own worry was that we were concentrating so much attention on the situation in Vietnam that we were not giving the pressing political problems in Europe the care which they must have.

This led into a discussion of the tensions in the Communist world, in which my interest was obviously greater than his. He was well aware of the dangers of those tensions. What he wanted to get straight in his mind was the skein of crosscurrents and tensions in the American world.

For example, he pointed out, it was often said that President Johnson would have difficulty in getting re-elected in 1968 if the war in Vietnam were still on. I conceded that this thought had been advanced by some American political commentators. But I noted that others, among whom I mentioned James Reston, held the view that if the war was on, the President would simply go to the voters on a basis of patriotism and probably this appeal would prevail.

In any event, I thought it was not a very solid reed for

Hanoi to lean on—the possibility that Mr. Johnson might run into election trouble over the war in 1968. Then, said my companion, what about the divisions in Congress? There had been a great rise in Republican strength in the November, 1966, elections. This should cause Johnson trouble. It might, I conceded. But not necessarily over the war. After all, it was known that the Republicans generally took a more hawkish view than the Democrats. I said it was my belief that a majority in Congress, of both Democrats and Republicans, would in a showdown support the President on the war.

It interested me that the Foreign Ministry man had not once raised the question often discussed in the United States—that is, the effect on the government and our war policy of the widespread domestic dissent and opposition to the President's course—the peace movement, the antagonism to the bombing policy.

I mentioned this now myself, saying that I thought it would prove illusory if the North Vietnamese pinned any hopes on a possible change in American policy because opposition to the war and to Mr. Johnson was so widespread that it might compel him against his will to modify his policies.

My associate said that I need not suppose they had any false notions on that score. They evaluated the American opposition to the war conservatively. They were under no delusion that it was strong enough or likely to grow strong enough to change the course of hostilities. But they were interested nonetheless in assessing the over-all balance of political power in the United States.

They felt that there were many factors which were working against the continuation of the war on its present scale or against its escalation. But they recognized that these influences were not great enough to cause any change. After all, the war, in their view, was a colonial war. It was, they held, motivated and directed by imperialist aspirations. The United States had, really, simply substituted itself for France. They were familiar with this pattern of motivation from their long years of experience with the French.

I said that I felt this also was a mistake. It would not do to draw analogies too closely from the French experience.

France, after all, had been a colonial power. She wished to regain her colony after the war, to hold on to it and to exploit it. As for the United States, I was convinced that we were entirely sincere in our declaration that we had no interest in the region, no desire to establish ourselves there and that we would like nothing better than to get out.

The Foreign Ministry man smiled cynically. He was sorry but he did not believe that. The United States, whatever mask it wore, was a colonial power of a new type. This was a colonial war of a new type.

I told him I thought he was badly mistaken. The truth is, I said—and you will find this hard to believe—there is nothing in Vietnam in which the United States has any material interest. There is nothing in your country which is worth our while economically. If the United States had to stay in Vietnam, it would simply cost us money. You have nothing for us to exploit. Vietnam isn't worth our while.

This shocked my companion. I could see it in his face. He had never expected to be told that his country had no value. To him, of course, and to his countrymen it had enormous value. He could not understand someone saying that it was without value. I do not know whether he thought I was being deliberately rude, eccentric or provocative. I did not tell him—although perhaps I should have—of the anxiety of so many Americans that their sons not be sent to fight in Vietnam.

I tried to explain about our economy and its organization. I said that I had not meant any slight against Vietnam. It was a fine nation with fine people. It possessed many excellent natural resources. It simply did not happen to fit into our kind of industrial establishment. I said he must understand that the American economy was so vastly productive that it created its own markets. All the foreign markets put together were only a fraction of the total. Not enough to matter a great deal to any American businessman except the comparative few directly engaged in foreign trade. It was not like France or the other old colonial countries which depended upon the exploitation of backward regions to maintain a high standard of living at home.

This brought our conversation to a natural pause. I complimented my host on the excellent meal. He smiled and then asked me another question. He had heard, he said, some talk of President Johnson's program for Asia. What was to be understood by that term? What was meant?

I wasn't exactly certain to what he had reference. I said I supposed he must mean the plans the President had discussed for the economic and social development of Asia, the plans for joint exploitation of the Mekong River Valley resources, the schemes he had advanced for an organized program to lift the economic standards and living levels of Asia once the war in Vietnam was over.

And what areas, said my companion, are to be embraced by this program?

All of Southeast Asia, I replied, and quite probably the whole of Asia.

Does it include all of Vietnam? he asked.

Yes, I said, I think it does, North as well as South.

A long silence followed. Then I thanked him for the pleasant lunch and the interesting conversation. We went out through the darkened main dining room, where the government banquet had long since been concluded, and rode back through the empty afternoon streets of Hanoi to the hotel, getting there just a few minutes before the customary afternoon alert.

It sounded that afternoon at 2:28 P.M. I responded quickly to the siren and the pounding on my door by the floor maid. As I passed through the back courtyard with its gilded cage in which three red and blue and black roosters lived, the SAM's began to go high in the heavens and the little kitchen helper, accoutered with his helmet and rifle, urged me to hurry into the shelter. I walked slowly, just to show that I was a veteran of the Hanoi war. Then the ack-ack batteries close at hand began to fire and I walked a bit more briskly.

The alert lasted about twenty minutes. I sat in the whitewashed concrete-walled bunker and thought about the conversation I had just had. It seemed to me that we had covered all the political possibilities which would have been considered in an analysis of why the United States might be compelled to slack off in its war effort. But none of the prospects had panned out. Not really. And I thought the Foreign Ministry man was shrewd enough to have sensed that. And then had come that final question—about the Johnson program for Asian development. I could not help but wonder whether somewhere in the Hanoi regime even that possibility was being analyzed—the possibility that once the war had been ended North Vietnam might join with the other nations of Southeast Asia in a Johnson plan. Frankly, I thought it was a pretty good idea.

The Mission of the National Liberation Front occupied the
only newly painted, newly redecorated building that I saw in
Hanoi—a large villa set in a spacious park not far from the
Foreign Ministry. It was, I was told, the former American
Mission in Hanoi and it had been completely done over and
put to the use of the N.L.F.

When I entered the villa, I was welcomed by a tall, pleasant man, speaking English, who described himself as chief of
the press section of the mission. He introduced me to a distinguished, gray-haired man with an air of quiet cosmopoli-
tanism who also had a considerable grasp of English. This
was Nguyen Van Tien, a former Saigon college professor, a
member of the Resistance movement since 1945, a member
of the powerful Central Committee of the Front and its dele-
gate in Hanoi.

It was not the smiles with which I was greeted or the hospitable way in which Tien and his aide offered me

coffee—not tea—which gave me a difficult-to-define impression. It was an impression which was deepened by the slight aloofness of the two aides from the North Vietnamese Foreign Ministry who accompanied me—one of them an interpreter and the other a functionary of the press department.

I had the feeling that the Front representatives in a subtle manner had created a common atmosphere which they and I shared and which, in a sense, excluded the two men from Hanoi.

Both of the Front representatives were from Saigon. The two Hanoi men were from the North. There was a distance in sophistication between the two groups which was wider than the thousand miles which separated Hanoi and Saigon. The men of the South acted like and seemed like men of the world. In their presence the two men from Hanoi appeared like country cousins. The men from Saigon gave the impression that they were accustomed to being with Americans, that they felt, perhaps, more at home with Americans than they did with their Northern compatriots.

Looking back on the afternoon I spent at the mission, I found it difficult to recapture the nuances which gave me these impressions. Yet when the talk had ended, it was the atmosphere which seemed to me more important, perhaps, than any single thing that had been said. I left the mission feeling that it might well be easier to arrive at understandings with the Front than with Hanoi, simply because of the Front's greater degree of sophistication and sense of accommodation to the world. I did not have this feeling about Hanoi. In talking to the North Vietnamese representatives I was struck by what seemed to me to be a kind of naïveté, a willfulness in clinging to positions when logic and reason dictated some modification. I did not have this impression with Tien. And I felt certain that this was no accident. He knew what he was doing, and there were moments when I looked at the men from North Vietnam and sensed that they were uncomfortable and a bit resentful at the empathy which had been created by the Saigon men.

But these were delicate and subjective shadings, which I sensed more deeply as I looked back on the conversation. The conversation in itself was particularly interesting to me because it opened a door to a new understanding of the role and the nature of the Front—one which I had not possessed until that moment. Later, when I had returned to the United

States, I spoke with persons who were far better informed than I was about the Front and who thought that my earlier ideas about the Front had been naïve. I had supposed when I went to Hanoi that the Front, or the Vietcong as we commonly but improperly called it, was largely the creation and creature of the North. I knew that it claimed a separate identity, but I thought this was probably a propaganda mask, worn for tactical purposes. I did not believe there could be any major difference of interest or policy between the Front and the Hanoi regime.

Before my meeting with Tien had concluded I began to have serious doubts of my notions about the Front—notions which I knew were shared by many of my countrymen. And before I left North Vietnam I was convinced that the nature of the Front, and specifically of its relationships to Hanoi and its probable role in a postwar Vietnam, had been badly misunderstood in the United States. I began to wonder what lay at the root of the misunderstanding—whether, indeed, we had really done our homework and whether, by chance, in our official passion and partisanship for the Saigon Government we had permitted ourselves to be misled. I found to my amazement that my ignorance of the Front's program and policy was shared by American officials with basic responsibility for our Vietnam policy.

The picture of the Front as it was sketched for me by Tien was one of an independent entity—possibly not yet exactly a government but certainly well on the way toward that goal. The Front now had established fifteen missions attached to governments abroad, including those of all the Communist countries and several in the Afro-Asian world, such as Algeria, the United Arab Republic and Indonesia. Tien himself for several years had been stationed in Cairo.

I asked him whether he considered himself an ambassador in Hanoi. He said his mission was not exactly an embassy but "a diplomatic post of a special form not seen anywhere else in the world."

He had diplomatic status, but his relationship to the Hanoi Government had a special intimacy which reflected a relationship more akin to that of the Commonwealth ties of the British than to the normal arm's-length position of the diplomat and government to which he was accredited.

Tien insisted that on all questions pertaining to the South he and Hanoi conducted discussions on an equal footing.

"The North cannot speak for the South," he said. "Anyone who has to discuss South Vietnam must speak with the Front."

I asked him how this worked out. Suppose, for instance, the Front needed some guns or ammunition. How did they get their supplies? Did they go to the Hanoi Government and ask Hanoi to obtain the guns from the Russians or the Chinese? Or did they go directly to Moscow or Peking with their request?

We go to the government from whom we hope to get the supplies, Tien said. The Front did not, he insisted, utilize Hanoi as a middleman in such transactions. If the Front needed a thousand machine guns, these were provided directly by the supplying government. The shipment was designated for the South. In the same manner goods for the North were designated for the North. Each handled its own business.

On the other hand, he emphasized that the North and the South were one people, one nation, and engaged in a common struggle and because of this each had the right to demand aid from the other. It was on this basis that the South came to the North for requests for assistance and these requests were honored by the North. The South would do the same for the North when, as and if needed.

I asked him who ran the war in the South. I pointed out that in the United States it was assumed that the orders to the Vietcong came from Hanoi. What was the truth of this?

"The direction of the struggle in the South is by the South and not by the North," he said.

I pressed him a bit on this question. I had heard repeatedly that there were Northern generals now in the South and that the command of a number of units, particularly of organized army units sent to the South by the North, was vested in Hanoi's officers, not those of the Front. He persisted in his affirmation that all military decisions in the South were the responsibility of the South.

I put the same question, later, to Northern representatives. They gave me the same answer. I must say, however, that I was not entirely satisfied on this point. Having observed the personality of the responsible officials of the Hanoi Government, it was hard for me to believe that they would put the command of Northern regiments or battalions entirely in Southern hands. It probably would be different with small groups which were incorporated into Southern guerrilla units. But with the large organized groups it did not make military sense to put them under Southern command. More likely, I thought, the Northern units were retained under Northern commanders, but the general course of operations was directed either by a nominal Front command or in close collaboration, more likely the latter. This conviction was deepened by reports and rumors which I heard among diplomats of differences of opinion between the Front and the Hanoi commanders as to the tactics, strategy and deployment of forces in the South.

The Front had come into being, Tien said, as a Southern organization. It was a natural outgrowth of the struggle against the French. After 1954 it continued to struggle by political means and went on in this fashion until 1959, seeking to oppose the Diem regime, but in the face of savage repression by Diem the Front had gradually come to the realization that only by armed struggle would it be possible to survive and to achieve its aims. In December, 1960, it had adopted a political program and reorganized itself for armed struggle.

It was Tien's contention that, contrary to American impressions, the Front had won increasing prestige and respect in the South and that it now held sway over areas in which about ten million of the estimated fourteen million people of the South were resident. I had no way of evaluating this picture of the Front's authority and influence. I found, however, that Hanoi officials, including Premier Pham Van Dong, assessed the Front in much the same manner and, indeed, contended that in 1966 it had increased the population under its aegis. This claim, I found, was supported by a careful analysis of the *Far Eastern Economic Review,* an independent and respected Hong Kong publication, which concluded that the Vietcong ended 1966 with more rather than less territory under its control. Whether the total area had somewhat increased, just held steady or fallen off a bit did not seem to me as important as the obvious fact that the Front was, like it or not, on the way to becoming a government-in-being which held sway over a very substantial portion of South Vietnam. It was from this circumstance that it derived its power, and it was this which compelled us to evaluate most carefully its nature and its program.

The program interested me intensely because I discovered

that it was not the same program as that of the North. Indeed, it differed from that of the North on a number of critical points.

The basic Front program had five points. These called for national independence, democratic freedom, peace, neutrality and reunification.

There were no surprises in the plans for national independence and peace. But on all the other points I found that the Front's program did not coincide with my impression of what the Front wanted nor did it mesh very closely with the program of the North.

The definition of democratic freedom, for instance, was not the same approach to politics that I found in Hanoi. The Front's Central Committee was made up of a diversity of political alignments. It had a hard core of Communists and, it was clear, the Communists provided the guiding force. In fact, I was told that the longer the struggle went on, the stronger the Communist influence had become. But in addition there were bourgeois non-Communist elements, nonparty intellectuals, leaders of the Buddhist sects and members of existing democratic parties. Some of the Central Committee members were Socialists. Others were non-Marxists. It was the Front's policy to permit the diversity of parties to continue after the war and after (as it hoped) it had come to power. It did not, or so it said, plan to establish a dictatorship of the Communist party such as existed in the North.

This was a major difference. Of course, I had heard this kind of talk before from Communist groups which were not yet strong enough to take power. For instance, in Eastern Europe at the end of World War II, in countries like Poland, Czechoslovakia, and Rumania, there had been coalition governments in which, in some instances, the Communists were minorities. There had been elections in which non-Communist parties had participated and parliaments with non-Communist majorities. But, after a few years, the Communists tired of this and with the aid of the Red Army established typical Communist dictatorships in all of Eastern Europe, simply suppressing all other political activity. This might readily occur later in South Vietnam. Only time would determine whether there was a political vitality in the South which could oppose the Communists. Or, of course, a settlement might in some fashion guarantee that they would not take over. But what was interesting to me was that the Communists obviously did not plan immediately to establish a power monopoly. In fact, they spoke very strongly of their feeling that the only stable kind of government in the South would be one in which all elements were represented.

The next point of difference lay in the kind of economy which the Front proposed to establish in the South. The North, to be sure, had a pure Communist economy. There was no private enterprise except for street vendors or a minority of the peasants, possibly 5 or 10 percent, who still tilled and owned their own land. All factories, stores, services, establishments and enterprises were owned and run by the state. There was a certain number of cooperatives in which artisans and handicraft workers banded together in something which superficially resembled private enterprise. But even these were not encouraged. In industry North Vietnam had followed closely the Soviet pattern. In agriculture it had set up a system of communes or collective farms which seemed to be more like the Chinese model than the Russian. But in this pattern there was no room or place or permission for private enterprise.

But the Front proposed to follow a different program. It was not going all out for Communism. Instead, it favored a mixed economy. It would include state capitalism or state socialism (I was unable to see anything but a semantic difference between the two) for large-scale enterprises. It would have mixed companies in which the state and private businessmen would share the capital and the profits. It would continue to encourage and protect private enterprise. Exactly how this mixture would work was something about which no one was too clear, but it seemed to me that the Front envisaged an economy which was far more like that established by General Ne Win in Burma or Prince Sihanouk in Cambodia than that of North Vietnam or North Korea. The retention of private business was an important part of the Front's program, and it appeared to be an essential one if it was to continue to attract those non-Communist elements which played such an important role in the society of the South.

The third difference between the North and the South arose in the sphere of foreign policy. The Front stood for establishment of a neutralist state. It would have no alliances with either the Communist bloc or the West and the United States. It would pursue a foreign policy similar to that of Burma and Cambodia, a policy akin to that which poor Laos supposedly was following. Its orientation would be firmly set against China, against the Soviet Union, against the United States. The only great power with which it might find itself in a sympathetic relationship was India, and even this was dubious due to India's hostility to China and strengthening ties to the United States and the Soviet Union.

In part, it seemed to me, this concept of a neutral South Vietnam grew out of the original provisions of the Geneva agreements which specified this role for Vietnam. In part, I thought, it might stem from an earlier concept of a Third Force community for Southeast Asia which might comprise the two Vietnams, Laos, Cambodia, Burma and possibly Indonesia.

But whatever the origin of the thinking which led the Front to espouse a neutralist role, the important thing was that despite the war, despite the involvement with the Communist powers (which now provided so much of the weaponry and supplies on which the Front depended), despite all this it clung to the concept.

The clash here between North and South could not have been more naked. For the announced policy of Hanoi was that it was part of the "camp of the Socialist powers." It was tied to the Communist world by the firmest of military alliances, which fixed its relationship not only with Moscow but with Peking. Granted that the "camp" of the Communist world no longer was united and was riven by the fiercest schism. Still, Hanoi was not neutral between East and West. And there seemed to be no present thinking among North Vietnam's rulers that they might move over to a neutral position. Indeed, in discussions with Hanoi officials I heard references again and again to the lost unity of the Communist world and nostalgic hopes that somehow it might be restored. I did not think Hanoi would lightly relinquish its role in the Communist world, no matter how divided that world became.

Thus, what did we have so far as the Front was concerned? Enormous differences between itself and Hanoi in three critical areas—internal politics, economy and foreign relations.

It was only by an evaluation of these differences that some light was cast on the next question which I put to Tien. This was the question of reunification. How did the Front envisage this? What would happen when the war was over?

He was voluble on this point, but I did not find him painting a very clear picture.

"We think," he said, "that reunification must proceed step by step. It will have to be settled between the Front and the North on a basis of equality. And, of course, the Front will decide all questions concerning the South in respect to reunification."

But what would actually happen?

He described the initial step. The first thing would be to restore postal service between North and South. It had been ten years now since people in the North and people in the South had been able to send letters back and forth—except by getting someone to mail them from outside the country. That came first. Then, the next thing was to permit visits and travel between North and South. He said I could not imagine how hard the division had been. It was worse than the Berlin Wall. Families had been divided. Mothers had not seen their children for a decade. This must come to an end. Everyone, North and South, wanted to end this feeling of being cut off, one from the other. Then the third thing was to get trade going again. North and South must exchange goods.

Very well, I said. That's the first step. What next?

What next—this seemed to trouble Mr. Tien a bit. The next steps, he said, would have to be worked out in agreement between North and South. There was no hurry. No one expected this to happen overnight. There was plenty of time. Maybe it would take quite a few years.

Quite a few years. This seemed to me to be a clue to the whole situation. Later when I talked with Hanoi officials and in particular with Premier Pham Van Dong, I found him speaking in the same kind of terms. No hurry about reunification. There are many complicated problems. We will decide these among ourselves. If it takes ten years or twenty years—that is our affair. The Premier displayed one of the few signs of anger which marked his lengthy discussion with me when he rejected the idea that the North wanted to "annex" the South. No one in the North, he insisted, had this "stupid, criminal" idea in mind. Reunification would only be by mutual agreement. And in the North they were as aware as in the South that each had different ideas on the future.

Indeed, they had. When these different ideas were examined, it seemed to me clear that not only would it be quite a few years before reunification occurred but that it also might never occur.

It did not seem to me that we in the United States had begun to explore the implications of these divergencies. Yet they lay at the core of any effort to work out a settlement in Vietnam; they were undoubtedly the most important factor in understanding what the possibilities were in the South. How could we be so ignorant of these remarkably vital matters? We were fighting a tremendously expensive war; we were investing billions of our substance in the conflict; we were expending the lives of thousands of our finest young men; we were disrupting the lives of hundreds of thousands of others. Was it not a matter of the most elementary prudence to understand in the most minute detail the political programs and relationships of the elements who were ranged against us?

During the time that I was in Hanoi a rally was held in the city for army cadets. It was addressed by Le Duan, the first secretary of the North Vietnamese Communist party. I did not get to meet Le Duan. So far as I knew, he had not been met by any foreign visitor. But he was an extremely important individual. There were many in North Vietnam who felt that if President Ho Chi Minh were to die he would probably be succeeded not by the much better known Premier Pham Van Dong but by Le Duan or another man hardly known in the West, Trong Chinh, a former party secretary, now head of the powerful Party Control Commission.

The most important point in the address which Le Duan gave to the army cadets concerned what would happen when the war had ended. He told them that the army must be ready for the transition to civil life, to the new tasks which would emerge. There would be many new challenges in peacetime. The country would have to be rebuilt. There would be the problems of moving the country onto civilian rails and in this the army would have a major role. There must be preparation for the problems and new alignments which would emerge at the end of the war. Peace would not bring a unified rule in North and South.

When the war ended, he said, there would be "Socialism in the North, democracy in the South."

This declaration was the talk of Hanoi. Everywhere I went the diplomats and correspondents were discussing it. Not that the thought was new. It had been expressed before. What

won attention was the fact that Le Duan had chosen this moment to emphasize this particular thought to the cadets—the
military élite.

It seemed to Hanoi that Le Duan's action had great significance. He was, in effect, preparing the cadets not for reunification of the country at the end of the war but for a continuance of division—for two radically different regimes, one in
the North, one in the South.

This seemed to flow with the greatest of logic from the
programmatic differences which I had heard expounded between the North and the South.

These differences may not have been perceived in Washington, but they certainly had been grasped in Peking. For, I
was informed, Peking was far from happy about the program
of the South. So unhappy was Peking that the Chinese had
complained to Hanoi about the Front, asking the North to
use its influence to get the Front to adopt a "Socialist" rather
than a "non-Socialist" policy. The Chinese were not the only
ones who expressed misgivings about the Front's program.
Other Communists were dubious, too. The North Koreans
thought it was a dangerous program, that it would lead to a
permanent division of Vietnam, that the differences should be
eliminated now while there was still time.

But—or so I was informed—Hanoi refused to intervene,
saying that the program was the responsibility of the Front.
If China wished to complain it should complain to the Front,
not to Hanoi.

Reluctantly the Chinese and North Koreans were said to
have yielded. But they had not withdrawn their objections. I
heard that Moscow was almost as poorly informed on the nature of the Front and its program as Washington appeared to
be. Not until comparatively recent times, according to this
version, had the Russians taken the trouble to learn the actual nature of the Front, its political composition and program.

None of this meant that the Front or Hanoi had given up
its hopes for reunification. The hotel where I was staying was
called Reunification Hotel. The new park which had been
built by North Vietnamese youths around the Hanoi lake adjacent to the Polytechnic University was called Reunification
Park. The propaganda line was not changed. Every official in
Hanoi with whom I spoke called reunification a basic objective of the war.

Yet no one, either from North or South, could give me any clue or timetable of how the reunification would come about. Premier Pham Van Dong said this was a question for North and South to work out "as between brothers." But, commented one tart-tongued diplomat, negotiations "between brothers" did not always run smoothly. In fact, brothers sometimes were those who found it most difficult to agree.

There was no way of proving how deep the differences might be between North and South. Possibly, if peace came, they would melt away like the spring snows and a completely unified Communist dictatorship would arise. But this hardly seemed likely. The programmatic differences were not mere quibbles—not when you were dealing with Marxists. Nothing is more important to a Marxist than a matter of program or principle. Moreover, there were subtle temperamental, environmental differences which I had sensed in the contrasts between the Southern representatives and those of the North, between the sophisticated, cosmopolitan, French civilization of the South and the "country cousins" of the North. The Southerner was a man of the world, the Northerner a simple, more direct, more blunt, more forceful, more naïve individual.

These differences might be put aside for the common goals of Communism. This had happened in other countries. But it also was notable that Communism did not erase all regional conflicts or divergencies. I had seen this again and again in the Soviet Union. There were no sharper differences than those between the Great Russians, for instance, and the Little Russians, or Ukrainians. It was still an open question whether these two closely related, ethnically similar peoples would ever over the years manage to maintain a basis for easy peaceful coexistence. In Eastern Europe this kind of difference had become more and more noticeable as time went on.

There was another factor. The Front had now been in existence for nearly ten years virtually as a *de facto* government. It claimed to speak for the fourteen million people of the South and to rule ten million of them against the seventeen million of the North. It had its apparatus, its bureaucracy, its customs of government. Its leaders had acquired the habit of authority and the familiarity of office. Was it likely that they would easily and quickly yield up their powers to the North? Or surrender the sweet perquisites of office to another set of officials? I did not think so. Communism might have changed many things, but it had not repealed the laws of human nature. I had never yet seen a bureaucrat who willingly surrendered power, especially not a Communist bureaucrat. I did not expect to see such a spectacle in Vietnam, and I thought that those specialists in Vietnamese affairs who overlooked this simple and obvious truth were careless indeed.

The Front had a government. It had a cabinet. It had its own network of diplomatic representation (though not yet diplomats accredited to it in its own capital, wherever that might be), its own troops, its own generals, its own petty officials, its own courts, its own tax collectors. It not only ruled in large rural areas. It had, or so I was told by its representatives, shadow governments and structures in all the regions of the South, ready to surface the moment the areas were liberated. It even claimed to rule large parts of Saigon. Quietly of course. I had heard that even the proprietors of bars and houses of prostitution which catered to the Americans paid taxes to the Front. It was safer that way.

The real nature of relations between the Front and Hanoi was hard to judge. Hanoi, for a year or more, had had a cabinet officer attached to the Front government. Was this man an ambassador or a boss? I thought he was more likely to be an ambassador.

Was it true that the Front ran the military show in the South? I had heard on excellent authority that there were very important differences of opinion about how the war should be conducted in the South. The Front preferred its own style of small guerrilla operations, hit-and-run tactics. It liked to conserve its forces and wait until the odds were strongly in its favor before striking. The North had sent in some regular army units. They preferred "main force" engagements, large-scale combat in which they involved substantial units of Americans. The South was not happy, it was said, about the Northern operations. The Northern troops were not conditioned to the kind of jungle warfare at which the South excelled. There had been losses, sometimes substantial losses, in the "main force" battles. There had been recriminations, so I was told.

There could be no confirmation of this kind of report. One had to trust one's instinct. In this case I thought it likely that there was substance to the rumors.

I had no doubt of the independent tendencies of the Southerners. The Front boasted of them. It insisted that it was its independence of outside influence which gave it political superiority over Marshal Ky and the Saigon generals. The Front took orders from no one. It said that Ky & Company were American puppets. This was the Front's line. Both Front and North stood as one in their view that the Front was the appropriate body to negotiate the settlement of questions relating to the South.

The Front was not yet ready to discuss in specific terms what kind of government it expected to emerge after peace was restored. But it was willing to declare that it did not expect to monopolize the scene. It was obvious that the Front expected a coalition to emerge, and it had specifically said it had no objection to elements of South Vietnam's Constituent Assembly and of the Ky regime (but not the Marshal) entering the government. Of course, it hoped to be the dominant factor in such a setup.

But the more I examined the situation, the more I wondered whether it would not be possible to construct around the Front a government which would possess precisely that element which all the Southern governments beginning with that of Diem had lacked—political viability. I was by no means convinced that given the appropriate circumstances this government need, necessarily, be dominated by the Communists. It would not be easy to put together such a structure. But it might be considerably easier than any other alternative which had yet been examined.

The more I scrutinized the actual programs of the North and the South, the more convinced I became that this was the field in which we should be concentrating our major attention. Here, if anywhere, existed overlooked potentials and genuine possibilities for constructing that durable and stable structure of Southeast Asia which thus far had so strikingly eluded even the reluctant architects of our massive policy of military intervention.

I was sitting one evening in the lounge of the Reunification Hotel when an East European Communist joined me for a cup of the excellent French coffee which was unquestionably the best product of the hotel's kitchen.

This was a man who had spent much time in North Vietnam and in the East. He was as familiar with Hanoi and Peking as with his own capital—possibly more familiar. He was fond of the North Vietnamese people and of their leaders, particularly Ho Chi Minh. He knew them well. He had been in Hanoi when the regime had been proclaimed after the Geneva Conference in 1954, and he spoke with sadness of those "wonderful days when we were all comrades together."

In those times, he said, everyone was working to make a success of North Vietnam—the Russians, the Chinese, the regimes in Eastern Europe and particularly the party of his own country. All wanted to make North Vietnam an example, a showplace, a model of what Communism could bring to Asia and particularly to Southeast Asia. Their hopes were grandiose. Speaking quite frankly, he told me that many of them had thought that Communism would spread from North Vietnam to the neighboring countries. There had been, of course, much fighting in the area and not a little subversion. In 1954 they believed that if they built up a strong Communist country in North Vietnam, the force of its example would sway the peoples of the neighboring countries.

"I wish you could have seen Hanoi then," he said. "The city was so lovely. Every building had been painted, the streets were spruced up and there were flowers everywhere."

The atmosphere had been as refreshing as the landscape.

"Everything seemed possible then," he recalled as he sipped his coffee. "There was no hint of a split in the camp. Russia, China, all of us were working shoulder to shoulder to help Vietnam, to enable the Vietnamese people to create a Communist future."

Now, he conceded, those days were far, far behind.

What had gone wrong? I asked. How had the split come about?

"It is very hard for me, a Communist, to say," he said. "Of course, we know all the polemics. We know the arguments. We know the disagreements. But what is happening now? I'll tell you frankly I just don't understand any more about it than you do."

Another Communist entered the lobby and joined us. He was from a West European party. We went on talking about China. This was the subject of much of the conversation and gossip in Hanoi while I was there—second, possibly, only to gossip about my own presence and what it might signify.

The second Communist was a young man. He was making his third visit to Vietnam. Each time he had come through Moscow and Peking.

"I have many friends in Peking," he said. "I am fond of them. We have many of the same ideas. Each time that I have come through Peking I have looked forward to our discussions. But last year things had begun to change, and this year it was very different."

He said that he had been in Peking for four days on his way to Hanoi in early December. He had spent most of his time in the hotel. His friends did not want to see him. The tourist people were polite but not communicative. He found it hard to grasp any understanding of the events that were going on.

"You knew that something was happening," he said. "You knew it was big, it was important. But just what it was you didn't know."

He said he had walked through the Peking streets, watching the Red Guards, and he had seen them putting up their posters on the walls.

"It is very interesting. Very colorful," he said. "They put up new posters several times a day. And they paint the walls. They paint them blood-red. Some walls are painted red from top to bottom. Then the posters are painted in red characters on paper and pasted on the red wall. In some quarters of the city all you see are the red walls. They are painted red in the morning. Then they are painted red again in the afternoon."

What was the stimulus of the Red Guard movement, I asked, and what seemed to be its objective?

"It is very powerful," he said. "You don't know who is directing it. But it is not just the young people. Once, for a time, it got out of control. The Red Guards began to put up posters and denounce people on their own. But they ended that quickly. The orders come down from the top. The question is, from whom at the top. You don't know who that is. But the Red Guards are being directed. It is not a question of anarchy."

Living in Hanoi against the background of daily reports of the Red Guards' activity and the constant stream of their demands, pronunciamentos, ultimatums, denunciations and mass meetings was like living under the brow of a volcano. Everyone in Hanoi was intimately aware of the Chinese crisis, intimately aware that it might grow more grave, intimately aware of the dire possibilities which it might bring to North Vietnam.

The problem of China was borne in upon Hanoi every day, and it was visible in the ordinary, everyday life of the community.

My arrival in Hanoi had stirred intense interest on the part of the diplomats in Hanoi—the Western diplomats, the diplomats from the neutral and nonaligned countries of Asia and those from the Communist bloc as well. And this was natural. Everyone wanted to know the significance of my trip. Was I, perhaps, carrying some message from President Johnson? Everyone wanted to know—everyone, that is, except the Chinese. They studiously avoided me. But not me alone.

One day the Foreign Ministry telephoned and asked if I would like to see an American drone, a robot plane, which had been shot down outside the city. They were making up a party of the accredited correspondents in Hanoi and would be glad to include me if I was interested. I was delighted and promptly went along to the Foreign Ministry, where I found the journalistic colony of Hanoi assembling, about thirty reporters in all. There was Jacques Moalic, the energetic correspondent of Agence France-Presse. There was an elderly but chipper lady from New Zealand named Freda Cook who called everybody "comrade." There was the Junoesque blonde from Radio Moscow and three other Soviet correspondents. There was a Polish journalist—very friendly. A Czech journalist—very friendly. There was also a group of Chinese journalists—very unfriendly. Everyone had come in his car, and all of them were ordinary machines except for that of the Chinese. They had a military-type command car. The five of them sat in their car with its side curtains and said nothing to their colleagues.

We drove out in a convoy to the site of the shot-down drone. The cars halted and we walked over the fields to the place where half a dozen North Vietnamese farm girls were digging in the mud to recover the engine of the drone. Already its wings and assorted parts had been retrieved from the muck and were piled up beside the hole. The Chinese came over to the site, brought out their cameras and took some pictures. They jotted down in their notebooks the few essential facts and figures. Then they snapped shut their notebooks, retraced their steps, got into their command car and whizzed away. If they said a single word to any newspaperman, I did not hear it.

This was not unusual. It was the ordinary way in which the Chinese behaved. They had nothing to do with anyone else. I saw them on two other occasions. One was a reception given by the Minister of Information and the other was a press conference given by a Japanese group which was investigating the results of the American bombing. Each time the Chinese attended in a small group, said nothing to anyone else and showed no interest in contact with any other foreigner.

It was not easy for the North Vietnamese to maintain good relations with the Chinese under these conditions of tension and isolation. It was a delicate task, filled with the most fragile of undertakings, apt at any time to break down.

One of the (to me) remarkable facts about reporting from Hanoi was that there was no censorship. I was aware that my dispatches were read by the Foreign Ministry before being transmitted, but they were sent along without a word being deleted. I wondered if this was special treatment for me, but I found on discussing the matter with Moalic that it was not. He had never been subjected to censorship in some six months of daily reporting—except once. He had been warned that he must not try to report a visit by one of the North Vietnamese party secretaries to Peking. "This is much too delicate," the Foreign Ministry told him. "We cannot allow anything about this visit to be published."

This seemed to me to be a fair measure of the sensitivity of Hanoi on the subject of China.

"I don't know how they do it," a Communist diplomat told me. "But the Vietnamese have managed so far to keep their relations with both Moscow and Peking. But, honestly, I don't think there is another man in the world who could have accomplished it. I give full credit to Premier Pham Van Dong. He is a miracle of tact—and he has had to be."

Of course, it was not only Premier Pham Van Dong. The fact was that many leading members of the North Vietnamese party had had long, long experience with the Chinese. President Ho, for example, after having been a member of the French Communist party, was for a long time a member of the Chinese Communist party. He served in the Chinese party during the period when Mikhail Borodin was Russia's agent there, at the time when Moscow's hopes were so high for the Chinese revolution, before Chiang Kai-shek turned on his Communist associates in 1927 and slaughtered them.

Ho had lived and worked in China for years. There he had set up the Indochinese Communist party, and there, in China, he had spent much time in prison during World War II. His associates in many instances followed the same career. They, too, had been members of the Chinese party. They, too, had long, intimate associations with China and the Chinese. Many basic themes of the North Vietnamese party line had been drawn directly from the Chinese, particularly techniques of organizing rural communes and methods of ridding the country of landlords. I was told that in North Vietnam, as in China, the peasants had been organized for group attacks on the "rich landlords" (often mere peasants a bit better off than the multitude), and in many cases they were incited to drive out the "landlord" or even murder him in the process of carrying the revolution to the countryside. Thus the peasants shared the guilt of the crime along with the Communist organizers. This was identical with what had happened in the Chinese rural areas.

There were other similarities. When I talked with the Vietnamese about their theories of protracted warfare, their ideas of retiring to the jungle and the caves and carrying on against the Americans for twenty years, I found them using almost the same terms as those used by the Chinese Defense Minister, Lin Piao, in his famous declaration of September 3, 1965, "Long live the victory of the people's war," in which he laid down the Chinese party line about the warfare of the "rural areas" of the world against the "city," about the battle that was starting in Vietnam and would spread through the backward lands of Asia, the Middle East, Africa and Latin America until eventually—fifty or a hundred years hence —the "city" areas of the world, North America, Europe and Russia, would be surrounded. When I taxed the Vietnamese with this, they merely said, well, there were similarities but each country evolved its own ideas.

Nonetheless, the intimate connections and associations of the North Vietnamese party with the Chinese were evident beyond a shadow of a doubt. The North Vietnamese certainly understood the Chinese and they had old friends among them. And this, I thought, made the task of maintaining relations easier. But, on the other hand, this might also make the task more difficult. Because there was, of course, a strong Chinese-oriented group within the North Vietnamese party, a group of Communists who felt that China was right and that North Vietnam should take its leadership and its doctrine from China and not the Soviet Union. It undoubtedly was helpful that Ho and Pham Van Dong and some others knew the Chinese so well, but it was probably a hazard that the relations of some North Vietnamese with their Chinese colleagues were so intimate.

The dilemma of the North Vietnamese was that they could no longer get along without either the Soviet Union or China. That is, they could not maintain the war effort at its present level without aid from both China and the Soviet Union. Of course, they got aid from the other Communist states. They even had a small general foreign trade with the non-Communist world. They had a trade agreement with France. They sold anthracite coal to Japan—their best foreign exchange earner. This brought them $2.3 million in 1964, and they carried on as much trade as they could with Eastern Europe. But none of this added up to much when faced with the voracious needs of the war, both to keep the North going in the face of the United States bombing offensive and to supply and provision the South.

This task required both the Soviet Union and China. And it required that Hanoi maintain good relations with both countries.

Supplies reached North Vietnam by two routes. They came in from China by rail and truck. All the goods provided by China came via this route. A great deal from the Soviet Union and Eastern Europe once came this way. But in recent times this had become an uncertain route although still a substantial one.

Haiphong was the other route for supplies. Now an increasing percentage of Soviet supplies came by sea via Haiphong. So did more and more goods from Eastern Europe. And this was the route for trade with Japan, Hong Kong, other Far Eastern ports and what shipping still arrived from Europe and the Middle East. The United States had attempted to choke off supplies through Haiphong with threats to blacklist traders who shipped to the port. This had eliminated a certain number of British-flag carriers and others. But the port was still jammed with the ships of several dozen nations.

China was North Vietnam's chief source of foodstuffs, principally rice, and without the 600,000 to 800,000 tons of rice which the North Vietnamese expected from China in 1967 they would find it difficult if not impossible to carry on. China was the chief provider of North Vietnamese rolling stock, rails and other railroad equipment. It was the supplier of equipment for the Gialam railroad works (badly damaged by American bombing) not far from the Hanoi airport. It provided almost all, or at least the major part, of the consumer goods to be found in Hanoi shops. It was a major provider of small arms, rifles, mortars, machine guns and ammunition. It provided some light antiaircraft weapons. It provided bicycles—probably the most vital single import.

All of this came by railroad or highway from China. The Chinese had given North Vietnam extensive aid in developing its internal railroads (which Peking itself used extensively for Chinese transshipment), and they continued to help the North Vietnamese keep the rail network going. They provided trucks as well. But their major contributions were in the field of railroad equipment.

Many of North Vietnam's light industries—its textile plants, rice mills, sugar refineries and cigarette factories— were installed and equipped with Chinese aid and machinery. Without spare parts and technical assistance these would quickly go out of operation.

But North Vietnam was dependent on the Chinese railroad not alone for Chinese supplies. For a long time it had been the major route for Soviet shipments. Over the previous year these shipments had repeatedly been held up by the Chinese. There were charges, which probably had some foundation in fact, that on occasion the Chinese had simply removed Soviet equipment—specifically MIG-21 fighters, SAM-2's and radar installations—from the flatcars and taken the weapons and equipment themselves.

I was told of another kind of harassment. The North Vietnamese would request the Russians to ship a certain piece of equipment—for example, conventional antiaircraft weapons. The shipment would arrive at the Soviet-Chinese frontier and be held up. Then the Chinese would come to Hanoi and ask whether the North Vietnamese really needed the equipment. Hanoi replied, certainly—it was vital. In that case, said the Chinese, we'll provide it. You don't have to get it from the Russians. Months would go by and no shipment from China would arrive.

The Russians, becoming increasingly irritated by the Chinese, began to take their quarrels into public, denouncing Peking's harassment and interruptions. The Chinese rejoined by asserting that the Russians were merely putting up a smoke screen in order to avoid sending arms to North Vietnam. In actual fact, the quarrel had been simmering behind the scenes for more than a year. All during 1965 the Chinese were trying to persuade the Russians to ship their supplies by sea. The Russians were insisting on sending them by rail. I asked a non-Asian Communist what lay behind that quarrel. He replied cynically, "Do you think perhaps that the Russians preferred that if the Americans got angry they would bomb the Chinese railroads whereas the Chinese preferred to have the Americans get angry and torpedo the Russian ships?"

Now the matter had gone far beyond that. A day hardly went by while I was in Hanoi that Peking or Moscow did not print or broadcast some vituperative comment about the other's lack of sympathy or cooperativeness with respect to the Vietnam war. The Chinese contended that they were providing 70 percent of North Vietnam's needs. The Russians called this nonsense.

The French Communist party secretary, Waldek Rochet, charged at a French Communist Party Congress that the Russians had sought in vain to persuade the Chinese to permit them to set up a special airlift to speed delivery of urgent supplies across China because of the interminable delays on the Chinese railroads. I asked a North Vietnamese official about this, and he sadly shook his head, remarking, "When people are angry with one another, they don't always tell the truth." The fact was that the Chinese had for some time been permitting the Russians to fly special planes, carrying key personnel, across China from Siberia to Hanoi. But even this facility was now being sharply reduced.

The principal result of the problems in transiting China was to divert more and more Soviet deliveries to Haiphong. This was now the route by which the North Vietnamese were getting their MIG-21's, their SAM-2's and their radar equipment. This was also the route being used for the vital petroleum shipments from both the Soviet Union and Rumania—the gasoline, oil and lubricants without which the truck routes to the South could not be maintained. This was how the Soviet trucks were being delivered.

Thus it now would be just as critical from Hanoi's point of view if she lost the supplies coming in through Haiphong, the Soviet matériel, as it would be if the China route was blocked. Both were required if the war effort was to be continued at the present level.

It was a mystery to me what financial terms might underlie the enormous shipments by both the Soviet Union and China. It was obvious that the spindly North Vietnamese economy, even under the best peacetime conditions, could not sustain such expenditures. An exhaustive analysis by Professor Jan S. Prybyla of Penn State indicated that North Vietnam was running a remarkable deficit in aid, probably in amounts equal to or more than its internal state budget. Soviet military assistance in 1965 was stated as exceeding 500 million rubles ($550 million). It probably went substantially higher in 1966. The Chinese aid would not equal that, since it was made up of less expensive items. What kind of bookkeeping was kept of these vast sums was not known. Yet, if precedent was a clue, the Soviet aid was being provided on credit with the tacit expectation of ultimate repayment. This was the case with Soviet military aid to China during the Korean War. However, the possibility of actual repayment of these vast sums seemed to me to be quite beyond question. North Vietnam had no means of generating the kind of cash flow which that would require.

How North Vietnam had managed to keep aid coming in view of the way the Soviet Union and China constantly watched for the slightest hint of favoritism to the other on which to base a complaint was a minor miracle.

The principal reliance of the North Vietnamese was a posture which came naturally to them. They persistently and aggressively asserted to both Moscow and Peking their complete independence of any advice on basic policy or strategy. They took a high-and-mighty attitude toward both the Russians and the Chinese.

A diplomat told me of a conversation he had had with an East European who mentioned a particular shortcoming in North Vietnamese military tactics.

"Why don't you tell them about it?" the diplomat asked.

His friend laughed. "Even the Russians don't dare give the Vietnamese advice on military matters."

This seemed to be correct. I heard many stories about the refusal of the North Vietnamese to listen to advice from any quarter.

There was criticism among East Europeans, particularly East European military experts, about the tactics and management of some of the sophisticated weapons which North Vietnam had obtained from the Soviet Union. Specifically, the critics contended that the North Vietnamese did not use their SAM's properly.

"If they had skilled technicians," I was told, "they would get a far higher total of U.S. planes with the SAM's. They really don't know how to use them."

A Western Communist who prided himself on his military experience said, "These people are incredible. We came to them and offered them our expertise. Particularly on missiles. We are very good on missiles. They refused. And they really aren't that good."

"Do you know what happens when a shipment of SAM's comes in at Haiphong?" I was asked by a Communist diplomat.

He said that the Soviet supply official came to the harbor with his North Vietnamese counterpart. They checked the invoices against the crates as the equipment was landed. Then the two men exchanged signed receipts and that was the end.

"The Russians never see the SAM again," my friend said. "They don't know where it is used or how it is used unless they learn by chance."

This was not true at the beginning. At the beginning the Soviet experts came in with the SAM's and instructed the North Vietnamese in their use. But once the North Vietnamese thought they had mastered the technique, they said thank you and that was that.

Much the same was true of the MIG-21's. There were plenty of foreigners in Hanoi who didn't think the North Vietnamese used these planes very well. The Russians had trained a batch of North Vietnamese pilots in flying MIG-21's in the Soviet Union. Now the North Vietnamese thought they had mastered the art, and they took no more guidance from the Russians.

But this was a calculated policy on the part of Hanoi, it seemed quite clear. The North Vietnamese simply did not wish to put themselves in a position where either the Soviet Union or China could contend that the other was being favored. It might cause some damage to the war effort. The North Vietnamese might (as they did one week while I was there) lose eight MIG-21's to the United States in a dogfight, probably because of faulty tactics, but at least they would avoid the fatal showdown between China and the Soviet Union.

In their internal propaganda the North Vietnamese deemphasized external aid. They were careful never to set up a separate exhibit for the Soviet Union or for China. When they showed the public something about their help, they began with Albania and went right down the alphabet.

It had been a hard fight. But thus far the North Vietnamese had managed to keep the balance. Whether they would be able to do so much longer was an open question. I seriously doubted it, and my doubts were shared by many anxious East Europeans. They were only too well aware of some of the turns which might lie ahead in China and Chinese-Soviet relations. Any one of these might suddenly confront Hanoi with the worst crisis of the war. No wonder the North Vietnamese were playing it as cool and cautious as they could with their two big allies. The outcome of the war and the very fate of their country might well hang on this balance.

When I went to Hanoi, there were three men with whom I
hoped to talk: President Ho Chi Minh, probably the most dynamic revolutionary personality then alive; General Vo
Nguyen Giap, the brilliant strategist and tactician of the Vietnamese Communist forces, the man who had been the archi-
tect of the Dienbienphu battle; and Premier Pham Van
Dong, the active, working chief executive of North Vietnam.

These three men had been intimately associated in Vietnamese revolutionary activities since the early nineteen-
twenties, when all had met at Canton during the exhilarating
days of the Chinese revolutionary movement. Here they had
formed bonds which had held together during the forty years
to follow. Here they had had their induction into revolutionary tactics and Marxist ways of thought.

Now, none of them was young. Ho's seventy-seventh birth-
day would be celebrated May 19, 1967. Pham Van Dong was
sixty. He was a Southerner, born and raised in Saigon. He

had been a student (and a leading soccer player) at the French Collège du Protectorat and then a teacher of history and geography. He became involved in student agitation and fled to Canton with the French authorities on his trail. There he met Ho, already a famous revolutionary under the name of Nguyen Ai Quoc (Nguyen the Patriot). In fact, Ho was so famous that when Pham Van Dong met him he was concealing his identity even from his fellow revolutionaries under the new *nom de guerre* of Vuong.

Pham Van Dong was one of the earliest of Ho's Vietnamese collaborators. After the collapse of the Canton movement Pham Van Dong went back to Vietnam and launched agitation in the mines and rubber plantations. The French arrested him in 1929 and cast him into Poulo Condor Prison, their worst, a place from which few men emerged alive. Fortunately he was released in 1936 by the French Popular Front Government, but for years his health was affected. Soon after the outbreak of World War II and the entry of the Japanese into Vietnam, Pham Van Dong went to China with the future General Giap. There with Ho they established a revolutionary headquarters for what was to become the Vietminh, the nationalist, Communist-oriented Vietnam liberation movement, which was formally proclaimed in May, 1941. All three, Ho, Pham and Giap, came back to Vietnam to build their underground organization. Ho soon left for China to try to enlist Chiang Kai-shek's support but was arrested as soon as he crossed the border and held as a French spy. Pham and Giap took over the Vietnamese leadership and managed to bring much of the North under their sway by the time Ho finally got back to his native land.

Pham Van Dong was a member of the National Liberation Committee, which proclaimed Vietnam's independence in September, 1945, and Minister of Finance in the first independent Vietnamese Government.

He made his first appearance in the West in 1946 when he was sent to negotiate with the French at Fontainebleau in an effort to get them to observe the agreement which they had signed establishing Vietnam's autonomy in March of that year. His next appearance was at the Geneva Conference in 1954 when he was serving as Acting Foreign Minister under Ho. Those who met him at that time recalled him as a gaunt man with burning eyes, a zealous revolutionary who had something of the appearance of an oriental Danton. His face was thin, his cheekbones high, and he seemed driven by inner fires of passion. His Western associates found him most difficult. They did not always understand his proposals and they felt he was more motivated by Marxist fervor than diplomacy. There may have been substance to this impression. But it was also true that he was still suffering chills and fever from malaria which he had contracted during his six years in the Poulo Condor Prison.

I devoutly hoped to see all three of these men. Ho was clearly one of the major figures of Asia. Giap was a brilliant general of a revolutionary school who had no exact counterpart unless it might be some of the Chinese commanders of the Long March. And Pham Van Dong, of course, was the leader of the government.

However, when I mentioned my desires to the Foreign Ministry, it was hinted that, in all probability, I would see only one of the three—just which one they did not know. I was advised to write letters to each of them, outlining the questions which I wanted to discuss. The letters would be passed on and we would await developments.

I wrote three letters, but I was careful to see that my questions, in general, covered the same ground. I did not know whether I would have an oral interview or merely receive a written response to my questions—as is often the case with touchy diplomatic inquiries, especially in Communist countries.

Bearing this in mind, I proposed these questions for discussion with Premier Pham Van Dong:

How have the North Vietnamese people been organized for the war against the United States? What has been the effect on the North Vietnamese economy?

What are the differences and the similarities between the struggle against the French and that against the United States? What, in general terms, is the nature of the plans and organization for an extended war—say, one lasting ten, twenty or thirty years—against the United States?

Does America's advanced technology and surplus of material means help or hinder the American military effort and, if so, how?

Are there any steps which third-party nations might take which would aid in bringing peace in Vietnam?

Both the United States and North Vietnam say they are prepared to discuss an end of hostilities under certain specified conditions, but neither side accepts the other's proposal. How can this deadlock be broken?

Under what conditions would North Vietnam accept volunteers from other nations to assist in its war effort?

What would be the results in terms of broadening the war if the United States were to cross the 17th parallel on land or by amphibious landings?

I submitted the same questions to Ho Chi Minh, with the addition of the following:

Has bombing in the North helped or hindered cooperation between North and South against the United States?

What is the present estimate of the civilian death toll in the North and of nonmilitary property damage?

How can arrangements be made for the exchange or release of American fliers now held by North Vietnam?

How does North Vietnam envisage the specific means for achieving reunification of the country?

My questions to General Giap included the following:

How would intense bombing of Hanoi and Haiphong affect the North Vietnamese military effort?

Can any comment be made on the American contention that organized units of North Vietnamese troops are engaged in the South?

I also asked him to compare the leadership, tactics and fighting capability of the Americans and the French.

The man whom I ultimately saw was Premier Pham Van Dong. I did not get to see President Ho (although he saw four foreign groups, including three groups of Americans, in a ten-day period that included the time of my visit) nor General Giap. When I met Pham Van Dong, I found that he had familiarized himself with the questions which I had submitted to all three men. He said he would try to answer them all and, in fact, he did touch on most, although some he skirted very lightly. He also spoke at length on other matters which I had not put into the written questionnaire.

I was a bit disappointed when the Foreign Ministry excitedly called me in on the morning of January 2 and Nguyen Diem, the information chief, told me that I would be received by the Premier that afternoon. I had hoped to see either Ho or Giap and I felt somewhat let down. But this feeling vanished in the course of my talk with the Premier, for it proved to be remarkably informative and wide-ranging. He turned out to be a man of brilliance and considerable wit, interesting to talk with, possessing a personality which ranged through a variety of emotions.

He met me in the Presidential Palace, a grandiose building which had been occupied by the French Governor General. President Ho, I knew, lived in a small cottage to the rear of the palace. I found that Pham Van Dong occupied another small suite in the former servants' quarters.

Our talk was held in the reception room, a formal drawing room in French style with a crystal chandelier, a fine parquet floor, an excellent Brussels carpet, Louis XVI sofas and a general atmosphere of elegance. The palace photographer was there to take our picture. The Premier poured out a glass of Vietnamese wine to toast our meeting and two palace servants hovered about, quick to refill our teacups. Two Foreign Ministry men, Mr. Diem and one of his assistants, sat silently throughout our talk. Pham Van Dong spoke in Vietnamese almost entirely, except for a few phrases of hospitality in French. The interpreter's English was poor. So poor, in fact, that midway in the interview a young man who was making notes had to take over the task of interpreting. No real damage, I thought, was done by the inept interpreter because I insisted on repeating any passage that was not clear or asking a question again when I was not sure of the response.

It would be incorrect to describe my meeting with the Premier as an interview. It was actually a conversation. Or, to be more precise, it was a long soliloquy by Pham Van Dong with brief interruptions by myself followed by some general conversation.

First the ground rules were laid down. The Premier would speak very freely. He disliked formal interviews intensely. He felt they were restrictive and he didn't feel comfortable in them. So he would talk and I would talk. Some of the talk would be on the record, some would be off. If I wrote anything about the conversation, I would submit it to the Foreign Ministry so that it could be checked for accuracy of quotation and also as to whether the material was on or off the record. The ground rules sounded fair and I told the Premier that I accepted them. He grinned and twisted himself around on the sofa to face me directly. Well, he said, who should start—you or me? I said I thought he should start and then if I had something to ask I would put the question. That was fine. He would begin. He had read my questions, not only those to him but those to President Ho and General Giap, and he would try to cover them all in his remarks.

"First we will talk about the war and proceed from that to talk about a settlement," he said. "Do you agree?"

I said I did. He then began to talk rapidly and easily, quite often punctuating his remarks with questions to me. Did I agree, for instance, with General de Gaulle's statement at New Year's in which he characterized the war as having been caused by the Americans, called it an unjust and a despicable war and concluded that the Americans should withdraw?

I told him that, in general, I agreed with that characterization but that the United States Government did not agree and that it was not my opinion which was important; it was that of the government.

If you agree, he smiled, then later on the government must arrive at that conclusion. If not now, they must agree next year, and if the Democrats didn't agree, then some other party would have to agree. Sooner or later that would have to happen. Didn't I agree?

No, I said. I don't necessarily agree on that at all. This question of attitudes toward the war involved very serious questions both of politics and of personality. I was not sure that events would necessarily follow the smooth train that he suggested.

I thought this response, possibly, brought him down to earth a bit. At any rate, he nodded his head eagerly and said, "I think politics is the main thing.

"I think you are right in expressing your doubts," he added. "It is a very big problem relating to us and to you. You and individuals like yourself must make a contribution to solving it."

What was it that Pham Van Dong wanted to tell me about the war? Essentially he wanted to give me a résumé of the American involvement in the conflict (as Hanoi saw it) and what had been the results of the fighting. With a few references to earlier times, he concentrated his exposition on events since 1964. As he related the story, the United States then had begun to commit itself to a policy of stage-by-stage escalation of the war. Pham Van Dong blamed this program on the American military commanders, whom he described as "shortsighted." He said they made repeated promises to the White House that they could bring the war to a successful conclusion. But each time they were not able to meet their pledge and were compelled to ask for more troops. He devoted some time to General Westmoreland's tactics, which he thought had proved no more effective than those of his predecessors.

"The situation is very bad," he said. "Worse than ever before. And they are now facing an impasse. What are they bound to do? Increase their strength in South Vietnam? How much? Where will they fight? And how to win victories?"

Thus, he said, the American military were really right back at the point they started from, unable to achieve a military victory and with no real choice but to escalate. He made clear it was this seeming inevitability of United States actions which had caused Hanoi to come to the conclusion that the continuing American policy could be nothing but escalation after escalation.

He did not believe that the great material superiority of the Americans provided the advantage which would assure victory. They had escalated once, twice, three times, four times. Why should victory come after the fifth escalation?

Then he turned to the questions which I had put to General Giap about the relative performance of the Americans and the French. He did not give me a comparison between the French and the Americans because he felt the essence of the situation was not in differences between those two military establishments. The problem was one of relative morale and spirit between the United States forces and those opposing them in Vietnam, and it was in this connection that he gave me an eloquent analysis of the spirit of Vietnam and its role in enabling his country to overcome the technical advantages of the United States.

"The military men of the United States," he said, "found that raising their force to 400,000 troops was not helping to solve the problem. They think that with half a million they can solve it. Some even speak of 600,000. Some say they may increase even more. I have told you the crucial problem does not lie in numbers."

He compared the excellent fighting capability of the National Liberation Front forces and the Northern troops with that of the South Vietnamese armies and insisted that the difference lay in the morale factor. As he described the situation in the South, the advantage was moving to the side of the Vietcong. Even in Saigon and the cities controlled by the Saigon Government, he felt, sentiment was flowing to the

Front because of the revulsion of the ordinary people against the moral corruption involved in the Ky Government and the presence of the huge American military establishment.

So far as the North was concerned he characterized the air war as a defeat for the Americans, both in a propaganda sense and in a military one. World opinion, he said, had clearly mobilized against the bombing and, so far as the military situation was concerned, bombing had not been decisive. It had not affected the situation in the South in any material way.

He did, however, indicate that there had been a crisis in Vietnam as a result of the bombing—presumably in its early stages when North Vietnam was not organized to maintain the movement of goods, supplies and manpower to the South in the face of bombing and before antiaircraft defenses had been brought to their present level of efficiency by the introduction of new sophisticated Soviet defense weapons. Now, he insisted, antiaircraft defense was growing stronger and stronger and thanks to the nation's youth—to which he gave full credit—the emergency had passed and they were moving into a stronger position.

He touched very lightly on the economic consequences of the bombing—so lightly that it was apparent that he did not care to discuss them. If he had done so, the conclusions would surely have been negative.

Now, he insisted, Vietnam had dug in. It was prepared. It had made plans. It was ready for anything which might come.

It was a people's war, and people's wars of necessity were long wars.

"That's why we are preparing for a long war," he said. "How many years would you say? Ten, twenty—what do you think about twenty?"

I smiled a bit wanly and said that I thought this would be a good year to stop the war.

He took no notice of my remark and went right on:

"What I used to tell our friends is that the younger generation will fight better than we—even kids so high. They are preparing themselves. That's the situation. I'm not telling that to impress anyone. It's the truth. That's the logical consequence of the situation. Our Vietnam nation is a very proud nation. Our history is one of a very proud nation. The Mongol invaders came. They were defeated the first time, the sec-

ond time and the third time. Now, how many times does the
Pentagon want to fight? So—how many years the war goes
on depends on you. Not on me."

That was the way he concluded his discussion of the war.
The impression he gave in sketching out the military situation, as he saw it or as he wanted me to see it, was of a man
who had the utmost confidence. He talked like the man he
was—a leader who had come through years and years of
fighting, who knew the art of war, who was well aware that
advantage flows now to one side, now to another, but who
was utterly confident that the long-term course of history, the
ultimate inventory of resources, favored his country rather
than the United States. I felt certain that he was overempha-
sizing Vietnam's strength. I did not think the balance was necessarily as strong in the South as he suggested. I knew the
economic consequences of the bombing were more severe
than he would have me think. Yet, over all, I did not believe
he had badly overstated his case. It was a piece of close-
grained reasoning. He might be wrong. We might find a way
of gaining a greater advantage from our manpower and technology. But thus far, based on actual results, the balance between this small, backward, underdeveloped country and the
world's foremost military power had been remarkably even.

"That's the first point," he said, smiling and reaching to
drink from his cup of tea. When he had noticed that I was
not drinking the Vietnamese wine, he had pushed his glass
aside and, like myself, took only an occasional sip of tea. We
paused a moment. My hand was tired from the furious
scribbling of notes. Outside the tall windows, which gave
onto the palace gardens, dusk was beginning to fall. I was
surprised to see that we had been talking for nearly two
hours without interruption. Of course, the necessity of interpretation slowed the course of the talk, but the time had
flowed by very swiftly.

The Premier smiled at me and resumed talking.

"Now, the second point," he said, "the question about a
settlement.

"Of course, you are interested in a settlement. I fully understand. I agree to talk with you about this. But to have a
good talk we must start with the origin of the war that we
were just talking about.

"For us the settlement is a very simple question. As far as
we are concerned it's a war of aggression, a colonial war, an

unjust war. So the settlement is to stop it. This kind of logic is flawless and irrefutable. Do you agree?"

"Many things in the world are not logical," I said. "I don't think logic is the main point here."

He nodded and went ahead with his exposition.

It would be fine if the United States halted the war, but, he agreed, we must live with reality; it was the real world that counted, not the one we hoped for. Nonetheless, it was clear in his mind that the proper thing, the proper course of conduct, was for the United States to cease hostilities. The moment that happened, he said, "We will respect each other and settle every question.

"Why don't you think that way?" he asked.

I let that pass. I decided it was the kind of rhetorical question which really could not be answered.

He then went into a discussion of the so-called "four points," the four points which Hanoi said constituted the "basis for a settlement of the Vietnam question."

There had been great controversy abroad about the significance of these four points. Were they to be considered preconditions for negotiation? Must the United States accept them before Hanoi would agree to sit down at a conference table?

The four points provided for (1) recognition of the peace, independence, sovereignty, unity and territorial integrity of Vietnam and the withdrawal of United States troops; (2) the noninterference of outside powers in the two zones of Vietnam; (3) settlement of South Vietnamese questions in accordance with the program of the National Liberation Front without foreign interference; and (4) peaceful reunification of Vietnam, to be settled by the people of both zones.

The attitude of the United States was that Hanoi was attempting to impose terms for a settlement before a conference, that the North Vietnamese insisted that the four points must be accepted first and that this meant talk at the conference table would be largely meaningless.

"These should not be considered 'conditions,' " Pham Van Dong now told me. "They are merely truths. The most simple thing is to recognize our sovereignty and our independence. It involves only recognizing the points in the Geneva agreements."

He said that the United States did not like to accept the four points and especially the third point about South Vietnam but, he insisted, "we must come to a solution on the basis of the four points.

"Whichever way you may go around, finally you must come to the four points," he said. These were not preconditions nor conditions for talks, he said, but "conditions for a valid settlement"—conditions necessary to reach a settlement which could be enforced.

When my dispatch reporting this discussion was published in *The New York Times*, it touched off a flurry of speculation, centering on the thought that Pham Van Dong had modified in some way the position of the Hanoi regime on the four points. This was not my understanding. I knew that on previous occasions the same interpretation had been presented by spokesmen for the North Vietnamese Government.

They had contended from the start that these were not "preconditions." However, the speculation in the West reached such intensity that the Foreign Ministry called on me and said they were going to issue a brief statement to dampen this down. They were careful to note that the faulty interpretation was not mine but that of Western commentators.

When this was done, the furor gradually died away because the essence of the situation was now clear. The four conditions did not have to be accepted before we sat down at the conference table, but they would be placed on the table as the key points of the settlement which was to be negotiated. To me the whole thing seemed to be a distinction without a real difference. I did not believe that Pham Van Dong meant that the four points were to be considered an agenda in the normal understanding of the term—four points which might be modified or compromised to meet the views of the two sides. I felt that he meant—as Hanoi had from the start—that the settlement must be constructed on this framework.

Whether there would be any give on the Hanoi side was another matter. There might well be in the end. But certainly there was no indication of it in the words he spoke to me about the four points.

He placed alongside his four points another one: that the United States halt unconditionally the bombing and all hostile activity against the North.

So far as the United States was concerned, he took the view that it was not really ready for discussions. It had not, in his view, given any sign of goodwill, and he felt this was essential if good-faith negotiations were to get under way. The pattern of American conduct, as he viewed it, was to talk peace only to mask preparations for escalation.

"Of course," he said, giving me a knowing look, "I understand this better than you because there are many things I can't tell you."

I did not know to what he referred specifically. I still do not. But it seemed apparent that he was making reference to some of the abortive efforts to get peace talks going which had ended, each time, in resumption of hostilities at a higher level. Indeed, he may have been referring to some such sequence in the very immediate past. He did not expand on this point, but he did emphasize that he felt it was up to the United States, if it really wanted peace—which he continued to feel was very dubious—to take the first step.

I pressed him hard on this. I was willing to concede that it was appropriate, perhaps, for the United States to act first. Indeed, we had said as much officially. But I felt that Hanoi should be prepared to take a second step. I did not know precisely what this might be, but it seemed to me that this would lend an element of equity to the situation.

The Premier reacted very strongly. He said that it was the United States which had started the bombing; it was the United States which was continuing to attack North Vietnam; this was an aggressive, illegal act; Vietnam should not be compelled to pay a price to get the United States to halt doing something which it had no right to do in the first place. This was a matter of principle.

I returned to the question. I said that even if one granted the justice of the North Vietnamese position, still one had to look at the practical consequences. I felt that it would ease the politics of achieving a negotiated settlement materially if North Vietnam would take some step. If Hanoi felt so strongly against the principle of reciprocity, it need not be invoked. North Vietnam could, on its own, independently, announce that it was going to take a certain step, possibly a standstill in force levels in the South. It could call this action its own contribution to international goodwill if it wished. The important thing was to make a move. If the United States acted, it would only be appropriate if North Vietnam acted also.

My remarks sent the Premier into a brown study. He paused for a good minute without saying anything—the first time in the course of our conversation in which he had halted the free flow of his ideas.

When he resumed, he said that he was ready to listen to anything I proposed in a spirit of friendliness but that he did not think it correct to raise the question in the fashion I had; that it implied some kind of "demand." He went on in this vein for some time, but before he finished speaking he had made clear to me in specific words that North Vietnam would not stand with folded hands if the United States actually were to halt the bombing unconditionally.

He talked a bit about the South—about the political program of the Front. Despite the differences in the Front program and that of the North, he said, Hanoi thought it was a "very sound program," a "clear-sighted and intelligent program fully conforming to the situation in South Vietnam." He thought it had the support of the people of South Vietnam. He believed that the United States was making a mistake in failing to recognize the Front and in continuing to take the attitude that it would not talk with the Front. For, he noted, it was the Front with whom the United States was fighting and in the end the war could only be halted by talks between those who were fighting.

So far as reunification of the country was concerned, he said there were many misunderstandings. The question would be settled between the North and the South. There was no hurry about it. They would do it in whatever way was most convenient.

"There are not many new things about reunification," he said, "so I don't want to elaborate."

I took this with a grain of salt. His remarks deepened my impression that neither North nor South had a clear picture of when or how reunification would occur—if ever.

Finally he went on to one of the key questions which I had put to all three men—Ho, Giap and himself. How and when would North Vietnam accept "volunteers." He prefaced his discussion with a strong reaffirmation of North Vietnamese independence.

"We are masters of our country, our affairs, our policy, our major and minor policies," he said. "This is very clear. If we had no independence, we could not wage such a war as we are now waging. We are independent and sovereign in all our foreign policy. That is the situation so far. And it will be the same in the future."

This was told to me, he made clear, in answer to suggestions in the United States that North Vietnam was a puppet—either of China or the Soviet Union or both.

As to the volunteers, this depended on the situation. Hanoi had made full preparations for volunteers. The volunteers were ready and waiting. All that was needed was the call. Volunteers would come—both for the armed forces and for the civilian services. North Vietnam could rely on this.

He did not specify the conditions under which the call might go out. But his words fitted the pattern of what I had been told by other officials: If the United States crossed the 17th parallel on land, if we made amphibious landings on the coast in the North, or if we carried our operations "too close to China"—whatever that meant—the volunteers would come in.

The Premier smiled now and said, "Now let us talk. On what do you disagree and have you any suggestions? I said at the beginning that I would speak frankly because I'm talking with a good-willed American. That is the basis of this talk."

I spoke to him with great frankness. I said that it was very difficult to end a war, far easier to begin one. That the basic problem, as I saw it, was lack of confidence on both sides. He thought the United States would use peace talks as a cover for preparations for escalation. Washington had the same fear—that the talks would be a cover for regrouping in the South. Both sides would have to make a major contribution if talks were to get going. It seemed impossible to me that public negotiations could be conducted at this stage. They would only lead to propaganda speeches and recriminations. The thing to do was to engage in private, secret, low-pitched discussions on a completely unofficial basis. Let diplomats or spokesmen for both sides explore. Let them see whether they could find any inclinations toward settlement. Let them advance proposals and counterproposals. If there was reason to believe that public talks could get somewhere, then—but only then—let the announcements be made.

We discussed these ideas back and forth until each had a precise notion of what the other had in mind. He had, I became convinced, no objection to the route of private unpublicized talks. It seemed to me that it was a worthwhile occasion to convey to the Premier some of the ideas current in the United States. I pointed out that President Johnson had repeatedly expressed his willingness to go anywhere at any time to engage in discussions. Rightly or wrongly, I said, the North Vietnamese had not given an impression of such willingness.

He was not inclined to accept Mr. Johnson's willingness. He felt that world public opinion had run strongly against the United States and its President and that the North Vietnamese position had strong support, even in the West. I suggested that it was not wise to exaggerate the role of public opinion. For example, the decisions to negotiate must in the end be made by the President. He was the principal spokesman on the American side and it was with the President that Hanoi must deal.

The Premier did not challenge my view but insisted that the key to peace lay in Washington.

"The party who has to make the first steps is Washington," he said firmly. "We have no doubt on this point."

When I indicated some disappointment that he had not been willing to take a more positive stand—in public—on the question of negotiation, he smiled and said:

"Everything must come in its time. We cannot press history forward. If this does not come today, it will come tomorrow. It is no use to make haste. If we show haste, it will be wrong and we will have to wait again.

"We must let the situation ripen."

I agreed. But I added that it was important not to pass the moment when the fruit was ripe. If one did, the fruit spoiled. It seemed to me that the fruit was ripe.

The Premier nodded. Apparently he was not quite certain about that. He rose now and shook my hand.

"I think that this has been a good talk," he said. "We understand each other. It is good that I understand you and frank talk is a good thing. We need frank talks to understand each other. If we do not agree today, we will tomorrow. Otherwise the day after tomorrow."

I walked out of the palace, pondering his remarks. It was nearly 8:30 P.M. We had talked for four and a half hours. But it had not seemed so long in the rapid exchange of thoughts. There was a great deal in what the Premier had told me, and not all of it was designed for public consumption. I only hoped that the talk would have the positive effect upon negotiations which, I was certain, it was intended to have. But the answer to that, of course, lay in Washington.

It was 3 A.M. on Saturday, January 7, 1967, when I followed the porter out of the deserted lobby of the Thong Nhat Hotel and into the black Volga which was to take me to the airport and my departure from North Vietnam.

At that hour there was no traffic on the central streets of Hanoi, but when we reached the Red River we encountered trucks moving out of the city and, entering the city, a procession of women, each with a *don ganh,* or carrying pole, balanced on a bowed shoulder. They were bringing a multitude of burdens into the city, big bundles of bulk paper, vegetables, wrapped packages which might have contained metal, machinery, flour—goodness knows what all the products were. Each bundle, judging from the bowed *don ganh* and the delicate half-step, half-shuffle with which the women walked, must have weighed fifty or sixty pounds, or even more.

There was nothing unusual about this sight. Every night

that I was in the Hanoi streets I had seen these long lines of human bearers, the long line of trucks. I had never crossed the almost-two-mile span of the Long Bien Bridge when it had not been crowded with traffic moving both ways, south from the north of the country or out of the city to the provinces.

It was natural that the bridge was crowded. It was Hanoi's only link between the north and south across the Red River. The railroad crossed on this bridge, and it carried two streams of vehicular traffic. At its eastern end the bridge ended in the industrial sections of Gialam and the western end rested close to the heart of Hanoi.

The long steel-girdered span could be seen for miles away from the air. It must, I thought, make a remarkably fine orientation beacon for the United States bombing planes as they approached Hanoi since, or so I was told, they customarily neared the capital flying very low, very close to the surface of the Red River, in order to avoid being picked up by the radar networks.

Not only was the Long Bien Bridge visible for miles; it was in all probability the single most important military objective in North Vietnam. Without the bridge the movement of traffic from north to south would be radically impeded. Loss of the bridge would not knock North Vietnam out of the war. But it would make Hanoi's war effort infinitely more difficult.

I knew, of course, that the bridge was heavily defended by antiaircraft batteries, both conventional guns and the Soviet SAM-2's. But this was generally true of the whole Hanoi-Haiphong area. This was where the North Vietnamese very naturally had concentrated their defenses.

The Long Bien Bridge was not the only important military objective in Hanoi. There were others—for example, there was the city's main power plant. This, too, presumably was heavily defended. But, like the bridge, it had not been attacked. It was situated in a region some distance from areas of heavy population.

There was in Hanoi and its environs other military objectives. None, perhaps, quite so vital as these two but many of substantial value to the North Vietnamese war effort. They also had not been attacked.

No aspect of the American war effort in Vietnam had been the subject of more controversy than our bombing offensive. There had been endless questions raised about it, passionate defense of its conduct and stronger denunciations of its concept.

The bombing program touched more nerves among supporters of the Vietnam war and its opponents than any other single factor. If I had not been aware of this before I went to Hanoi, it quickly became apparent during my stay there. I could not tune in the BBC or the Voice of America on my short-wave set without hearing the pros and cons widely debated, largely stimulated by my reports of the results of our bombing in North Vietnam.

It was plain to me from my first walk through Hanoi and my first day or two driving about the country that it was impossible to make an intelligent evaluation of the United States bombing without an on-the-spot inspection of the results, both physical and spiritual. The same thing had been true of World War II bombing. Not until the postwar ground survey of strategic bombing results was it revealed that many Nazi war production centers actually increased their production under the impetus of our total bombing. It was, to my way of thinking, unfortunate—but hardly surprising—that in the din of debate over the bombing and over my reports almost everyone lost sight of some central factual observations which, of course, were the only valid contribution which I was in a position to make.

What I did in North Vietnam was to see what had happened, report so far as I was able to on where the bombs had hit, what damage they had done, what they seemingly had been aimed at and how this was affecting the war effort and will to resist of the North Vietnamese people.

I had been given a most unusual opportunity. It is not often in wartime (in fact, it is almost without precedent) that a trained observer from one belligerent is permitted to go behind the lines and evaluate the results of the military tactics and strategy of his government.

Yet this was precisely what I had the opportunity of doing. If I was not the best military observer in the world, at least I had seen a great deal of war and of bombing and I had years of experience in reporting under Communist conditions. I may not have seen everything; I may not have reported it with the precision of an intelligence operative. But I did have a pair of bright eyes.

It was unfortunate and a detriment to our national interests that when I began to send back my reports some United

States officials, notably civilians in the Pentagon, felt called upon to turn loose a barrage of invective which diverted some attention from the essence of what I was able to garner. They made much of the fact that I had not always specifically attributed casualty figures to the local Communist officials, although what other source one might have in a Communist country I really don't know.

But, perhaps, they wanted to twist attention away from what I was reporting. If so, they did themselves and the country a disservice. My impressions centered not only on what we had done and what we apparently had tried to do. They also centered on what we had not done and had not tried to do. Some of the second category of questions were those which puzzled me most—for example, the Long Bien Bridge. We had not attacked it. It was possible that some bombs and rockets which hit close to the ends of the bridge in the attacks of December 13-14 were designed to show that we could attack it if we wished. If these small bombings were a suggestion to Hanoi of what we could do, then this was an example of our use of bombing as a psychological or propaganda weapon. It hardly seemed to make sense to me. Every day the people of Hanoi crossed the Long Bien Bridge. They could not help but think how vulnerable it was. I never crossed it without that thought in mind, and I mentally kept hurrying my driver because it seemed to me that any moment an F-105 might appear overhead and give the Long Bien Bridge the *coup de grâce*.

The same concept applied to the power station and to a half-dozen other really *important* targets. They were not and had not been attacked. Why?

The question would not be worth raising if we had attacked nothing in the Hanoi area. But we had. We had sent our bombers to objectives much much more difficult to bomb than the bridge or the power station. We had instructed our airmen to zero in on extremely small targets, targets of the most trivial military value, but targets which compelled them to undergo just as serious antiaircraft punishment as they would encounter around the bridge or power station. Why?

Supposedly we attacked for purely military reasons. But if military values were the criterion, then why not attack the Long Bien Bridge, the power station, the MIG-21 airfields?

It could not be contended that these important objectives were being spared because of fear of civilian casualties. They were situated in areas where there were far fewer civilians than the regions of the small objectives against which we were sending in our fliers.

What was the rationale of this kind of decision—to attack insignificant targets in heavily defended regions but spare the big ones?

If there was an answer to this, it must, it seemed to me, lie in the realm of psychological warfare. Or politics. Not military tactics.

There was another shining target in North Vietnam— Haiphong. The port, jammed with shipping, crowded with supplies, with undistributed munitions and war matériel, was a prime military objective. It could, of course, be devastated by bombing. It was heavily defended by SAM-2's and conventional antiaircraft weapons. But militarily the operation was entirely feasible. We had made very effective attacks in that region, especially the initial operations in late June and early July when we destroyed the Haiphong petroleum storage facilities.

But here there was a logical and understandable reason against air assault (or blockade) of Haiphong. Such action would inevitably involve the United States with the Soviet Union and many other powers. The harbor was filled with Soviet shipping and Soviet citizens. It was crowded with ships of many other Communist countries and shipping of some of our allies (despite our efforts to blacklist it).

Thus an attack on Haiphong would be fraught with the most obvious dangers of escalation and involvement in military confrontation with the Soviet Union and severe diplomatic consequences.

The decision against bombing Haiphong, therefore, could be understood in diplomatic terms even if it obviously had very high priority from the military standpoint.

But take another example. We constantly attacked the railroad to the south. This made good military sense. But why did we so often attack the railroad at points where it ran through villages and small towns? Granted that there were sidings at these points where two trains could pass. Granted that there probably would be some small freight platforms. What difference did that make if the road could be interdicted equally well out in the open countryside away from civilian habitations and presumably away from the antiaircraft installations which were placed in the villages and towns to protect them against attack? Why program our fliers to hit the railroad where casualties almost certainly would occur among civilians and where our planes would almost certainly encounter stronger antiaircraft fire?

Did this, too, involve psychological reasons?

I could not answer these questions, but it seemed clear to me that they must be raised and discussed. These were issues which cut to the bone of the bombing offensive.

There was another which flowed logically from the problems of our targeting.

Our bombing attacks had a scatter pattern. They were being conducted all over the North—from close to the Chinese frontier down, in increasing intensity, to the Demilitarized Zone, at the border with the South. We scattered our effort and we flew, on a good day, scores or even hundreds of missions, a bomber here, a bomber there, all over the map. We had different and complicated rules for our airmen. In certain zones (in the south and the Demilitarized Zone) they were free to fire at anything that moved, to bomb anything they thought might be a target. No holds barred. These were called "Free Strike Zones." In other areas—and I was not precise as to exactly which these were—we conducted what we called "armed reconnaissance." This meant that we sent our fighter-bombers into the countryside looking for trouble. Again, it usually meant, as I understood it, that they could attack transport moving on roads, anything that looked like a military aggregation. They were reconnoitering for targets which might or might not appear.

Then there were precise targeting areas. These, as I understood it, included most of the northern part of North Vietnam. Here the airmen were severely restricted. They could only aim for authorized targets. This did not mean that they could not jettison their bombs if closely pursued, if necessary to carry out evasive action or to save their own lives.

And finally in the inner circle around Hanoi and Haiphong the President himself reserved the specific right to approve targets and operations.

There was thus a series of gradations which governed the pattern of the air operations in North Vietnam. This was complex and confusing. It seemed to me that it inevitably would give rise to honest pilot errors. Again and again it seemed to me that the commanders of the air operations were placing on their men burdens which were beyond the ability of the best technology and the best trained men.

What was the reason for this elaborate pattern when it would have been so simple and effective to concentrate our bombing on a simple line in the South, a special zone of interdiction which would run across the narrow waist of Vietnam and extend into Laos and thus cut off all movement of men and supplies into South Vietnam? Such a bomb line, reinforced with a zone of defoliation, a mine barrage and a picket line of American and South Vietnamese forces, would bring the whole problem under control with a minimum of effort. There would be no civilian casualties, no civilian destruction. From the military viewpoint, it seemed to me, it would be effective and virtually airtight.

So far as I knew, this expedient had not been considered. Instead, we involved ourselves in the most elaborate, difficult, controversial and costly kind of maneuvers. What was the reason? Did it lie, again, in the realm of psychological warfare? Were service rivalries involved?

There was a question about the air effort which was raised not infrequently by the North Vietnamese and had been advanced by others.

This was the extent—if any—to which the Vietnamese war was being utilized as a laboratory for the testing of weapons and techniques. This was a frequent charge by Hanoi. Hanoi contended that all kinds of chemical warfare had been experimented with in the South—defoliants, aerial weed-killers to render agricultural regions barren, the intensive application of napalm and fire weapons against villages and personnel and the introduction of an arsenal of new types of planes and new kinds of bombs. The North Vietnamese were particularly exercised over the use of antipersonnel bombs of which the so-called "lazy dog" was cited as a fearsome example. I saw a number of "lazy dogs" which had been recovered whole. They were, indeed, an ingenious and, I had no doubt, effective weapon. They were devised for use against antiaircraft gunners, machine-gun nests or other military groups occupying exposed or semiexposed positions. The weapon consisted of a canister about twice the size of a milk can. This was filled with three hundred iron balls a little smaller than a baseball, called guavas. The canister was designed to explode a short distance above the earth, scattering the guavas in a circle. The guavas were fragmentation bombs with a fuse which permitted them to roll across the ground before exploding and hurling hundreds of tiny steel fragments through the air. The weapon was supposed to destroy any living being within a radius of three hundred yards, and it looked to me as though it would probably achieve its purpose if the people were unprotected.

The lazy dog had been introduced in North Vietnam some time in the spring of 1966, replacing an older type of antipersonnel device called a pineapple.

I supposed that the lazy dogs and the pineapples were dropped by our planes on what they presumed were antiaircraft batteries, radar installations or military outposts. The trouble was that in heavily populated North Vietnam they inevitably took a toll among civilians.

Was the military utilizing the air war in the North to experiment with devices and tactics? Some experimentation was inevitable. It was part of warfare. Devices were constantly tried, improved or rejected. The contention of Hanoi that its country was being made a laboratory for military experiments, as the Spanish Civil War had been by the Nazis and Italian Fascists, was not one which could readily be proved or disproved. The only test was whether the tactics, weapons and targeting seemed, generally, to be designed for the military results which they were supposed to achieve.

Proof was difficult. But it seemed to me there were enough oddities so that questions might be raised.

Most of America's public attention had been focused on the bombing in Hanoi and in other cities and towns like Namdinh and Phuly. But I had more questions about the theory and practice of bombing in the countryside.

For instance, there was the remarkable phenomenon of the attacks which in many rural areas seemed to have hit every building that was two or three stories tall, every structure which appeared as consequential on the landscape. What was the military purpose of this? Was this the result of random "armed reconnaissance" or was it deliberate targeting which presumed that any structure more than one story tall had a military value?

I could not tell from the ground in Vietnam. I could see that many bombed buildings had not actually been military objectives, but I could not read the mind of the pilot who bombed or rocket-blasted them or that of his superior officer who gave the orders.

What about the dikes? We had said repeatedly that they were not being officially targeted. That they were prime military objectives was perfectly obvious. Their destruction would, in large measure, destroy the country, make it impossible for it to feed itself, wipe out millions of acres of rice land, starve or drown millions of North Vietnamese. The dikes were easy to attack. They lay at hand all along the Red River. They could be destroyed with far less loss of life and United States aircraft than, for instance, small truck repair yards in the Hanoi area.

But we had not targeted them. Why? What was the military or psychological reasoning behind this? Without being targeted the levees had been in fact repeatedly hit. I had seen the bomb craters with my own eyes in several parts of the country. Accidents? Possibly, although the pattern of craters lying along a levee looked far from accidental. How was this to be interpreted? Was this more aerial psychological warfare? A signal to the North Vietnamese of what we might do if we really get serious? But if we were not serious about our bombing offensive after two years, if we were still, in effect, half in, half out, what was the logic of that?

There were other questions which lay behind the façade of bombing which urgently struggled for elucidation, it seemed to me. What was the effect of competition between the Strategic Air Force and the Seventh Fleet for participation in the air war in the North? What effect had this on the tactics and strategy of what we did in the North?

And behind it all lay the great unresolved question of whether, as some of our air strategists privately suggested, the bombing was just a dry run in preparation for the ultimate air war against China.

The bombing program had been criticized throughout the world and particularly in the United States on a variety of grounds. It had been attacked as antihumanitarian, immoral, illegal, ineffective in military terms and a factor in lengthening the war and preventing the achievement of peace rather than the reverse.

Its supporters contended that it was the "most humane" military technique yet evolved, that it was the only method for containing the Communist threat in Southeast Asia, that it was economical in terms of matériel and manpower, that it had reversed the balance in Vietnam and put us on the road to victory, that it had stiffened the resolve in the South and weakened it in the North and that its relentless pursuit would enable us to achieve all our objectives without the need for diplomatic haggling or compromise.

The bombing offensive began February 7, 1965. At first it was announced as an act of retaliation for a Vietcong attack on the Pleiku air base in which eight Americans were killed. Then on March 2, 1965, the United States command began general air attacks on North Vietnam, no longer on a basis of "retaliation" but as a matter of military policy.

What was the original aim and purpose of the air operation? According to McGeorge Bundy, President Johnson's assistant who made an on-the-spot assessment of the Vietnamese situation before the President authorized the inauguration of the air strikes, the action was undertaken because it was felt that "it was only a matter of time before the Communists would win, unless something was done about it."

On the evidence of another of Mr. Johnson's assistants, Richard Goodwin, the President was advised that the morale of South Vietnam could be revived only by bombing North Vietnam and that this action would keep Saigon in the war and so weaken Hanoi's will to fight that the commitment of large numbers of American ground forces would not be necessary.

The air action, thus, apparently had three main purposes at the time it was started early in 1965:

1. The bolstering of the morale of the South Vietnamese Government.

2. The weakening of the will to fight by Hanoi.

3. The avoidance of commitment of large United States ground forces.

It seemed to me that it had been successful on the first count. The Saigon Government had endured a number of crises since the winter of 1965 but survived them all.

On counts two and three the record seemed less impressive. Certainly I found no measurable weakening of the will to fight by Hanoi. And as for the commitment of United States ground forces—within a month, in March, 1965, they were being committed to battle and the enormous escalation which zoomed their numbers in two years from 25,000 to 400,000 got under way with a rush.

But these original objectives had been succeeded by others. It was now said that the purpose of the U.S. air offensive was to "bomb" Hanoi to the conference table and to interdict the movement of men, munitions and supplies to the South. The wonder of this offensive was that we were accomplishing our purpose without inflicting the usual kind of casualties on civilians and nonmilitary objectives. Our bombing techniques had been so improved that, as McGeorge Bundy said in the January, 1967, issue of *Foreign Affairs,* "The bombing of the North has been the most accurate and the most restrained in modern warfare."

The advocates of bombing now based themselves almost entirely on the new arguments: Hanoi was being "bombed" to the conference table because, as Mr. Johnson put it, the level of pain was being steadily increased (to a point at which they inevitably would holler "Uncle"—hopefully not "Uncle Ho"); the movement to the South was being interdicted, and this was being accomplished with the barest minimum of non-military death or destruction.

Into this cozy dream world my reports from Hanoi had burst like a chilling blast of winter wind.

What did I, in fact, observe in North Vietnam?

A stiffening of national will rather than its weakening. This was not only my own observation. This was supported by the foreign diplomats, both Western and Eastern, who had been continuously resident there during the whole period of the bombing. There was remarkable unanimity in the views of these observers. They likened the phenomenon to others which they had seen, the morale of England of 1940 under the Nazi blitz, the spirit of the Russians under Hitler's total war, the spirit of Berlin and Hamburg under the devastation of the R.A.F. and the United States Air Force.

So far as the Hanoi Government was concerned, there was no sign that it was staggering toward the conference table. On the contrary, it appeared to have drawn upon the resources made available to it by its great Communist allies, China and the Soviet Union; it had mobilized its own population with remarkable skill and was carrying on the war fairly effectively. Moreover, it seemed to be ready to carry it on into the indefinite future if the United States resolutely refused to negotiate. Presumably this came as no surprise to Secretary McNamara. He had said flatly that the bombing was not expected to destroy Hanoi's will to fight and had added that since only 15 percent of North Vietnam's gross national product was provided by industry it was not possible to bomb the country to a standstill.

So far as the supply, reinforcement and provisioning of the South were concerned, I saw every day during my visit to Hanoi that this was going forward at a substantial rate. It was costing Hanoi a great deal—in diversion of man and woman power, in investment of time and matériel, in genuine hardships, particularly in the agricultural sector. But the price was not beyond Hanoi's means. It was being paid. Were the North Vietnamese sending south as much as they wanted? As much as the South needed? I could get no precise figures on this. But it seemed to me that they probably were. Our own statistics on the movement of men from the North to the South appeared to be thoroughly confused. General Westmoreland insisted that the movement of Northern reinforcements into the South was going forward at a *higher* rate despite the bombing—a remarkable testimony, if true, to the endurance and energy of the North. In Washington the Pentagon contended that the rate had gone down in the course of 1966. This was cited as an argument of the effectiveness of the bombing program.

I got no statistics at all on the question while I was in Hanoi. My guess, based on the attitudes expressed to me in conversations with North Vietnamese (and other Communist) officials, was that the movement of men and matériel was being carried on at about the rate needed to maintain effective force levels in the South.

Would more men and materials go to the South if it were not for the bombing? Possibly. But my estimate and that of non-Vietnamese Communists was that it would not make much difference. There was, they thought, a decided limit on the men and war equipment which could be effectively absorbed in the South.

The argument was made that our bombing was a cheap, efficient method of applying pressure to the enemy—cheap in total costs, cheaper in manpower and more effective than the use of land troops.

This argument could not be proved one way or the other from the ground in Vietnam. The North Vietnamese contended that they had shot down more than sixteen hundred aircraft, including robots and drones. Our official figure was around four hundred planes. Soon thereafter Hanson Baldwin of *The Times* obtained statistics showing that the true losses of United States planes in Southeast Asia, including damaged planes, planes lost on take-off and in accidents, were over seventeen hundred. The cost in aircraft was not estimated. But most of the planes cost $1.9 million or more each to build—some of them as much as $3 million. The manpower losses were impressive also.

The North Vietnamese held possibly two hundred or more American airmen prisoner. I tried in vain to see these men. I was not granted permission. I submitted a list of names of men missing in action over North Vietnam and asked for information on their fate. I got none.

Diplomats in Hanoi told me that they heard that the men were fairly well treated but that they had complained of the rice diet. The North Vietnamese professed themselves unable to change this as they did not have bakeries for producing bread. They told me the men were no longer held in Hanoi, that they had been dispersed about the country because of fear of American bombing. Most diplomats doubted this. They thought they were still in or around Hanoi.

The airmen had been subjected to at least one indignity. They had been paraded through the streets of Hanoi on August 2, 1966. There was one incident. A Communist diplomat struck a wounded airman. A diplomat who witnessed the occurrence said he lived in hope of a chance to retaliate against the other diplomat.

I heard only one military argument in support of our bombing offensive which sounded plausible. I was told by some foreigners in Hanoi (and the argument was made by military men with whom I later spoke in the United States) that the attacks had prevented the North from providing the South with large-caliber artillery and possibly tanks.

I was not convinced from what I saw of the North Vietnamese roads and railroads that it would be impossible to move heavy guns to the South. In fact, I was not entirely convinced that some heavy artillery might not have been moved to the South. Heavy tanks, however, certainly seemed out of the question because of the condition of the bridges. But I did not think heavy tanks were suited to the terrain and the tactics being employed in the South.

It was my own judgment, possibly a subjective judgment, that on balance the bombing of the supply routes had had a modest effect on the course of the war. It had made it more difficult to move stuff to the South. It had not prevented these movements but it had compelled the investment of very large quantities of men and supplies. Were it not for the bombing, presumably this manpower would have been available for other purposes—agriculture, for instance. So far as matériel was concerned, the picture was more confused. The matériel came from the Soviet Union, China and Eastern Europe. Had it not been so badly needed, would other kinds of goods have been sent? I wondered. My guess, and again it was a guess, was that the Soviet Union would never have sent SAM-2's and MIG-21's to North Vietnam had they not been needed to counter the United States air attack. From this viewpoint the air offensive was placing a slight strain on Soviet capacity and Chinese capacity. But not one which was meaningful.

So far as the point about the precision of our bombing was concerned, its validity had dissolved after inspection of the ground results. United States bombing techniques might have advanced in some degree over those of World War II. Hopefully, they had. But they had not acquired the advertised accuracy. Civilians were dying in North Vietnam. Homes, houses and purely civilian areas of cities were vanishing under the impact of American air power. The "humaneness" of the American air effort produced the same desolated countryside, wounded, injured and mangled men, women and children which had been the inevitable characteristic of the air war in Europe and Asia during World War II.

War was not a pretty business. And the Pentagon's façade of soft, reassuring verbiage had not made it so in the rice paddies and mud-and-thatch villages of Vietnam.

It was true that by great efforts at organization, dispersal and civil defense the casualties in North Vietnam had been held down, often to figures which seemed remarkable to me. They seemed remarkable to the Pentagon, too, and after roundly attacking me for using "Communist statistics" the Defense Department then proceeded to cite the same figures to show how accurate and careful our bombing had been.

These did not exhaust the questions which swirled around our bombing policy. But they were enough to convince me that taking all the factors into consideration—the ground swell of world opinion against the United States, the intense antagonisms bombing had produced within the United States, the remarkable welding together of the North Vietnamese people under the impact of the bombs and the availability of better (I believed) alternatives—the air program had been counterproductive. It had produced negative consequences for the United States. It had cost us far more than we had originally estimated (or even now would admit). It had not produced military, political or psychological results to justify its continuance.

But it had encouraged Marshal Ky and his associates. There was no doubt of that.

I strongly suspected before I arrived in Hanoi that the North Vietnamese authorities would not have taken what was for them the giant step of authorizing my visa unless they had decided that the time had come for active exploration of the possibility of peace-by-negotiation in Southeast Asia.

I departed from Hanoi with that suspicion transformed into positive conviction.

No other sensible interpretation could be placed on the conversations which I had with the Premier and other North Vietnamese officials.

It was apparent that the war was approaching one more of those crossroads which had marked its development over the years. It could proceed in one of two totally opposed directions: down the arduous but productive path of negotiation toward settlement and peace; or it might be precipitously escalated and carried far beyond Vietnam, suddenly to embrace vast areas of Asia or the world.

This evaluation was not contained in what anyone in Hanoi was prepared to say publicly. In fact, even in private, there was a tendency to fall away from declaring explicitly what was expressed implicitly. But that North Vietnam was prepared to explore actively and seriously the possibility of bringing hostilities to an end was no longer a matter of doubt.

What had produced this attitude in Hanoi? Obviously, I had not found that our bombing had achieved this result.

I thought that a circumstance far more dangerous to Hanoi, and quite probably to the world, lay in the background of the changed thinking. That circumstance was the chaos in China.

Here in Hanoi one felt the hot breath of the Peking crisis like a fiery draft from a suddenly opened furnace. The events in China were like some terrible charade. Everyone's attention was riveted on them. Everyone knew the fateful consequences which might flow from them. But no one knew how to influence them.

A year earlier I did not believe Hanoi had been especially eager for negotiations with the United States. At least I did not think that North Vietnam was then prepared to talk in terms of a settlement which would have been acceptable to the United States. Earlier than that, I believed, negotiations would have been even less productive.

Going back over the course of events from 1945—the struggle against the French, the victory at Dienbienphu, the Geneva settlement and the gradual transition from political struggle to warfare—it seemed to me that Hanoi's ambition had undergone great changes.

In the early period, and probably as late as 1958 or 1959, I thought that Hanoi and the other Asian Communists, with Chinese encouragement, had been thinking in grandiose terms. They had dreamed of the creation of a great Asian Communist movement which would have the sympathetic guardianship of Peking. Peking would help with ideological support, material means and possibly even the kind of logistic and tactical support which had aided General Giap to succeed at Dienbienphu. The fulcrum of the movement would be Vietnam. There was every reason for Hanoi to think that political evolution in Vietnam favored the North and specifically favored Ho Chi Minh, who then (and now) was the only national leader which the country possessed. Communism or quasi-Communism might then readily spread from Vietnam and possibly from Indonesia to Malaya and to Vietnam's companion successor states of French Indochina, Cambodia and Laos.

This had been a dream and possibly more than a dream in those years.

But with the steady rise of conflict within the Communist world this goal had begun to appear less and less realistic.

By the early nineteen-sixties, I believed, it must have seemed quite impossible. By this time the polemics between the Soviet Union and China had begun to affect the world Communist movement radically, and no Communist regime was more caught in the middle than that of North Vietnam.

During this period it was still possible for Hanoi to dream of political domination of Vietnam or at least a close working partnership with the South under Liberation Front leadership. There had not been demonstrated up to that time (nor to the present) any political vitality in the Saigon Government which was likely to last once the war ended or the United States removed its props.

The inauguration of the American bombing offensive had not changed Hanoi's evaluation of the probable outcome in Vietnam. It still seemed that Hanoi and the Front would survive long after Marshal Ky or his successors had vanished. The bombing would make it harder for Hanoi and the Front. It would prolong the struggle. It would cost North Vietnam most, if not all, of the restricted socioeconomic gains achieved since establishment of the regime. But the gains were not essential and the losses would not be decisive. The country was still too primitive, too poorly developed. Even if all the industries, all the improvements were destroyed, even if all the towns and cities were wiped out, the country, its essential peasant life and rice culture, would endure.

There was nothing about the bombing of the North which, in the long run, was likely to add to the political viability of Saigon. On the contrary, in the end the results would be the same except that the North Vietnamese would suffer more, the casualties would be higher, the losses greater.

On the other hand, the United States would also suffer. It would begin to cost America a great deal to maintain its war effort. Those members of the Hanoi Government who took ideological guidance from Peking did not think this was at all bad. They shared the view of the Peking Marxists, who held that the more places in the world in which the United States could be mired down in grinding, endless, expensive, frustrating conflict in formerly colonial areas, the more the United States would be bled, the more her resources would be expended, the greater the burden on her social and political structure, the more intense the strain on her relations with other nations and the greater the political defeat for the United States through loss of world support, particularly among the former colonial peoples who possessed the majority of global population, who dominated the United Nations and who, in the future, would have to be reckoned with.

China was playing the long game. It was counting on the Vietnam war as the first in a series of skirmishes in which the United States would be entrapped. When enough United States forces had been tied down in Asia, in Africa and in Latin America, Peking would come out on top.

It was an attractive theory. It would require decades to work out. But Asia had more time than anything else. It would cause considerable loss of life and destruction of property. But the Chinese were not too concerned.

Eventually this strategy might involve the United States in war with China. But that too would be endured. Indeed, the Chinese had already worked out the tactics whereby they believed they could survive American nuclear attack.

Here the strategy of Peking and that of Hanoi showed a remarkable concordance. Ho Chi Minh talked about the inevitable escalation of the United States war effort. He and his associates noted how we had first bombed only a little way above the 17th parallel, then gradually widened out until the whole country was attacked. At first we did not hit Hanoi and Haiphong. Then gradually we moved on the two big cities. Eventually, Ho contended, the worst would happen—Hanoi and Haiphong would be attacked in a systematic and sustained fashion. But, he insisted, this would not mean the end. North Vietnam would retire to its caves and its jungles and struggle on for ten, twenty, fifty years and finally the United States would be defeated.

Long before that another thing would have happened. The volunteers would have come into the war—the manpower of China and possibly of the Soviet Union and of Eastern Europe which stood ready to come at Hanoi's call.

Did Ho really think that events would take this course? That the destruction of his country, the involvement of all the Communist world, was virtually certain? Possibly not. Quite possibly he thought that the prospect of total involvement would, in time, bring the United States to discuss terms acceptable to the Communists.

But now history had taken a turn which not even the least sanguine North Vietnamese had anticipated. The brooding quarrel between the Soviet Union and China had boiled over. The consequences already were disastrous for the orderly conduct of North Vietnam's defense. Month by month and week by week the problem grew more grave. North Vietnam was spending more effort now trying to maintain relations with its two great neighbors, trying to keep the flow of supplies coming through, than on any other aspect of the war.

And the possibility daily heightened that graver disaster lay ahead.

China could at any moment erupt into civil war, which would mean the diminution or cutoff of the supply route. The intraparty conflict in China might reach such bitterness that one faction would halt supplies or close the roads. The Chinese already were hampering the movement of Soviet goods. They might stop them entirely. The conflict between Moscow and Peking might move into open warfare. This would make deliveries impossible.

Any one of these combinations might produce the worst of consequences for North Vietnam. The country and its leadership might be drawn into the intra-China dispute through the simple fact that so many of Ho's associates had intimate relations with the Chinese. Many in his entourage had connections as close with Peking as they had with Ho. Suppose Peking thought that Soviet influence was coming to the fore in Hanoi—might it not instruct its friends in Hanoi to intervene? Might Peking already have intervened through third parties to try to affect Hanoi's policies?

It was possible the Chinese would try to confront Ho with a *fait accompli* and subvert his government if they thought he was beginning to side with the Soviet Union. In their present hysteria almost any act of Hanoi's could be interpreted in Peking as hostile to China or pro-Soviet.

Hanoi had stated flatly that it would not receive "volunteers" from China or any other Communist state except in certain specified instances and only when it called for them. But could Ho be certain that Chinese "volunteers" might not suddenly pour over the frontier in response to a demand from a member of the North Vietnamese Government acting on the instruction of Peking?

There was not a diplomat with whom I talked in Hanoi who was not sensitive to these potentials. They had changed the whole aspect of Hanoi's attitude toward peace and nego- tiations. There was not a diplomat from Eastern Europe with whom I talked who did not strongly favor negotiations at the earliest possible moment. Not all of them favored this course because of fear of China. Many had strongly favored it be- fore the Chinese crisis. But the Chinese crisis strengthened their feeling that the war represented a grave fissure in the world political structure, that it created a situation which under the stress of events in Peking might lead the world to nuclear catastrophe.

And a nuclear war, they pointed out, was regarded with horror by all the world—except Peking, which had prepared a strategy for dealing with the nuclear devastation of China. Peking, they noted, was talking about the inevitability of American nuclear assault, the wiping out of Chinese nuclear centers, the destruction by nuclear weapons of all China's large cities. Peking thought this would merely create a trap (killing, incidentally, possibly 300 million Chinese) into which the United States would fall. Because, said Peking, after the bombs had done their work the Americans would still have to enter the nuclear-poisoned countryside and seize the land, and there they would find the Chinese, 400 million strong, emerging from caves and bunkers, ready to fight with primi- tive bombs and grenades at a range of two hundred yards or so—closer than America's technology could be effectively employed.

The European Communists were familiar with this Chinese thinking. They were chilled by it and by the consequences it might bring to themselves and to Southeast Asia.

I could not find many North Vietnamese who relished the idea, but they were so accustomed to talking of protracted war, of retreating into the hills, of fighting through decades while the Americans exhausted themselves, that the prospect did not fill them with so much horror.

But I did not believe that Ho wished to lead his country down that avenue. I thought that he and his leaders had taken the measure of what the next year was likely to bring. And the year after that. It must look to them that the chances for bringing more strength into a negotiation in 1968 were less than the chances in 1967. Beyond 1968 lay more and more question marks.

I did not know whether Moscow, in seeking to free its hands for the China crisis and in its hopes of uniting the West in a common front against Peking, had sought to persuade Hanoi of the desirability of negotiation. Perhaps not. The Russians had found themselves in a delicate position vis-à-vis Hanoi and the Communist world. Every Communist knew Moscow had no deep interest in Vietnam. Everyone knew Moscow wanted the war settled. But that made it difficult for the Soviet Union to take a direct hand. Possibly, with the rapid deterioration in Peking, Moscow had finally spoken more directly.

Whatever the event, now, at this late hour, Hanoi was interested in talking terms. But even so there was a grave impediment. It could not talk openly or directly lest this provoke the very intervention and reprisals by the Chinese of which it was most fearful. At a hint that Hanoi was ready to talk peace Peking was apt to intervene forcibly—by closing the frontier and cutting off supplies, by bringing political pressure to bear within the North Vietnamese Government or by sending in the "volunteers" to shift the balance back toward war.

I had felt before going to Hanoi that the only effective method of exploring the possibilities of negotiation was by private, completely secret talks, far from the spotlight of world opinion. It was not hard to see the futility of publicized techniques. Some efforts occurred while I was in Hanoi. The British Foreign Secretary, George Brown, made a public appeal for talks, putting the weight of his stress on Hanoi. He added for good measure the suggestion that the talks be held in Hong Kong, oblivious of the fact that the Chinese two days earlier had charged that Hong Kong was a base for the aircraft carriers whose planes were bombing North Vietnam. It was incredible bumbling. Or possibly it was not intended seriously except to ease the pressure on the Labour party at home to take some action toward ending the war.

The Pope made appeals and U Thant made appeals. None of these received a very enthusiastic welcome in Hanoi. There had been suggestions that General de Gaulle might make a good mediator. There was no doubt in my mind that De Gaulle was well regarded in Hanoi. But the attitude of the North Vietnamese officials suggested that they much preferred such a delicate business to be carried on without the intervention of third parties. They had had considerable experience in the past—a bit more than I was aware of when I was in Hanoi—of the difficulty of making and maintaining contacts with the United States. Publicity was the one thing they did not want. The intervention of a third party merely increased the possibility of a leak, with the unpleasant consequences which might follow.

The talks could not stand publicity. Of this I was certain. The North Vietnamese had to see the light at the end of the tunnel before they started down the passageway. Until they could feel, privately, that there was a real possibility of an agreement they could not afford public negotiations. Because the moment they entered public negotiations they could expect the China route to be cut and they could expect active Chinese efforts to upset the talks. This would be fatal unless they knew that they were going to be able to reach a peace agreement. If they started out on negotiations and failed, they would find themselves in a critical situation, compelled to renew the war against the United States but with their principal source of supply cut and the possibility that their government might have been severely weakened internally.

They had other fears, which paralleled the fears with which the United States approached the idea of negotiation. They feared that if they started to talk their people would be convinced that peace would inevitably follow. If the talks stalled and war was resumed, it would not be possible to restore the remarkable fighting morale which they now had and which constituted their chief resource against the powerful United States. They did not have many assets and they did not feel they could jeopardize this one. They also feared that if they entered talks without a clear notion of the agreement which lay at the end, the United States might utilize the period of negotiations to increase its force levels in the South and prepare for resumption of hostilities when the talks came to an inconclusive end. This fear paralleled two great fears of the United States—that if bombing once halted it would not be possible (because of public opinion) to resume it and that the North might enter into talks simply to utilize the period for reinforcement and regrouping, which would then enable it to emerge from a deadlocked negotiation in a far stronger position.

These were the dangers which lay in the minds of the

North Vietnamese and the Americans as they gingerly approached the idea of negotiations. The only way in which they might be removed was for each side to attempt an exploration in complete secrecy. They would have to see what each side was prepared to do; whether the ingredients of a deal existed. This was by no means certain. But the possibilities could be assessed through this process. I recommended it strongly to Hanoi, speaking as an interested observer. I had no diplomatic role. Anything I said was said just as an American newspaperman who happened to be in Hanoi. Therefore I could talk with a freedom which a diplomat would not possess. The same held true on the other side. When I returned to the United States, it was possible for me to talk to Washington with the same frankness and lack of reserve that had marked my conversations in Hanoi.

It seemed obvious both in Hanoi and in Washington that each side was aware of the critical moment which had arrived. If the turn toward negotiation was not taken, what was the alternative? On Hanoi's side, the deterioration of the situation in its rear would bring an inevitable turn toward radical expedients. On the American side, the pattern surely would follow the channel of escalation to higher and higher force levels. What specifically would we do? I was in no position to guess. But the speculation in military quarters had been fairly precise: intensification of bombing, sustained air attacks on Hanoi, blockade or bombing of Haiphong, land operations north of the 17th parallel, amphibious landings in the Gulf of Tonkin, all of the ominous developments which would produce the entry into the war of the "volunteers." Chinese volunteers.

The options were epochal. Peace or a land war, very possibly a nuclear war, with China. Possible Soviet intervention.

To say that events had arrived at a turning point was an understatement.

I returned from Hanoi convinced that a settlement of the Vietnam war by negotiation lay within our grasp. I was convinced it would not be easy to negotiate, and I was by no means convinced that we were prepared to understand or undertake this difficult and complex task. But that the ingredients of a settlement, one which would be viable, enduring and relatively favorable to our objectives in Asia, at least as I understood them, now had come within reach I had no doubt.

This, I must say, came as something of a surprise to me. I had explored the ground in Southeast Asia with some care only a few months earlier, in the late spring and early summer of 1966, in a trip which led me all around the periphery of China. I had gotten the impression then that the establishment of a secure and comparatively stable Southeast Asia might be impossible on terms which Washington would consider acceptable.

As I understood our objectives in Southeast Asia, they comprised the following:

We had no desire to overthrow the Communist regime of North Vietnam. We accepted the continuance of Ho and his successors in that country.

We had no territorial aspirations in Vietnam and none in Southeast Asia. We had no desire to remain in South Vietnam or any part of Vietnam.

We desired the establishment in South Vietnam of a viable regime which would not be Communist-dominated, Communist-oriented or Communist-threatened, but we did not insist that this regime be necessarily that which now held power in Saigon.

We desired to reduce the Communist threat to all Southeast Asia and to increase the security of the area, particularly that of Laos, but we had not spelled out specific aims so far as this point was concerned.

We were prepared, once peace and stability had been restored, to withdraw our armed forces and to offer economic and technical assistance on a massive scale, which would help to create the material foundations for a rapid advance in standards of living and development.

We were prepared to assist in cooperative multi-nation projects such as the Mekong River development.

If these were, in fact, our objectives in Southeast Asia, it seemed to me, on the basis of my conversations with representatives of the Hanoi Government and of the National Liberation Front, that with hard bargaining we could come reasonably close to fulfilling them.

So far as the public record went, the chief difficulty concerned the future status and regime of South Vietnam. The problem centered on Hanoi's support of the Front as the appropriate spokesman for the South. We did not recognize the Front, although we had said cryptically that there would be "no difficulty" about a place for the Front at the negotiating table. The existing Saigon Government of Marshal Ky was our ally-of-record, and while we had not committed ourselves to perpetuating his regime, our inclinations naturally went toward the Saigon Government, with all its faults, rather than the Front, with which we had done mortal combat.

Was there room for maneuver on this point?

I suspected there was, although I did not expect the Front or Hanoi to put this on public record or even to agree to it in the first round of private discussion. But both sides had publicly agreed that they would back a "coalition" government. The Front had spelled this out to include members of South Vietnam's Constituent Assembly and some members of the Ky Government (but not Ky). We had not gone so far, but the Saigon Government had at least intimated that it looked toward a coalition. The sentiment for a coalition certainly was strong among members of the Constituent Assembly.

The problem here was balance. Who would have the majority? Was there some nonaligned or moderate figure around whom a coalition government might be constructed? Would a coalition government possess durability or would it, even if headed by a non-Communist, quickly fall apart or succumb to Communist intrigue? We did not wish to see repeated in Southeast Asia the history of Eastern Europe's postwar coalition governments, which quickly fell under Communist pressure.

I believed that the vital ingredients of the Liberation Front program (at least as described in Hanoi)—a mixed economy, free rights for all parties, neutral foreign policy, no alliances—would permit construction of such a government. Its stability could be insured by United States economic aid, guarantees by Asian powers and the Great Powers, guarantees by Hanoi. There was an armory of factors which could be utilized to give the structure strength if it possessed the vital ingredient of political virility.

What about the North? It seemed clear that the moment was appropriate to restore the North to the situation which had been envisaged by the Geneva agreements, to try to cut its military links to Peking and to Moscow. The divisions within the Communist world favored such neutrality. It would ease the pressures on Hanoi enormously. Of course, Hanoi, even more than Saigon, would require guarantees. Not only of support (against Chinese intervention) but of economic aid and assistance in rehabilitation. The situation had developed in an appropriate manner for the achievement of aims which had lain far beyond the horizon of possible diplomacy a year earlier.

It was an unequaled opportunity for the United States, one which might not recur and which might slip away in certain eventualities, such as the reduction of political tensions in Pe-

king or a *rapprochement* between Peking and Moscow, both
of which might occur.

But establishment of neutralized regimes in Saigon and
Hanoi would only be the start. It seemed to me that Laos represented an equally dangerous problem. Laos had become a
mere fiction—a land which was in the hands of an uncertain
number of guerrilla operations, some sponsored by the
United States, some by the Communists, some of purely Laotian origin.

Unless Laos could be quieted and sanitized, the whole
theater of struggle might simply shift westward from Vietnam, with the warriors of the C.I.A. and the Chinese International going at it hammer and tongs (or hammer and sickle).
This would undermine the area dangerously. Cambodia had
managed to stay out of the war, but it needed economic and
probably political support as well. Thailand would be in trouble if it lost its burgeoning war-boom prosperity. Many considerations dictated the creation of a strengthened International Control Commission with a broader mandate and genuine powers not merely to police these countries but to aid
and guide development. What political form this might take I
did not know, but it should not lie beyond the competence of
American diplomacy to establish a structure in Southeast
Asia which would make the region a going concern.

This would create what the United States had so long
hoped for—a strong and viable Southeast Asia, resistant to
the spread of Chinese influence and Chinese Communism.
Certainly China was going to be a power in the area. It always had been. It was unrealistic to suppose it could be shut
out. But if we built on the strong factors of nationalist sentiment such as had been invoked in North Vietnam, such as
would surely develop in South Vietnam, the same force
which had caused Indonesia to throw off the Chinese and the
Communists, we would see emerging not a series of poor,
weak client countries, not a region dependent into infinity
upon a huge American military garrison and the expenditure
of United States funds, but a progressive group of countries,
internally strong, resolutely independent. Independent of us.
Independent of China. A healthy Asia, it seemed to me, must
be an independent Asia.

This was the chance which had been created by the unexpected developments in Peking and their repercussions in
Hanoi. It might well be the chance of a century.

But I was not certain that Washington could grasp the opportunity. Washington was tired and Washington was stale. Washington, I feared, was filled with too many men who had committed themselves to so many past mistakes that they lived only for some crowning disaster which would bury all the smaller errors of the past. Washington was filled with politicians who were concerned with what would bring in votes in the next election or what would discomfit a possible election opponent. In that atmosphere it was difficult to get men to indulge in imaginative statesmanship. Too many were afraid to take a chance. The old policy might be a mistake. It might lead to catastrophe. But change was dangerous and uncertain.

And there were competing counsels.

For instance, there was the military. The military, not unlike the French who had been there before, had not had a good time in Vietnam. Their record was poor, partly because it was not a situation which yielded readily to the application of military power and partly because the politicians were always trying a teaspoonful of this, a teaspoonful of that. When a general finally got the dose increased to a tablespoonful, this was not enough and he should have recommended a swig. No general won glory by telling his president to turn the job over to the diplomats. So they called for more of whatever it was and hoped for the best. If the Vietcong were stubborn this year, maybe double the force next year would do the job.

I was told when I was still in Hanoi by someone who had been very recently in Saigon that the American military establishment there would not accept negotiations at this time, no matter what Hanoi said.

"They think they have Hanoi on the run," said this man. "They are not going to quit now. They want to pour it on. If it is poured on hard enough, there won't be any Hanoi to bother with."

I didn't know if that accurately reflected the thinking of the American military establishment in Saigon, but I encountered this line in Washington in some quarters on my return. The reasoning was simple. If Hanoi was in trouble, if China was about to blow up, if the North Vietnamese were about to lose their supply line—why talk to them? They will have to crawl to us later on. Let's hit them with all we've got.

From the standpoint of total military victory I found a grim honesty about this argument.

But—and this was a large "but" to my way of thinking— this policy led straight to the confrontation which was most dangerous of all—confrontation with China's land forces, and quite possibly involvement with the Russians. We might crush Hanoi only to find ourselves locked in a fatal nuclear embrace which would eliminate all problems in Vietnam by eliminating the world of which Vietnam was a part.

I thought this to be a counsel of utmost recklessness. But, of course, its advocates never mentioned the cataclysmic potentials. They limited themselves to talk about clobbering Hanoi. But, curiously, Hanoi could have been clobbered at any time in the last two years. And had not been. Why do it now when Hanoi was ready to talk peace?

A strange way to reason. Or so I thought.

But, perhaps, there lay behind this reasoning a hidden factor which governed our whole Southeast Asian strategy. Or a half-hidden factor, one which was often discussed by the Pentagon strategists and the ideologists of war-game theory, the men who created the logical structure against which much of our strategic air policy was elaborated.

This was the line that the real enemy in Southeast Asia was not North Vietnam. It was China. We were there not because we worried much about the regime in Saigon or that in Hanoi but to draw a line against China. This was what much of Asia thought.

I had heard this thesis advanced in Asian capitals in the summer of 1966. The Asians simply did not believe that the United States was investing the sums we were putting into Vietnam or the manpower we were stationing there or the enormous bases we were building in South Vietnam and Thailand simply to fight Ho Chi Minh. No. China was the objective. That was the way they calculated it. We were preparing to fight China. Some thought we were trying to provoke China so that we would have an excuse to bomb it, to destroy its nuclear facilities. After all, had not some of our generals proposed that line? Did it not possess a certain grim sense? If we were going to fight China ultimately, would this not be a good time to do it—before China got too strong, when we could still be sure of knocking out its atomic production centers?

If this was, indeed, our basic, secret, unstated strategy, if

Vietnam was a holding operation or a maneuver to try to draw in China, if we were going through the motions of fighting North Vietnam but really were preparing for an assault on China—then, of course, the question of peace in Vietnam became moot. What was the point of it? It would run counter to our genuine intentions and would make it more difficult to cope with China.

For those who believed along these lines—and I had no doubt that many thoughtful men in the Pentagon and perhaps some not so thoughtful men in the Senate shared these ideas—there was nothing more strongly to be resisted than talk of peace or of ending the conflict in Vietnam. Each time peace talk arose it must be strongly rebuffed. We must not take yes for an answer. We might indulge in a little rhetoric to soothe the ruffled feelings of the world. But we must not let it interfere with the war. This must be remorselessly pressed and escalated to the limit. China must be compelled to intervene. According to this thinking, the very thing which Hanoi most feared—the possibility of Peking's moving volunteers over the frontier—was devoutly to be hoped for since this would enable us to trigger the nuclear offensive which would eliminate China from the map.

It seemed preposterous to suppose that men like President Johnson, Secretary Rusk or Secretary McNamara considered the war in such terms. I had no doubt that they were as eager as anyone to find a solution. But they were also determined that it would be a solution which would stand the test of time and trouble. They did not wish, having made so major a commitment of American treasure and manpower, having so deeply staked their prestige and reputation, to enter a cul-de-sac which would lead to another Panmunjom or to embark upon a negotiation which would create a ramshackle settlement from which would emerge the next world crisis.

Skepticism was natural. Outright antagonism was another thing. There seemed to me to be one great difficulty about getting talks going. Both the United States and North Vietnam were still in the ring. Neither side was staggering toward collapse. The dangers which Hanoi envisaged were dangers of the future, not the present. In such a situation it was difficult for either side to give the ground which would make compromise possible.

Yet it was plain that the situation had reached precisely the point of development at which the most effective kind of solution could be achieved. It was not easy to end a war, and it was remarkably difficult to end one without laying the train for a new war only a few years in the future. This we had done in our settlement of World War I. It was the ruthless terms ruthlessly imposed on the Central Powers which set the stage for World War II. I was not convinced that the unconditional surrender imposed upon Germany and Japan at the end of World War II did not contain the seeds of World War III, although this might have been averted by the extraordinary aid rendered by the United States. Yet in Europe many observers felt that if World War III came, Germany would again be the instigator and that the cause would lie in the World War II settlement.

We now were at a striking point in history in Southeast Asia. Hanoi had not been defeated. The United States had not been defeated. Each was conscious of the strength of the other. Each had suffered. But not irretrievably. We could, therefore, if we utilized our instincts for statesmanship, construct a settlement which would have the elements of equity, honor and reasonableness and which might endure.

Were we to follow the course of obliterating Hanoi, of hitting it with everything in the book, of driving North Vietnam back to the caves, would we not create a vacuum—even if we escaped nuclear war with China and/or the Soviet Union? Might we not then find ourselves with nothing but a vast grayland in which not even Marshal Ky would manage to reign supreme? What of neighboring Laos and Cambodia? Would not total defeat in Vietnam, even if obtainable, create a situation in which for a hundred years we would be committed to maintain costly and numerous garrisons to police the marches of the devastation which we had created, the vast and evergrowing jungles, uninhabited by man, beast or bird, which would be our inheritance?

These speculations arose inevitably as one pondered the alternatives.

To my way of thinking the arguments ran strongly toward an effort at negotiation.

The task of negotiating a durable Southeast Asian settlement was difficult. But it was a fascinating one, the kind to evoke a challenge to any diplomat, the kind which would be a monument to the statesmanship of the man who accomplished it, something far beyond the transient triviality of so many postwar diplomatic settlements. This could be the foundation for a whole new epoch in Asia, one which would contribute to the strength and stability of a world which would endure whatever passing crises might come to China or even to India.

I hardly needed to think about the consequences which would flow from it: the release of American energies and resources to cope with the problems of Latin America and Africa, to turn once again to the raveled threads of Europe, to the critical negotiations over the atom, the détente with Russia, to the world population explosion and, finally, to the problem of China itself.

Perhaps those generals were right who believed that the only way to deal with China was to atomize it. But I thought that there must be another way. China was the world's most talented nation, the reservoir of more human skills than any other existent, a people of infinite capabilities, possessor of the world's longest history, the world's most complex culture, inventor of so many of the great technologies of the human era. Was it true that we could not find a way to live with China? Must the globe be turned into a poisonous desert because of China? I did not believe so. Surely America's heritage, Yankee ingenuity and the democratic imagination of our great people could devise a better course.